FRIENDS OF MEN

FRIENDS OF MEN

BEING A SECOND SERIES OF

GUIDES, PHILOSOPHERS AND FRIENDS

BY

CHARLES FRANKLIN THWING

D.D., LL.D., LITT.D., L.H.D.

PRESIDENT EMERITUS OF WESTERN RESERVE UNIVERSITY
AND ADELBERT COLLEGE

CT119
.T54

ESSAY INDEX

Essay Index Reprint Series

BOOKS FOR LIBRARIES PRESS
FREEPORT, NEW YORK

First Published 1933
Reprinted 1968

LIBRARY OF CONGRESS CATALOG CARD NUMBER:
68-8500

PRINTED IN THE UNITED STATES OF AMERICA

CONTENTS

Contents

I
PHILLIPS BROOKS

Born Boston, December 13, 1835; died January 23, 1893. He was a great grandson of the founder of Phillips Academy, Andover, Mass. Prepared for college at the Boston Latin School, graduated Harvard, 1855; taught in the Boston Latin School; studied for the ministry in the Theological Seminary at Alexandria, Va., where he did some teaching in the preparatory department. In 1859 ordained deacon and became rector of the Church of the Advent, Philadelphia. In 1860 ordained priest, and in 1862 he became rector of the Church of the Holy Trinity, Philadelphia. In 1869 became rector of Trinity Church, Boston; consecrated bishop of Massachusetts in 1891. He was overseer and preacher of Harvard University for many years.

Author: Volumes of sermons; Lectures on Preaching; the Bohlen Lectures on The Influence of Jesus; and of a few poems, including the Christmas hymn ''O Little Town of Bethlehem.''

FRIENDS OF MEN

I

PHILLIPS BROOKS

FROM my desk as I write I look up and see two pictures: one of Phillips Brooks and one by its side of Cardinal Newman. Each of these men, in different ways, has great meanings for one who was young fifty years ago.

There was a man sent from God whose name was Phillips Brooks. He was sent into my life as early as my Freshman year at Harvard. Quite by chance, early in that year, I heard Brooks preach. For the next seven years I heard no other preacher if Brooks could be heard. On many Sundays I heard him preach no less than at three services. For in the evening of a Sunday of each month he was preaching in the St. Johns Chapel at Cambridge. Even after my theological student days began I often went from Andover to Boston just to be a grateful and thrilled worshiper in Trinity Church. I knew it was my last chance to hear great sermons.

As I look back, and listen back, more than fifty

3

years, I ask, what was the origin of the power of
Brooks as a preacher? I might add the clause "over
me," for, be it said, that power is still present and
moving in mind and heart, in conscience and in will.
Such a reference is not unfitting, for these interpretations are, and are designed to be, personal.

It is seldom that we have the advantage of a full
statement of the plan and method by which an intellectual master comes to, or exercises, his mastery. It
is also more seldom that we are able to unite with
the plan and method an example of the work itself.
We do know, however, the method by which Webster
prepared his speeches either for a jury, for the court,
for his fellow senators or for the general public. We
have many examples of each type. We also have as
personal memoirs the methods by which Grant
mapped out his campaigns and his interpretations of
his carrying out these campaigns. With equal clear-
ness we know the methods by which Brooks made his
sermons; for those sermons the multitudes have heard
and studied and by them been inspired. His Yale
Lectures on Preaching give his theories, and his theories represent and present the foundation of his sermons spoken and heard.

To Brooks, preaching was a union of both personality and truth. In his *Lectures on Preaching*, he says,
"Preaching is the communication of truth by man to
men. It has in it two essential elements, truth and
personality. Neither of those can it spare and still be
preaching. The truest truth, the most authoritative

statement of God's will, communicated in any other way than through the personality of brother man to men is not preached truth. Suppose it written on the sky, suppose it embodied in a book, which has been so long held in reverence as the direct utterance of God that the vivid personality of the men who wrote its pages has well-nigh faded out of it; in neither of these cases is there any preaching. And, on the other hand, if men speak to other men that which they do not claim for truth, if they use their powers of persuasion or of entertainment to make other men listen to their speculations, or do their will, or applaud their cleverness, that is not preaching either. The first lacks personality. The second lacks truth. And preaching is the bringing of truth through personality." [1]

And further, "However the Gospel may be capable of statement in dogmatic form, its truest statement we know is not in dogma but in personal life. Christianity is Christ; and we can easily understand how a truth which is of such peculiar character that a person can stand forth and say of it, 'I am the Truth,' must always be best conveyed through, must indeed be almost incapable of being perfectly conveyed except through personality." [2] "Even if we look at preaching only, it must still be true that nothing can ever take its place because of the personal element

---

[1] *Lectures on Preaching,* delivered before the Divinity School of Yale College, in January and February, 1877, p. 5.
[2] *Ibid.,* p. 7.

that is in it. No multiplication of books can ever supersede the human voice. No newly opened channel of approach to man's mind and heart can ever do away with man's readiness to receive impressions through his fellow-man. There is no evidence, I think, in all the absorption in books which characterizes our much reading age, of any real decline of the interest in preaching. Let a man be a true preacher, really uttering the truth through his own personality, and it is strange how men will gather to listen to him. We hear that the day of the pulpit is past, and then some morning the voice of a true preacher is heard in the land and all the streets are full of men crowding to hear him, just exactly as were the streets of Constantinople when Chrysostom was going to preach at the Church of the Apostles, or the streets of London when Latimer was bravely telling his truth at St. Paul's." [8]

These generous quotations I have made chiefly because of their own worth, and also because they prepare the way for asking and for trying to answer the question, what was the personality of Brooks which was fused in and through his interpretations of truth?

For more than fifty years the personality of Brooks has seemed to me to stand, first, for fullness of life. He embodied Christ's purpose, "I came that ye might have life, and have it more abundantly." Whatever was, or is, life or in life, either in itself or

[8] *Ibid.,* pp. 11-12.

in its relationships, was found in him. The height and breadth and weight of his body were type and symbol of this interpretation. Colossal, he moved as a giant, yet without the cumbersomeness of the giant. The life of the former generations, and they were the best of New England, seemed to stand forth in face and form, and to speak in voice, a voice which united strength, pervasiveness, persuasiveness, and mellowness. The disciplines of the scholar had not chiseled his face into refinements and sharp outlines, but life's experiences had helped to emphasize a certain impression and expression of strength in the face. To this strength was added a certain peculiar witchery of the eyes. All of life some way seemed to have contributed to his life. The diverse offerings which make up our racial compounds had given to him all of their best. The thoughts and feelings of the great thinkers had made their contributions. The undertones of the literatures possessed his soul. Each man is both a unit and a composite. Brooks was indeed a composite of many lives, and they were united into the noblest unity in his personality. This personality teemed with life. He once remarked that he had never known the grace of sickness. He did, indeed, know the grace of full health of every part of his composite being. Men who influence other men are usually blessed with a surplus fullness of life. But in Brooks this surplus fullness seemed more full, more overpowering, of a higher degree, than usually obtains.

Quite akin to this fullness, or perhaps a form or expression of the very fullness itself, was what I shall call a certain personal responsiveness, or sense of freedom. It was the cubical quality or element; it was breadth, but it was not breadth only, for breadth might be superficial or thin. It was depth, but not depth only, for depth might spell unhuman profundities. It was height, but not height only, for height might represent a superhuman remoteness and sublimity. It was all these elements fused and united. The breadth was joined with the depth and with the height. The depth was one with the breadth and the height, and it was also free from remoteness. The height was united with the depth and the breadth, and while sublime and lofty, it was yet human. There was in Brooks the Emerson quality of character of which he spoke in one of his last addresses. "Character, and character only, is the thing that is eternally powerful in this world. Character is the divinest thing on earth. It is the one thing that you can put into the shop or into the study and be sure that the fire is going to burn. Character now, and character forever!" *

In this cubical relation of his manhood filled with life was also a certain intellectual alertness. The intellect was as a steel spring, wound up tense, ready to leap on call. Of an illustration of this quality, I was once both a spectator and an auditor. At the

* *Life and Letters of Phillips Brooks,* by Alexander V. G. Allen, Vol. II, p. 931.

morning service of the first Sunday of a December Brooks went into the pulpit during the singing of the last verse of the hymn before the sermon; and, standing in the pulpit, opened his sermon case. Having opened the case he closed it, returned to the chancel, and taking a Bible went back to the pulpit. Opening the Bible, he found, as it proved, a text from which he proceeded to preach. The text was the words of the Philippian jailer addressed to Paul and Silas: ''What must I do to be saved'' [5] The sermon was a threefold answer to the question: first, consciousness that one is lost; second, consciousness that there is a way of being saved; and third, the use of the way found in Christ. I well recall the powerful interpretation. To myself I said at the time, ''Brooks found that he had no manuscript of his sermon or else a wrong manuscript.'' Within a few days thereafter the New York *Tribune* printed a paragraph to the effect that Phillips Brooks found, upon going into his pulpit last Sunday,—he had with him the sermon which he had preached the preceding Thanksgiving Day. Alertness and the power to seize immediately, fully, firmly, constructively, on the facts and truths of an emergency, and to bring forth a rich result, were dominant and constantly controlling in his vital personality.

There was also in Brooks a keen and full appreciation of values. This appreciation was both moral and intellectual; it was emotional as well. He recognized all values as precious, the less as less, the least

[5] Acts, 16:30.

as least, the more and the most as more and most.
These values were intrinsic and consisted also in relationships. The more numerous the relationships, the
more precious were these worths. He sought at once
to render to God God's things, and to Cæsar
Cæsar's. He was a pastor. He carried his people in
his great heart of love. His social life was broad and
intense, but his sermons represented his chief method
and force for helping men. Never meticulous, he
yet was concerned with individual duties. Ever
catholic in judgment and tastes, he was never guilty
of visionariness.

There is a fifth quality which I wish to name. I
shall call it tolerance. More specifically it stood for
the enlargement and application of the sense of appreciation. Brooks' tolerance was neither compro-
mise nor indifference, neither intellectual blindness
nor hardness of heart. It was based on loyalty to
essentials and on a proper adjustment to incidental
forces. It recognized the inter-mixture and the inter-
weaving of the good and of the bad. It understood the
truth of Christ's remark that the wheat and the
tares better grow together. The tolerance was endowed with patience and was supported by love. Not
foreign to the quality of tolerance was another quality which I shall call graciousness. Graciousness is
favor to the ill- or un-deserving. It is not love. Love
may be an affection existing between equals. Graciousness is a relation existing between unequals.
The acts of grace came from his hand, the words of

grace from his lips as the dew from heaven, unconsciously and beneficently. The mood of the unconscious principle of graciousness belonged to his whole life and complete character as blueness belongs to the sky and the ocean.

These six qualities in Brooks seem to me to be peculiarly constructive: fullness of life, responsiveness, intellectual alertness, appreciation of life's values, tolerance, and graciousness. I want to lay down by their side the elements which Brooks tells the Yale students should belong to the preacher as a person. They are first, personal piety. "It is personal piety, a deep possession in one's own soul of the faith and hope and resolution which he is to offer to his fellow-men for their new life." [6] The second quality is mental and spiritual unselfishness. "I mean that kind of mind which always conceives of truth with reference to its communication and receives any spiritual blessing as a trust for others." [7] The third quality is hopefulness. The fourth quality is health. "The ideal preacher brings the perfectly healthy body with the perfectly sound soul. Remember that the care for your health, the avoidance of nervous waste, the training of your voice, and everything else that you do for your body is not merely an economy of your organs that they may be fit for certain works; it is a part of that

[6] *Lectures on Preaching,* delivered before the Divinity School of Yale College, in January and February, 1877. By the Rev. Phillips Brooks, p. 38.
[7] *Ibid.,* p. 39.

total self-consecration which cannot be divided, and
which all together makes you the medium through
which God may reach His children's lives.'' [*] The
fifth quality which he tells the Yale men should belong to the preacher is ''in every man who preaches
there should be something of that quality which we
recognize in a high degree in some man of whom
we say, when we see him in the pulpit, that he
is a 'born preacher.' Call it enthusiasm; call it eloquence; call it magnetism; call it the gift for
preaching. It is the quality that kindles at the sight
of men, that feels a keen joy at the meeting of truth
and the human mind, and recognizes how God made
them for each other.''   But, in addition, Brooks
tells the Yale theologues that they should have not
only these five qualities, but also other qualities
which seem to lie in a yet higher zone, and to be yet
more formative than this quintette of elements. The
first of these superior forces bears the broadest,
deepest, and highest name of character. The second
stands for freedom from self-consciousness. The
third element is genuine respect for the people to
whom one preaches. A fourth element is what
Brooks calls gravity. ''Perhaps there is no better
name than Gravity. I mean simply that grave and
serious way of looking at life which, while it never
repels the true lightheartedness of pure and trustful
hearts, welcomes into a manifest sympathy the souls
of men who are oppressed and burdened, anxious

[*] *Ibid.*, p. 41.   [*] *Ibid.*, p. 41.

and full of questions which for the time at least have banished all laughter from their faces."[10] "The gravity of which I speak is not inconsistent with the keenest perception of the ludicrous side of things. It is more than consistent with—it is even necessary to—humor. Humor involves the perception of the true proportions of life. It is one of the most helpful qualities that the preacher can possess."[11] "But humor is something very different from frivolity."[12] "The smile that is stirred by true humor and the smile that comes from the mere tickling of the fancy are as different from one another as the tears that sorrow forces from the soul are from the tears that you compel a man to shed by pinching him."[13] "Pure gravity is like the hinges of the wonderful gates of the ancient labyrinth, so strong that no battery could break them down, but so delicately hung that a child's light touch could make them swing back and let him in."[14]

A fifth quality which Brooks counsels the Yale men to possess is courage. "The timid minister is as bad as the timid surgeon. Courage is good everywhere, but it is necessary here. If you are afraid of men and a slave to their opinion, go and do something else. Go and make shoes to fit them. Go even and paint pictures which you know are bad but which suit their bad taste. But do not keep on all your life preaching sermons which shall say not

---

[10] *Ibid.,* p. 54.   [11] *Ibid.,* p. 56.   [12] *Ibid.,* p. 57.
[13] *Ibid.,* p. 57.   [14] *Ibid.,* pp. 58-59.

what God sent you to declare, but what they hire
you to say. Be courageous. Be independent. Only
remember where the true courage and independence
comes from.'' [15]

The qualities named in these two groups of
Brooks' interpretation seem to me to be inter-
changeable. Character and courage belong to the
first group as fully as to the second. Piety and mental and spiritual unselfishness may be as fittingly
included in the second as in the first group. These
several qualities, too, are essentially one with the six
qualities which in my own independent judgment
seem to characterize Brooks himself. Do not fullness of life, responsiveness, intellectual alertness,
appreciation of life's values, tolerance, and graciousness belong to the great elements and forces which
Brooks names as characteristic of the minister?

His own interpretation one likes to think of as
autobiographic. In his interpretation of what the
preacher at least must be, or of what at his highest
he will be or may become, is a portrait of Brooks himself, painted not from a superficial mirror but from
the depths of his own soul. I venture to think that
my own interpretation is not therewith inconsistent.
And yet, after all, one must not analyze the man as
the botanist analyzes the flower, tearing it in pieces.
Brooks was more than each element or than all elements united. Brooks was himself.

But to Brooks preaching was not only personal-

[15] *Ibid.,* p. 59.

ity. It was also truth. The truth which Brooks held
and preached is, for the present purpose, best seen,
heard, felt in the subject and treatment of the subjects of his sermons. In this interpretation one
might almost make a Homer's catalogue of ships. Yet
the titles are not meaningless. I do venture to
name a few of them, together with their texts. For
Brooks' texts were real points of interpretation and
of application, and not points of departure in thinking. *Visions and Tasks*—"While Peter thought on
the vision, the Spirit said unto him, Behold, three
men seek thee." Acts x. 19. *The Mother's Wonder*—
"Son, why hast thou thus dealt with us?" Luke
ii. 48. *Brotherhood in Christ*—"Simon, called
Peter, and Andrew, his brother; James the son of
Zebedee, and John his brother." Matthew x. 2. *The
Earth of the Redemption*—"The heavens, even the
heavens are the Lord's: but the earth hath he given
to the children of men." Psalm cxv. 16. *The Man
with Two Talents*—"To another he gave two talents." Matthew xxv. 15. *The Safety and Helpfulness of Faith*—"They shall take up serpents, and
if they drink any deadly thing it shall not harm
them. They shall lay hands on the sick and they
shall recover." Mark xvi. 18. *The Great Expectation*—"Let your moderation be known unto all men.
The Lord is at hand." Philippians iv. 4.[16]

In the development of Brooks' sermons there were
to me two relationships of peculiar worth: first, the

[16] Taken from Contents of *Twenty Sermons*.

personal testimony of the preacher himself. This testimony stood for closeness to life. Life was intimate to and with him. The life which overflowed in Brooks was presented in each sermon. The sermon gripped one through a vital force. This grip came out of and through himself. It was close, intimate, personal. His witness was a personal testimony. A second element, too, was the power and use of contrasts. A single volume illustrates this worth. *The Duties of Privilege, the Little Sanctuaries of Life, the Mitigation of Theology,*[17] are among the titles of great sermons. His use of contrasts is well set forth in a picture of two rivers. "One is a great, broad, quiet stream, ever moving swiftly but smoothly on, unbroken by rapids, majestic in its calm and noble monotony, each mile of its great course seeming like every other mile, so perfectly and evidently is it everywhere itself. Its great thought is continuity. The other river is a mountain torrent. Broken and stopped perpetually, it is always gathering itself up in a pool, at the foot of the rock that stopped it, for a fresh start. It is always full of new beginnings. It is different in each mile of its course from what it is in every other mile; when it grows calm for a moment it seems as if it had wholly stopped, until it finds an outlet and plunges down another precipice, and with a new cascade begins its life again. Like the first stream, like the majestic and continuous river, is the life of

[17] Taken from Contents of *New Starts in Life*.

God. Continuousness and identity is our great
thought of Him. 'From everlasting to everlasting
thou art God,' we cry. Full of movement, the impression of His life is stillness, like the impression
of the vast and solemn Nile. But like the mountain
torrent is the life of man. With a true continuity,
so that it is the same life from its beginning to its
end, it yet forever is refreshing its vitality with new
beginnings. It loves to turn sharp corners into unseen ways. It loves to gather itself into knots and
then start out with the new birth of a new resolution. It loves to take into itself the streams of new-
born lives that its monotony may be refreshed with
their freshness.'' [18]

But more comprehensively one can say that all of
Brooks' sermons are living. They are incarnations
of himself. They do not have the massiveness, the
sense of glory of the French preachers. They are not
primarily ethical, apologetic, argumentative, or evangelistic. They defy exact classification. They are
living, and they are as hard to put into homiletical
or philosophic classifications as is life itself. They
grip life, and life grips them. They wrestle with
life, and life wrestles with them. The topic of an
early discourse, *The Eternal Humanity*, voices the
whole life of man. The topic of a later sermon, *The
Withheld Completions of Life*, also springs up from
and into life. In their oneness with life lies their
power over life. Both as cause and as result they are

[18] *New Starts in Life,* pp. 2-3.

a witness. Dealing with truth, they also deal with life. Concerned with man's life, they are based upon truth. Concerned with truth, they also deal, and must deal, with life.

The consummate truth which is thus declared in closeness of life and in personal testimony is what? It is nothing less than knowledge of God. Of this comprehensive truth he says, "The knowledge of God lies behind everything, behind all knowledge, all skill, all life. That is the sum of the whole matter. The knowledge of God! And then there comes the great truth, which all religions have dimly felt, but which Christianity has made the very watchword of its life, the truth that it is only by the soul that God is really known; only by the experiences of the soul, only by penitence for sin, only by patient struggle after holiness, only by trust, by hope, by love does God make himself known to man." [19]

Brooks was the priest of a church, and the minister of individual parishes. But perhaps more than either priest or minister, he was a preacher of the pulpit. The two Philadelphia ministries, important in themselves as they were, were yet a prelude to, or a preparation for, the richer ministry in Trinity Church of Boston. Yet his preaching to the students of American colleges formed a constituent and lasting part of his whole service. For many a year he was the most beloved and most eagerly expected preacher in many a college pulpit. To his own college he gave

[19] *Sermons Preached in English Churches*, p. 110.

himself as a member of its board of preachers, and at its 250th anniversary he preached on "Jesus Christ, the same yesterday, today, and forever." At Yale, at Vassar, at Brown, at Johns Hopkins, and many other colleges he was the great preacher. His service was as unique as it was lasting. It has no parallel. His influence over college men and women is probably the most personally lasting of his influences over individuals, for these sermons were addressed to those who were young, and in that part of life in which they are most responsive to the best intellectual and other inspiration.

Still further, I wish to compare Brooks with another apostle, who was also a great preacher. I began this study with an allusion to Cardinal Newman and to Brooks. Likewise I close it.

Brooks and Newman were both alike and unlike. The similarities and identities are perhaps more fundamental and impressive than the differences, and yet the differences are not insignificant indeed. At any rate it is important, first, to interpret the likenesses, and to try to evaluate them.

Brooks and Newman were youths of little or of no promise. Neither Harvard nor Oxford gave intimations of their future. So far as any forethought was taken, Newman was designed, being the son of a banker, to become a banker, and Brooks' first experience in active life was in teaching, wherein he at least partially failed.

Both Brooks and Newman became by common con-

sent great examples and interpreters of the religion
of Christ. They were devoted adherents to the common faith, and devout worshipers at the altars of
the church universal. On the basis of this understanding and service they embodied a noble sense of
what is connoted in the word "gentleman," a word
which Newman has so greatly defined. Newman's
manner was of Oxford, refined, gentle, said to be of
a half-effeminate diffidence. Brooks' was direct,
forcible, but without undue forcibleness, appreciative, altruistic. Each possessed insight, both broad
and keen, into the human mind and heart. Each
possessed what is called, in English speech, character. In this character were embodied not only power
and resource intellectual, but also what may be described as the emotion of the intellect. There was
also in each a certain perception of the heart, em-
bodying Pascal's undying phrase, "the heart has its
reasons which the reason knows not of." Each was
gifted with a fair degree of self-confidence, and yet
this confidence was consistent with a deep degree of
humility. Neither was influenced to any extent by
German learning or German theology. Each was a
liberal, one for the liberal branch of the Catholic
Church and the other for a liberal Protestant faith.
Each was a product of his own country and of his
own time. Each was an outstanding, and some would
say the most outstanding, preacher of his generation
or generations. With Brooks it was a typical single
generation of thirty-three years. With Newman it

was generations, covering three score of years. Newman's career was divided into two almost equal
parts, measured by time. In the first part he became
the most revered of Englishmen. In the larger share
of the second part he was forgotten by most of his
countrymen, even if remembered by the chosen few.
Brooks' career was one of undivided, noble ascent.
Each was devoted to the cure of souls in personal
relationships, and each also, and more especially
Brooks, through preaching. Each was inclined to
choose for his sermons themes very definite. *Brotherhood in Christ, Timeliness, The Knowledge of God,
The Sufficient Grace of God,* illustrate the breadth
and the narrowness of Brooks' selections, but always
definite. *Willfullness—the Sin of Saul, Love—The
Safeguard of Faith against Superstition, The Influence of Natural and Revealed Religion Respectively,*
also illustrate the character and characteristics of
Newman's. The writing, too, of each preacher,
whether of the sermon for delivery or of the essay
(and Brooks' essays outside the sermon were
few), was of the best type. Newman helped Whately
to make his Rhetoric and text book, for generations
of students, and Brooks had been trained by great
teachers of English at Harvard College. The style
of each is flexible, fluid, flowing, full, though Newman's has greater richness, nobler beauty, and an
element of subdued splendor. Each sweeps the
hearer or the reader on and on through great atmospheres, toward great conclusions. Each is a mas-

ter of form and loyalty through words, a minister
to the angel of truth and of truthfulness. Each
sometimes gives the impression through the force
and rush of words, through sentences, through paragraphs, that the utterance is the mother of ideas
quite as completely as that the ideas form the force
which makes utterance. Whether either could be
called an orator depends for its answer upon the
definition of oratory. But it is certain that each
could stir the emotions and move the will through
the intellectual presentation of truth and could affect the imagination by mental illuminations unto
great pictures, and the will unto forceful and definite action. Neither founded a school. The oratory
at Birmingham has not the dominance or the beauty
of Assisi; yet Birmingham's disciples have become
apostles to the world. Newman, it must be added,
had his Manning. Brooks also had his opponents,
especially in relation to his becoming a bishop.

On this foundation of similarities it is fitting to
build a statement of the unlikenesses. Newman came
of a Dutch Jewish family, Brooks of a pure and
best New England ancestry. Newman's life was one
of vicissitude, Brooks' of calmness, and progressiveness. One was the mountain torrent, the other the
calm river. Newman was the more interested in self.
One half of his score of volumes are essentially
autobiographic. Brooks is the more interested in
humanity and in general religious truths. His dozen
and chief volumes are largely sermons. Newman, to

make a rather superficial distinction, is a believer
in, and a follower of, dogma. Brooks is a believer in
doctrine. Newman's intellect is bathed in symbol-
ism; Brooks' is founded on emotional rationalism.
Newman is rather a man of action, the administrator; Brooks the practical philosopher. Newman is
both a mystic and a skeptic in many relations;
Brooks a mystic, his skepticisms being absorbed and
forgotten in his beliefs. Newman's intellect is subjective and analytical; Brooks' objective and synthetical. Newman is never a modernist; Brooks is
a modernist from the beginning. Newman is a mystery almost from his earliest years, as such he continued, and is so called scores of years after his
death. Brooks is never an enigma. His life lies open
like a book to be read of all men. It was indeed
transparent, yet it had its reserves. Newman's intellect is subtle. He is the *doctor subtilis*. Brooks'
is built on cardinal principles of virtue. In Newman
subtlety of intellect seems to overcome the soul. In
Brooks the soul absorbs and incorporates subtleties
and dialectical discriminations. If John Wesley's
preaching in Oxford belongs to the eighteenth
century, Newman's preaching, in St. Mary's, belongs to the nineteenth: Brooks is more akin in spirit
to the earlier master. Brooks is primarily and princi-
pally the preacher; Newman primarily the historian,
the critic, the theologian, as well as the preacher. Newman is concerned with what seems to be technicalities, historical rituals; Brooks with the broad domain

of truth. Brooks belongs to Jerusalem and to Athens; Newman to Athens and to Rome: on both Hymettus and the Vatican he builds altars. Newman is more ecclesiastical, Brooks more religious; Newman more devoted to works, Brooks to the truthfulness of faith. Brooks is the more positive, aggressive; Newman the more defensive. Brooks seldom if ever uses the double-edged tool of irony. Newman uses it not infrequently as a great power and of consequence. Gladstone described Newman as, "a wonderful man, a holy man, a very refined man, and (to me) a most kindly man." [20] Thorold of Manchester, in dedicating a volume of sermons to Brooks, said of him,

> "Strong, fearless, tender, eloquent
> Incapable of meanness
> Blazing with indignation at all kinds of wrong
> His heart and mind deep and wide as
> The ocean at his door
> Simple and transparent as a child
> Keen with all the keenness of his race." [21]

Newman's style has the more of music, and it is the music of the violin, sweet, tender, entrancing, beautiful, with deep strains of passion quieted, of hope calmly realized, of sorrow comforted. Brooks' style is of the organ and orchestra, each part contributing its offering of beauty, of strength, of imagination,

[20] *The Life of William Ewart Gladstone*, by John Morley. Vol. III, p. 422.
[21] *Life and Letters of Phillips Brooks*, by Alexander V. G. Allen. Vol. II, p. 946.

yet at times all parts uniting in halleluiahs and Te Deums.

Perhaps these likenesses and these contrasts are fittingly summed up in placing side by side two sermons of the great preachers, preached from the same text. But identity ceases with the text. The very titles of the discourses proclaim their essential differences. In Brooks' the title is the transcription of the scripture text: *I am the Light of the World.* In Newman the metaphysical or psychological reference is immediately made: *The Philosophical Temper First Enjoined by the Gospel.* The primary difference is continued in the succeeding paragraphs. In Newman the following may be selected as representative interpretations: The objections to Christianity are answered by the fact that the greatest philosophers of modern times have been obliged to submit their reason to the Gospel; The general principles which Revelation presupposes are coincident with the research into nature; Seeking for truth is regarded as an indispensable requisite for finding it; Modesty, patience, caution are requisite in philosophical inquiry; Excessive attention to system may hurt science; Certain philosophers regard Christianity as a slavish system, prejudicial to freedom of thought and to the aspirations of genius—such are a few intimations of the chief paragraphs of Newman's sermon. Many of these propositions and the general method of reasoning seem to suggest the great *Analogy* of Butler or the *Logic* of Whately, a book which, like the *Rhetoric*, Newman helped to make.

Newman is thus metaphorically suggestive of the school of Athens. Brooks' treatment of the same text which Newman used is direct, simple, orderly, progressive, suggestive of the charge at Balaclava. What is the meaning of these words, first asks the American preacher. After using a simile of the power of the sun over the material world, he answers the main question by saying, "A thousand subtle, mystic miracles of deep and intricate relationship between Christ and humanity must be enfolded in those words; but over and behind and within all other meanings, it means this,—the essential richness and possibility of humanity and its essential belonging to Divinity. Christ is unspeakably great and glorious in Himself. The glory which He had with His Father 'before the world was,' of that we can only meditate and wonder; but the glory which He has had since the world was, the glory which He has had in relation to the world, is all bound up with the world's possibilities, has all consisted in the utterance and revelation and fulfilment of capacities which were in the very nature of the world on which His Light has shone." [12] "The truth is that every higher life to which man comes, and especially the highest life in Christ, is in the true line of man's humanity; there is no transportation to a foreign region. There is the quickening and fulfilling

[12] *The Light of the World, and Other Sermons*, pp. 4-5.

of what man by the very essence of his nature is.'' [23]
''It is redemption and fulfilment which He comes to
bring to man. Those are His words. There is a true
humanity which is to be restored, and all whose un-
attained possibilities are to be filled out. . . . Is it
not all a claiming of man through all his life for
God? Is it not an assertion that just so far as he is
not God's he is not truly man?'' [24] Applications to
the broad, high, and deep truth follow: first, to
character; secondly, to conversion; and third, to the
naturalness of the new life and also to service to all
men of purity and to other great conditions of the
individual, to reality, to the revealing of the mystery of man, to the revelation of the highest possibilities of the soul, to the satisfaction of men's minds
about the Bible. It also applies the truth to the
present age, in the vastness of the varieties of life
in this age and to the deepest yearnings of humanity. Among the last paragraphs of the sermon he
gives this interpretation of religion. ''Our religion
is not a system of ideas about Christ. It is Christ.
To believe in Him is what? To say a creed? To
join a church? No; but to have a great, strong,
divine Master, whom we perfectly love, whom we
perfectly trust, whom we will follow anywhere, and
who, as we follow Him or walk by His side, is always drawing out in us our true nature and making
us determined to be true to it through everything,
is always compelling us to see through falsehood and

[23] *Ibid.*, p. 6.   [24] *Ibid.*, p. 7.

find the deepest truth, which is, in one great utterance of it, that we are the sons of God, who is thus always 'leading us to the Father.' " [35]

And what shall the interpreter say of the comparative worths and the results of the life and service of these two men? The results are, I believe, above every other form of value embodied in their books. Their voices ceased within the last eleven years of the last century. The number of those who heard these voices rapidly lessens. The memories of those who yet remain normally become dim. These books are for Brooks, books of sermons or of addresses which are virtually sermons. For Newman these books are not only sermons, but also essays autobiographic, as the *Apologia*, as doctrinal dissertations, like *The Development of Christian Doctrine*, as interpretations of education, like *The Idea of a University*. His poems also and hymns are, and will remain, regnant and moving. Certain parts of *The Idea of a University* enlarge the mind, thrill the heart, fire the imagination. Newman's school still lives in the oratory which he established at Birmingham in 1847. It is at once his altar and his grave. Brooks lives in his church in Boston against whose wall is placed his statue. Both still live above all other forms in their books. Brooks has a smaller but a more loyal audience for his sermons; Newman has a larger and more diverse audience for writings which are also more diverse but ever appealing to the emotional intellect

[35] *Ibid.*, p. 23.

and to the thoughtful heart. Each, indeed, is sure to live in his own human domain so long as humanity welcomes thought suffused with deepest feeling, in interpretations of life which inspire, and in a guidance of life which points to noblest destiny.

II

GEORGE EDWARD WOODBERRY

Born in Beverly, Mass., May 12, 1855; died January 2, 1930. Received A.B., Harvard, 1877; Litt.D., Amherst, 1905, Harvard, 1911; LL.D., Western Reserve, 1907; professor of English, University of Nebraska, 1877-78, 1880-82; professor comparative literature, Columbia, 1891-1904. Fellow American Academy of Arts and Sciences; member American Academy Arts and Letters; hon. fellow Royal Society Literature. Author: History of Wood Engraving, 1883; Edgar Allan Poe, 1885; Studies in Letters and Life, 1890; The North Shore Watch, 1890; Heart of Man, 1899; Wild Eden, 1900; Makers of Literature, 1900; Nathaniel Hawthorne, 1902; America in Literature, 1903; Poems, 1903; The Torch, 1905; Algernon Charles Swinburne, 1905; Ralph Waldo Emerson, 1907; The Appreciation of Literature, 1907; Great Writers, 1907; The Life of Edgar Allan Poe, 2 vols., 1909; The Inspiration of Poetry, 1910; Wendell Phillips, 1912; A Day at Castrogiovanni, 1912; The Kingdom of All-Souls, 1912; Two Phases of Criticism, 1914; North Africa and the Desert, 1914; The Flight, 1914; Shakespeare, 1916; Ideal Passion, 1917; The Roamer, 1919; Collected Essays, 6 vols., 1920-21.

Editor: Works of Lamb, Shelley, Poe, Tennyson's *Princess*, Bacon's Essays, Coleridge's *Ancient Mariner,* and collected Poems of Rupert Brooke, and of many other volumes.

II

GEORGE EDWARD WOODBERRY

TEACHER, POET, ESSAYIST

WOODBERRY, like his master, Lowell, was triple-starred. He was teacher, poet, essayist. His teaching began on his Harvard graduation in 1877 in the University of Nebraska. With a brief interruption it continued till 1882. His richest contribution as a teacher, however, was made in and through Columbia University from 1891 to 1904. In the first eight years of his professorship his subject was "literature," in the last five "comparative literature." To his teaching he brought general and technical knowledge; but above all else he brought a sense of life and also devotion to his students. His personality gave a glow to his interpretations. His following was marked by both numbers and loyalty. To the Columbia students of his time he was, and still is, known and felt as the "Old Man." This loyalty did not vanish with his retirement in 1904. It continued to show itself in many forms. Perhaps the most personal and indeed unique form was the Woodberry Society, an associa-

tion of loyalists of both Columbia and Harvard, to
whose annual meetings he occasionally came. Its
members propose that it shall still exist, to promote
the ideas and ideals which he loved.

For teaching Woodberry was prepared, not by the
later technical processes, but by a rich and enriching
undergraduate course and by private study. His chief
studies at Harvard were Greek, Latin, Philosophy,
and English. In each of them, and in other studies
as well, he won distinction. In the two middle years
of his course he was the first scholar in his class, in
the Freshman year the fourth, in the Senior the fifth.
His rank for the whole course was third. In Philosophy he received highest honors. Among his teachers
were Goodwin, Lane, Bowen, Palmer, and Child.
Among his fellow students were men who subse-
quently made rich contributions to American and to
world life.

But it is as a writer that Woodberry makes the
worthiest and apparently the most lasting appeal.
Whether as a poet or as an essayist this appeal is or
will be the stronger it is quite vain to prophesy. One
can hold, and easily, a brief for either side. As one,
however, I am obliged to accept Wordsworth's ver-
dict, wiping out a commonly accepted distinction between prose and poetry. For Woodberry's imagination, whether voiced in prose line or poetical, is one
and the same. One and the same is his essay on the
historic glories, shames and natural beauties of
Taormina, with his verses upon *Gibraltar.* The sweep

and the swing, the lift and the largeness, belong almost equally to paragraph and to stanza. Each is bathed in the atmosphere of beautiful appreciation. In each one feels a sense of timeliness and of majesty. Is "the round of heaven greatens as it goes" clipped from essay or from sonnet? Is "all is silent save the surge" a line taken from sonnet or from essay? Each is touched with the sublime. "Art is secondary to matter." As Frederic Harrison said of a passage in De Quincey's *Opium Eater*, "not poetry, but as fine as any verse."

For in both essay and verse Woodberry deals with the great themes, the greatest. I might make a catalogue of them taken from the table of contents of his volumes. It is more fitting and more expository to interpret these themes as they appeal to me, reading his paragraphs.

Woodberry writes of democracy, of democracy not as Bryce wrote of it, great as that writing is, but of democracy as "a mode of dealing with souls." For "men are souls, and this is a fundamental concept of democracy." He writes of religion in its simple elements, "faith, hope, love—these three," and also of pantheism as the "great mood of the human spirit which it is, permanent, recurring in every age and race." He writes that intellectual education "as an element in life is always overvalued; and, within its sphere, which is less than is represented, it is subject to error, prejudice, and arrogance of its own; and, being without any necessary connection with love or conscience, it has often been a reactionary, disturbing, or selfish force in politics and events, even when well acquainted with the field of politics, as ever were any of the forms of demagogy in the popular life.'' He also says, ''having been much in colleges and near to education I must bear my hard testimony—the brain thrives and the head; but the soul dies.'' He writes of law, ''It is not, like conscience, a searcher of men's bosoms; its knowledge extends no farther than to what shall illuminate the nature of the event it examines; it makes no true ethical award.'' He writes of fraternity as giving many benefits, in particular in establishing toleration, ''not in religion merely, but of opinion and practice in general; and thereby largely [it] has built up a mutual and pervading faith in the community as a body in all its parts and interests intending democratic results under human conditions.'' He writes of equality as ''the identity of the soul, the sameness of its capacities of energy, knowledge, and enjoyment.'' He writes of ''the universal faith, in which we are bred, that we are children of a common Father, and saved by one Redeemer and destined to one immortality, and cannot be balked of the fullness of life which was our gift under Divine Providence.'' ''Do not the heavens still declare the glory of God as when they spoke to the Psalmist? and has the light that lighteth every man who is born into the world ceased to burn in the spirit since the first candle was lit on a Christian altar?'' Universal faith is found in ''the intimacy of

God with his creation and with the soul of man."
Other elements of this universal faith are "the immanence of sublime power" as found in Wordsworth,
the "immanence of transcendent love" as found in
Shelley, and the "immanence of mystery" as found
in Tennyson. He writes of idealism, and of the race's
dream of truth hovering between two worlds, the
world of salvation and the world of damnation,—"The
method of idealism is that of all thought, that in its
intellectual process the art of the poet, so far from
being a sort of incantation, is the same as belongs to
the logician, the chemist, the statesman." He writes
of art as everlasting, of beauty as timeless, and as
"the solvent of the nations" and of the essential oneness of all the arts.

There are, moreover, two commanding fields of
which, directly and indirectly, suggestively or comprehensively, he ever writes. They are literature and
life. These two fields lie in close and vital nearness.
If one is the reality, the fundamental source, the inspiration, the other is the expression.

How diverse, how full, how vital, how pregnant,
is Woodberry's interpretation of literature! "That is
his [the poet's] gift—the power to live. . . . They
[the poets] lived before they sang. Emotion is the
condition of their existence; passion is the element
of their being; and, moreover, the intensifying power
of such a state of passion must also be remembered,
for emotion of itself naturally heightens all the faculties, and genius burns the brighter in its own

flames. . . . The poet is the leader in the dance of life." "Literature is an art of expression. The material which it employs is experience; or, in other words, literature is the expression of life. Action, emotion and thought are the three great divisions of life, and constitute experience. Literature undertakes to represent such experience through the medium of language, and to bring it home to the understanding of the reader." "It is useful to recognize at once the fact that literature is not an object of study, but a mode of pleasure; it is not a thing to be known merely like science, but to be lived." Literature is an introduction of ourselves to ourselves. "Literature, then, is the key to your own hearts; and going out with the poets you slowly or swiftly evolve new life after new life, and enter partially or fully on that race-inheritance which is not the less real and sure because you must reach out your hand and take it instead of having it stored in your nerves and senses at birth; predispositions to appropriate it are stored even there, but it is a thing of the spirit and must be gathered by the spirit itself." Literature was to Woodberry an emptying of self into the vessels of verse or of prose. To it he held himself in the mood of "true reverential piety," to use a happy phrase of Professor MacCallum of the Australian University of Sydney. His offerings were "solid and noble" as Wordsworth said of two poems of Tennyson, and of "diction stately." Through literature he made his richest contribution to humanity. In his last days he said and said repeatedly, ''he had accomplished what he meant to do.''

But literature has its basis in life. This basis in life meant quite as much to Woodberry as to Matthew Arnold. In Arnold, however, it has ever seemed to me to contain a bit of artificiality. It savors of an Oxford lecture or of an Oxford Common room. The sea, an ultimate reality, is in Woodberry's soul. His forefathers were ship captains, who took the ''long voyage''—to India and to China. His life is realism touched by imagination. Emotion, too, social emotion, moves him in both stanza and paragraph. Writing of Shakespeare he says, ''The fullness of life in all its forms, which makes the plays great, has as its underlying basis this life-force, the affirmation of life, in its energies, its desires, its revelations, in the conscious spectacle of being, and with the more brilliancy because of the transcendent idealization to which the scene of life here has been subjected.'' In literature the youth ''first comes in contact with the large life of mankind.'' Comprehensively, ''Life is the matter of literature; and thence it comes that all leading inquiries to which literature gives rise probe for their premises to the roots of our being and expand in their issues to the unknown limits of human fate.'' Fundamentally, he says, ''Life impresses me less as a birth initially out of the divine into mortal being than as birth into the divine at each step of the onward way.'' Summing all up, he adds, ''The subject-matter of literature is life in the forms of per-

sonality and experience.'' The literature with which
Woodberry deals, of which he is the creator, is, therefore, the literature founded upon, inspired by, and
pervaded by life itself.

So far I have tried to bear to my reader an interpretation, inadequate as I know so well it is, of
Woodberry's treatment of the great themes of our
being and especially of literature, and of life itself.
I now wish to seek to interpret his treatment of the
great men of our own English literature, and of other
worthies in other domains of thought. Their number
is large. They may be counted into the hundreds.
His consideration of many is limited to a paragraph,
or to a part of a paragraph. But the interpretation
of the greatest belongs to the page, the section, the
whole essay, the volume.

Perhaps the first to be named is James Russell
Lowell. For Lowell was, in a sense, Woodberry's
schoolmaster. Both were sons of New England, the
one rooted on the left bank of the Charles, and the
other on the Beverly shore. The noblest traditions
of town and state, of war and peace, belong to each.
Lowell is put by Woodberry among the great in the
temple of humanity. He is ''the only critic of the
highest rank that our country has ever produced.''
Woodberry knew better than most; for he made a
catalogue of the library at Elmwood. Although the
larger part of all that Lowell has to say relates to
literature, he is primarily the American patriot.
''There can be no doubt that Lowell had faith in

our national destiny, as perfect as was ever possessed by a patriot aware of dangers, yet supremely
confident of mastery over them.'' For ''he em-
ployed well-nigh all the resources of his mind in the
service of his country.'' Lowell's mind is that of the
constructive critic, his mind is also that of the idealist. He emphasizes the human worth of the imagination. Lowell was to Woodberry a patriot above party.
His *Commemoration Ode* gives ample and more than
ample proof. ''He (Lowell) found in the 'Commemoration Ode' (1865) his loftiest subject and most
enduring fame.'' To the author of *My Country*
Lowell was a great patriot, as well as a great master
in literature.

The place next to Lowell's in Woodberry's grateful devotion, both in formation of character and in
allegiance, is held by Charles Eliot Norton. This devotion is indicated in many ways. The letters of Mr.
Norton give evidence. In 1879 Norton writes to
Lowell of Woodberry, ''He is growing fast in power;
the experience of life is serviceable to him; and if he
keeps his health, and has sufficient energy, much that
is good may be fairly expected from him. He has no
successors in College with literary gifts that approach
his in quality.'' To Woodberry himself he writes in
1886, criticizing *My Country,* ''The poem as a whole
seems to me too absolute in singing the praise of the
beloved land. We are men; we know the good and
the ill of the world; we love our country, but with
keen-eyed and disciplined passion, not blindly exalt-

ing her, not feeding our imaginations on unrealities, on what might never and nowhere be. The dreams of a perfecter state are gone. We are awake, and see the shadows as well as the sunlight. To do justice to the America that may be, we must not exalt the America that is, beyond her worth. Moderation is strength. We do not care for a 'fourth of July' ode!'' He also in general writes to Woodberry, ''You have one more lesson in philosophy to learn, in the real philosophy—that of life; not to be saddened by the imperfection of men and of nature. In the very cherishing of ideal aims, in the clear recognition of the rarity and preciousness of beauty and of joy, an equal recognition is implied of the solitude, the weariness, the prosaic course of daily life. Before we win the last victory, we must be content to be without hope,—and to be ready and cheerful for the day, *Even though* the struggle nought availeth.'' Such were the lessons which Norton read to Woodberry four years after his graduation. But a few years after, in 1887, Norton writes to Woodberry of what Woodberry himself has done for him. He says, ''I should try to make you understand that you have helped me to keep something of the spirit of youth through the sympathy which you have evoked, and that your regard has been an encouragement to me to believe that I might be rendering some service to others. One can accomplish so little in comparison with what one desires to accomplish, and in my case strength so often fails for the doing of what with a little more strength one would do easily, that there is need of philosophy not to allow what might be to make one discontented with what is. Such affection as yours comes in to reinforce and illumine my philosophy. I am grateful for it." The debt in turn which Woodberry feels he owes to Norton is beautifully and nobly expressed in the Harvard Phi Beta Kappa poem of 1913:

"Envy me not, whose hand the Master took,
    His firstling charge, boy-leader of the host
Of those who followed in the after-time;
Meet is it that I praise him, who forsook
All else to travel the steep heavenly coast
Where what he told me of is won or lost,
And aye the lone soul to its sun doth climb.
He hardened me to breathe the burning frost
Where Truth on all things pours its naked ray;
He taught me to neglect all worldly cost
And through that shining element make way
Where Reason doth the spirit of light obey.
Yet, with prophetic forecast, evermore
He brought forth things of beauty from his store;
And in my bosom fed love's fiery core
With wisdom sternly tender, warmly high,
That through love only doth man live and die,
Howe'er his nature may through art refine;
Thus had he from the deathless Florentine
Intelligence of love, the poet's power;
And oft he led me to the Muse's bower."

On general grounds, however, one anticipates that Woodberry's deepest devotion will be paid not to his teachers, be they never so formative and inspiring as

were Norton and Lowell, but to Shelley.[1] For, at
times he seemed to be almost ''Shelley-mad.'' The
flights of Shelley and of Woodberry seem to lie in the
same atmosphere, a highly rarefied atmosphere indeed. Woodberry writes of Shelley, ''No poet ever
put such unreserved trust in the human spirit. He
laid upon it the most noble of all ideal tasks, and inspired it with faith in its own passion. 'Save thyself,' he said, and showed at the same time the death
in which it lay, the life of beauty, love, and justice
to which it was born as to a destiny.'' For of himself one would say, as he says of Shelley, ''he would
stand preëminent and almost solitary for his service
to the struggling world, for what he did as a quick-
ener of men's hearts by his passion for supreme and
simple truths.'' Likewise it may be said of Woodberry as he again says of Shelley, ''he put persuasion
in the place of force, and love in the place of hate,
and the genius of victory which he invoked was the
conversion of society by the stricken cheek and the
lost cloak.'' This partial service, moreover, takes on
the form and force of the imagination. In *Prome-
theus Unbound* it becomes the ''millennium of mankind.'' Other poems, like the *Adonais*, are filled with
these and like and unlike emotions: ''personal pathos,

[1] This interpretation of Shelley's influence over Woodberry
is confirmed by the recent issue of a volume entitled *The
Harvard Shelley Note-Book*. It contains Woodberry's first
and last writing on Shelley. Its worth for the present purpose, however, is more precious as a personal memorial than
as a literary presentation.

of meditation on life, of divine philosophy, . . . under the spontaneous and unreflecting impulse of poetic passion." But all are held in both the elder and the younger poet within the bounds of beauty.

Yet I have both a feeling and a judgment that it is not to Shelley, but to another quite as unlike to Shelley in time and environment as he is in poetic creativeness, that Woodberry feels himself in deepest kinship—Virgil: whose two thousandth birthday the world of scholars is commemorating. For in point of fundamental relation he writes thus of Virgil: "This presence of Virgil in his verse is elementary. He was a lover, and through love disengaged from life its moment of beauty, of sentiment, of millennial hope; but this beauty, sentiment and hope are seen under that almost atmospheric charm which has coined for itself the name Virgilian and is breathed from himself." In a like spirit, a classmate at Harvard, Theodore Chickering Williams, wrote in an introduction to his great translation of the *Æneid:* "Virgil's has been a living name to every generation since his own. He outlived the Rome he sang; and during the long eclipse of pagan literature survived as a Christian poet. His influence upon European letters has been vast and continuous." The *Æneid* is indeed a world poem more than the *Iliad,* and apparently it is a timeless work as really as the *Iliad.* Yet, despite this lasting and world-wide imperialism of the great poem, it has another power which rules in Virgil and which most influences Woodberry. It is the power of love.

"He was a lover of life; only an immense love of life could have so revealed to him the pity of it. At every touch he shows a spirit naturally dependent; teachable, yielding, hospitable, responsive, sympathetic, appealing, his heart flows out upon things, uniting with them at every contact, from his early loves of nature, romance and antiquity, his long passion of patriotism, on to his brooding over the fates of men."

The quest for the men who influenced Woodberry and whom he interpreted might well go unto unhorizoned fields, a field which bears the greatest names, names unlike in origin, time, experience, and offerings to humanity. Among them are Lucretius, a pantheist of the imagination; Milton, who inspired liberty and wrote immortal verse; Wordsworth, who "illustrates, and amplifies the experience of the race in its direct relation to nature"; Keats, who "died on the promise of the fruit"; Browning, the moralist, the psychologist, the realist, the idealist; Swinburne, the master of lyric power, meditative and passionate; Tennyson, the interpreter of his own time and the prophet of immortality; Hawthorne, the psychologist, the artist, the moralist; Poe, that weird figure of American and of world literature; Emerson, living for God and for his fellows of the race. These masters of literature represent the personalities who ministered to Woodberry, and to whom he paid devotion. But why continue? Enough has been said, and perhaps more than enough, to intimate a few of the great ones who entered into Woodberry's constitution, intellectual, ethical, imaginative, emotional. Enough, too, has been said to suggest the chief priests of the altars to whom and through whom he worshiped.

Woodberry is known in and through his books. He was personally shy. He seemed to welcome, and at times to seek, solitude. About him there clustered a certain wistfulness which spelled aloneness, meditative and pensive.[2] One of his teachers at Exeter, Mr. J. A. Tufts, writes me that even in the early Exeter years he was "quiet." The mood continued. He ever seemed, both early and late, to elude one. But in his books he spoke out. In his odes he sang forth in notes clear, strong, resounding, free. The world he could take into his heart, even when he closed its doors to his classmates.

His books are great in their themes; themes which thrill the heart, absorb the intellect, command the will, and, rightly interpreted and obeyed, guide and

[2] President Warren of Magdalen College, Oxford, in his Dramatic Narrative, *The Death of Virgil,* voices a similar sentiment.

> "The poet's life may oft seem indolent,
> Inactive, uneventful, self-absorbed,
> Yet must he gain the mastery of his art
> Like other craftsmen by incessant toil,
> And steel himself to suffer if he would see
> Fair offspring of his travail of the soul,
> Or skill to ken, what only quiet may
> In noontide meditation, watch of night,
> —For still the Muses haunt the brooding mind—
> The one in many that makes the many one,
> Something that underlies our rainbow dreams,
> The pattern of the web of all the world."

The Death of Virgil, by T. H. Warren, p. 53.

quicken man's going forth unto perfection. They are the embodiment of the noblest art. They incarnate the idealism which he ever preaches and praises. But so complete and perfect are they that the art is hidden. They are like to nature in nature's highest naturalness. His is an art which is free from cycles and zones. It comes as near the universal in time and nation as can be given. It is Greek.

In the style in which these great themes are treated is a largeness, a freedom, an amplitude which belongs to nature and its phenomena, and especially to the sea. The sea which entered into and remained in Woodberry was the atmosphere in which he ever thought and wrote. The horizons are far-off, and the paths to these horizons are numberless. Such a style, of course, necessarily lends itself to the dignities, to the nobilities, to the worthiest glories, of literature. The exact phrase is built into the well-wrought sentence. The sentence, completed and complete, is laid as polished stone to stone into the self-sufficient paragraph. The noble paragraph is united with the interpretative and quickening chapter of the cathedral-like volume.

In writing thus of his work and of the man, I conclude with yet another interpretation which seems to me to be elemental and fundamental. It concerns the deepest, broadest, highest relation. It is the element which appeals to me representing the secret of this man. By no means am I sure I have caught the clue. Others will find another talisman of the labyrinth.

To me, however, the secret of Woodberry is spelled by the word—love.

The word has at least two connotations: good will and sentiment. In each of these meanings the word applies to Woodberry. Good will was a permanent, constructive element of his manhood, and also the sentiment of love was fundamental and formative. It was a godly gift of a godly ancestry. Sentiment was, further, a personal mood. Good will, too, was a personal mood. Both formed the atmosphere of his soul; both belonged to his writing as well as to his character.

The good will and the sentiment took on frequently the form of deepest sympathy with man, sympathy with man in his lifelong centuries of sufferings, sufferings inflicted by nature and by brother. Hear this, taken from one of the closing paragraphs of the essay *Taormina:* ''Sum it all, pang by pang, all that Etna ever wrought of woe to the sons of men, the agonies of her burnings, the terrors of her living entombments, all her manifold deaths at once, and what were it in comparison with the blood that has flowed on this hillside, the slaughter, the murder, the infinite pain here suffered at the hands of man.''

Evidence for this general conclusion of the secret of Woodberry's life and work is of many sorts and is cast in diverse molds. Perhaps the most moving of the confirmations is found in his poetry, poetry as diverse as *The North Shore Watch,* as the *Phi Beta Kappa Poem,* and as the sonnets of *Ideal Passion.*

The North Shore Watch is in memoriam to a youth
by a youth. It is Tennyson again writing of
"A. H. H." I do not quote, for I should yield to the
temptation of excess. But from the *Phi Beta Kappa*
poem I extract the simple line, "Now he is gone, O
how the heart grows still!" The forty-two sonnets
of *Ideal Passion* give evidence too which is indeed
proof. Out of them I select lines from the thirteenth
and the thirty-seventh:

"Love opened to me the deep infinite,
  Sphere beyond sphere, seas after rolling seas;
Where swam the world, my soul companioned it,
  And in its comprehension was my peace;
On the eternal vague did, brooding, sit,
  And from creation knew not how to cease."

"But so doth love within my bosom swell,
And in my eyes such wondrous tidings are,
I kneel, expectant of what heaven shall tell."

A field quite unlike the imaginative gives further
evidence and illustration. It lies in the feeling of,
and for, the race. The importance of the race belongs
to Woodberry's evaluation of literature; but it also
belongs to his personal affection for humanity, for
humanity in its diverse zones and diverse castes. The
depressions which the Great War gave to his spirit
are perhaps the saddest proof. Art, moreover,
broadly and intensely human, bears its individual-
ized messages and applications. "Each school, each
age, each race has its own art, often highly indi-

vidualized and peculiar to itself." One of these applications is found in his address on Wendell Phillips, given at the first meeting of the Woodberry Society in 1911. Woodberry declares that Wendell Phillips was "one of the masters of my life—the ideal American." Wendell Phillips stood for the negro as a suffering slave, as a free citizen, as an aspiring spirit.

The sentiment and the will of love, be it also said, were consistent with another feeling, which is often found in highly organized poetic natures: It is the feeling which is called moodiness. For Woodberry was at times a creature of moods. In fact, one of his dearest friends, of fifty years, writes me that he was the victim of "moody moods." But, be it at once said, such moods were not characteristic. Be it also affirmed that his friends looked, and rejoiced to look, above and beyond the occasional cloud and storm to the starry firmament of the man himself. For the man himself lived for, of, and by love, both as a good will and as an emotion.

To one further source of support of love as standing for the secret, I turn at once, and with reluctant eagerness. It is found in personal letters. Scores of the letters written through many years have I read; some written to me, some written to friends even more intimate. Not a few of them are so self-revealing, so full of feeling, that after much reflection they were not printed as was first proposed in the biography of one of the dearest of his friends, Henry T.

Finck. With what affection does he write of "Allie" Wheeler, of Charlie Barrows, of "Jim" Byrne, and of "Dick" Norton. "I suppose you noticed Dick Norton's death in Paris. He was one of the loveliest souls I ever knew, and, thank heaven, I knew him long." (Letter of 1918.) The affection for the father was continued in the son. Near his last birthday he wrote to a friend, saying, "It's nice to feel the atmosphere of love round once in awhile." The letters teem with special affection for his boys who fell in the Great War. They are voices out of the past, both near and far away, all speaking the deepest of love, of sentiment and of good will.

What beauty was to Keats, what love was to Shelley, that was love to Woodberry. Other principles and other elements were also constant and constituent. A sense of justice possessed him. Though he felt that he had suffered injustice at a crisis in his life, the feeling neither hardened his heart nor seared his conscience. In idealism he lived. Art was his passion. Truthfulness was an ideal. Duty was his master. But pervading his whole being, constructive as a force, conscious and unconscious, guiding as a star in the darkness, a support in the daily task, was the principle, the mood of love. "The greatest of these is love."

III
ARTHUR JAMES BALFOUR

BORN July 25, 1848; died March 19, 1930; educated at Eton, and Trinity College, Cambridge; in 1874, he became M. P. in the Conservative interest for Hertford and represented that constituency until 1885; 1878, became private secretary to Lord Salisbury, foreign minister, and accompanied him to the Berlin Congress. Released by the general election of 1880, he began to take a rather active part in parliamentary affairs. In 1886, was appointed secretary for Scotland with a seat in the cabinet; later appointed chief secretary to Ireland; 1891, he became first lord of the Treasury and leader of the House of Commons. During the illness of Lord Salisbury in 1898, and again in Lord Salisbury's absence abroad, in charge of the foreign office. In 1902, became prime minister; resigned on Dec. 4, 1905. Elected for the City of London in 1910 by enormous majority; announced his decision to resign Nov. 8, 1911; 1915, became First Lord of the Admiralty under Asquith; 1916, appointed foreign secretary under Lloyd George; April, 1917, head of the British mission which visited America in order to arrange for regular coöperation between the two countries; invited to address the House of Representatives on May 5. In 1920 appointed chief representative of the British government at the first assembly of the League of Nations, and also at the international conference in Washington, D. C., in 1921-22. In 1922, created an earl; resigned office.

Author: Defence of Philosophic Doubt; Essays and Addresses; The Foundations of Belief; Theism and Thought, a Study in Familiar Beliefs.

III

ARTHUR JAMES BALFOUR

COMMONER, ARISTOCRAT

A DECADE ago at the Travellers' Club in London I was presented by a family friend to Arthur James Balfour. As Balfour passed on I said to my friend, "We in America think that that man has the best brain in England." His reply was, "We in England think so too." He had a right to think and to say so, for his was the judgment of an experienced statesman.

It was the right, perhaps even the duty, of Balfour to have such a brain. How could he avoid such a gift of nature? For Arthur James Balfour was a part of the Cecil family. The family of Cecil has for almost four hundred years been a power, and a power of many sorts, in the government of the British people. The devotion to affairs of state, the quiet courage of matured convictions, the influence of official position, the strength of character belonging to rich personalities, have been illustrated in the family in each generation. Even as I write this paragraph I hear of a Cecil taking a first-rate prize at Oxford. In

55

Arthur James Balfour the great qualities of his great family were incarnated.

The course or method of his education was almost as inevitable as were his personal inheritances and abilities. To Eton he went as a boy of fourteen. Eton did not give to him what it gives to boys at the present time, an accurate knowledge of Latin and Greek. For many years after he left Eton, and when indeed as chancellor of Cambridge, in conferring degrees he put a false quantity on the word *doctoris*. But more important than false or true quantities in Latin citation, Eton did give to him a worth far greater than an acquaintance with classical syntax or even literature. Eton gave to him four friends, three of whom are known as Lansdowne, Cawdor, and Rosebery. The fourth in the quartette was his tutor, the brilliant and fairly unknown William Johnson. Johnson was one of the score of assistant masters of the upper school. Balfour acknowledged that it was to Johnson he owed the opening of his mind. Of Eton and of Eton education he afterward said "as natural, and therefore as inexplicable, a growth of our English soil as the British Constitution itself." [1]

From Eton, in 1866, Balfour went to Trinity College, Cambridge. At Cambridge the chief experience lay in coming under the direct and personal influence of Henry Sidgwick, Sidgwick who was to be his brother-in-law. (It may be noted that Sidgwick also had great influence over William Everett.) Of Sidg-

[1] London *Times* Educational Supplement, March 22, 1930.

wick's power he himself has written at length. It is
a passage which deserves full quotation, both for
personal and general academic reasons. "My philosophic equipment when I first became his pupil was
but slender—being, indeed, little more than what I
had acquired at Eton for my own entertainment. Nor
did I find it easy to increase this modest stock of
learning by attendance at ordinary lectures, which
others besides myself have found a somewhat irksome
and ineffectual means of increasing knowledge. Few
teachers would, in these circumstances, have taken
either much trouble or the right kind of trouble with
so unsatisfactory a pupil, and certainly any teacher
would have been justified in leaving me to my own
devices. Fortunately for me Henry Sidgwick took a
more tolerant view. In addition to his other lectures
he had at that time a small class for those specially
interested in the metaphysical side of the 'moral
sciences' Tripos, a class so small indeed that it consisted, if I remember right, only of one other student
besides myself. We met in Sidgwick's own rooms.
The teaching was largely in the nature of conversa-
tional discussion; and though I cannot, at this distance of time, recall it in detail, I retain a vivid recol-
lection of the zest with which these hours were
enjoyed.

"This was partly due to the method which Sidgwick adopted. In the first place we were allowed to
forget that we were preparing for an examination, an
oblivion which may or may not be desirable in other

branches of study, but is almost essential if the pleasures of speculation are to be enjoyed without alloy.

"In the second place he did not unduly force upon us the historic method of studying philosophy. The history of thought is doubtless of the first importance to the philosopher as well as the historian, but its importance is secondary and derivative. Nor is it likely to be fully appreciated by the youthful student. To him the subtleties of metaphysics are mere weariness unless the problems he is asked to consider are problems which he wants to solve. What some eminent person thought two hundred or two thousand years ago, and why he thought it, are matters which seem of small moment unless and until their bearing on the questions which call for an answer to-day becomes more or less apparent. This, at least, was my own feeling at the time; and either because he agreed with the sentiment or because he thought it wise to take account of it in dealing with his juniors, Sidgwick never drove us into those arid regions of speculation where, to the modern mind, the arguments seem without cogency and the conclusions without interest.

"I greatly regret that at this distance of time I am not able to give the precise details of his method of teaching. This is partly due to a very defective memory, but partly also to the fact that the relation of tutor and pupil rapidly ripened into a warm personal friendship; and I find it quite impossible to

disentangle the impressions he left on me, and to
assign some to official teaching, others to private conversation. But this is, I think, in itself a high tribute
to his qualities as a teacher. What most people want
in order to do their best is recognition; and the kind
of recognition from a distinguished man of eight-and-
twenty which is most valued by a boy of eighteen is
the admission that his difficulties are worth solving,
his objections worth answering, his arguments worth
weighing. This form of conveying encouragement
came naturally to Sidgwick. Of all the men I have
known he was the readiest to consider every controversy and every controversialist on their merits. He
never claimed authority; he never sought to impose
his views; he never argued for victory; he never
evaded an issue. Whether these are the qualities
which best fit their possessor to found a 'school' may
well be doubted. But there can be no doubt whatever
that they contributed to give Sidgwick a most potent
and memorable influence, not so much over the opinions as over the intellectual development of any
who had the good fortune to be associated with him,
whether as pupil or as friend. I was doubly happy
in that I was both." [2]

This passage serves to intimate what, after nature's
gift, served to make the mind of Arthur James
Balfour.

There were also other personalities or groups of

[2] *Henry Sidgwick—A Memoir* by A. S. and E. M. S., pp.
309-311.

personalities which made rich contributions. The first in time, as well as in worth, was his mother. Balfour's mother died at the age of forty-seven. Her death was, as he says, an irreparable loss. To her he declares his debt was the greatest. It was at the home in Whittingehame in East Lothian, where he was born and where he is buried, that she lived from the time of her marriage to her death. "It was there that she brought up her eight children, all of whom came into the world between 1845 and 1854. It was there that through sixteen years of failing health she devoted herself with the most enlightened energy to their welfare, and the welfare of all connected with the estate. Our debt to her is incalculable; and it is largely through the working of her spirit that the close-knit continuity of our family life remained unbroken by her death, and has so remained to the time of her great-grandchildren." [3] His debts to his friends computed, however, as one will "are as nothing compared to what I owe to her love, her teaching, and her example." [4]

But as he intimates in the making of his mind Balfour does give a large and vital place to his friends and family associates. These friends and associates formed the best of Cambridge life of the middle decades of the century. Lord Rayleigh, like Sidgwick, a brother-in-law, his own brother Frank, Professor of Morphology, and a brother Gerald, a Fellow, were

[3] *Chapters of Autobiography* by Arthur James, First Earl of Balfour, edited by Mrs. Edgar Dugdale, p. 3.
[4] *Ibid.*, p. 68.

among these formative influences. For no less than
fifty years members of his family held great posts
and had vital influences in the University of Cambridge. But his friends, too, outside the family made
worthy contributions. He says, ''Not the least important elements in the educational machinery of an English public school are the boys; and not the least important elements in the educational machinery of an
English University are the undergraduates.'' [5] Among
these friends were Austen-Leigh, a Fellow of King's,
and afterward its Provost, George Darwin, Spencer
Lyttelton, and indeed other members of the great
family all of whom save one were of Eton and Cambridge.

But life itself above every other force gave education to Balfour. Life touched him at every point,
intellectual, æsthetic, social, ethical, religious. Every
noble force and every noble condition of English society made its offerings. To that society he gave
much, as well as received much from it. There was a
sort of contemporaneous or coöperative giving forth
from him and a coming into him of the diverse
wealths of English and Scottish life. His was a mind
full, as his was a manhood rich, to give and to
receive.

At the first meeting or other meetings of Balfour,
one had a certain deep feeling, and a feeling rather
more than a definite idea, though the idea was not
lacking as a chief element—the feeling was that this

[5] *Ibid.*, p. 33.

man is a great gentleman, a great gentleman in whom
rich traditions and inheritances are lodged, for
whom the noblest places in life are reserved, not by
his claims, but rather by conferrings which he could
not avoid. Dignity of manner was joined with simplicity, the dignity was as remote from assumption
as it was from apparent humility. Consideration
of your intellect and of heart was manifest, without
any intimation of condescension. Suavity without
softness, seriousness without gloominess, a noble trifling without trivialness, self-possession without coldness, sympathy without effusiveness, respect for the
other man consistent with self-respect, and a gentleness which seemed to spell a certain form of greatness, were both visible and audible. All these intimations give evidence that Balfour was rather a
thinker than an executive, rather a philosopher than
an administrator, as one devoted rather to reflection
on life's and death's infinite problems than as one
who, glorying in achievement, sought to solve them.
The instinctive judgment was that he was not simply
a nature's nobleman, but also a nobleman of humanity.

Balfour's written and spoken words concerning
subjects of fundamental values and of vast variety
are as windows which let one behold and interpret
that mind. Primarily it was a philosophic mind. Its
interest in philosophy began early. As he himself
says, "It has been continuously in my mind—I've
worked at it off and on—well! since I was at Eton.

No! really *before* Eton, I believe I began muddling about with those ideas. You know—when I look back at myself, I'm appalled by how little I have changed in eighty years." [6]

One might call his the English philosophic mind. English philosophy is not given to the development of distinguished and distinct schools of philosophy as is the German mind. Balfour had no such allegiance to any one school as Haldane had for Hegel. His reason and his reasoning were rather of a general type which found truth in the experimental school of Locke and of Mill, as well as in certain types of idealism. Of the reason he himself says, "there can yet be no doubt that reason is, or appears to be, the cause over which we have the most direct control, or rather the one which we most readily identify with our own free and personal action. We are acted on by authority. It moulds our ways of thought in spite of ourselves, and usually unknown to ourselves. But when we reason we are the authors of the effect produced. We have ourselves set the machine in motion. For its proper working we are ourselves immediately responsible." [7] Of reason also in a practical way he says, "To Reason is largely due the growth of new and the sifting of old knowledge; the ordering, and in part the discovery, of that vast body of systematised conclusions which constitute so large a portion of scientific, philosophical, ethical, political, and theo-

[6] *Ibid.*, Foreword, p. xii.
[7] *The Mind of Arthur James Balfour.* Selected and arranged by Wilfrid M. Short, p. 21.

logical learning. To Reason we are in some measure beholden, though not, perhaps, so much as we suppose, for hourly aid in managing so much of the trifling portion of our personal affairs entrusted to our care by Nature as we do not happen to have already surrendered to the control of habit. By Reason also is directed, or misdirected, the public policy of communities within the narrow limits of deviation permitted by accepted custom and tradition. Of its immense indirect consequences, of the part it has played in the evolution of human affairs by the disintegration of ancient creeds, by the alteration of the new external conditions of human life, by the production of new moods of thought, or, as I have termed them, psychological climates, we can in this connection say nothing. For these are no rational effects of reason; the causal nexus by which they are bound to reason has no logical aspect; and if reason produces them, as in part it certainly does, it is in a manner indistinguishable from that in which similar consequences are blindly produced by the distribution of continent and ocean, the varying fertility of different regions, and the other material surroundings by which the destinies of the race are modified.'' [8]

With Balfour's allegiance to the reason is to be joined his loyalty to authority. Authority and reason he calls rival claimants. Yet he adds, ''we must not forget that it is Authority rather than Reason to which, in the main, we owe, not religion only, but

[8] *Ibid.*, pp. 29-30.

ethics and politics; that it is Authority which supplies us with essential elements in the premises of science; that it is Authority rather than Reason which lays deep the foundations of social life; that it is Authority rather than Reason which cements its superstructure. And though it may seem to savour of paradox, it is yet no exaggeration to say, that if we would find the quality in which we most notably excel the brute creation, we should look for it, not so much in our faculty of convincing and being convinced by the exercise of reasoning, as in our capacity for influencing and being influenced through the action of Authority.'' [9] Yet, while Balfour thus acknowledged the value of authority, it is proper to ask who is to judge of the authoritativeness and authenticity of authority? Is not the reason the supreme court of interpretation and of decision?

Of the general philosophic worth of the mind of Balfour, William James wrote to his brother, Henry, April 26, 1895, saying, ''I have been reading Balfour's 'Foundations of Belief' with immense gusto. . . . If I mistake not, it will have a profound effect eventually, and it is a pleasure to see old England coming to the fore every time with some big stroke. There is more real philosophy in such a book than in fifty German ones of which the eminence consists in heaping up subtleties and technicalities about the subject. . . . B. is a great man.'' [10]

[9] *Ibid.*, p. 31.
[10] *Letters of William James.* Edited by his son, Henry James, II., p. 20.

In the judgments, beliefs, and believings of Balfour, there stands fundamentally an acknowledgment of a Supreme Being. ''When once we have realised the scientific truth that at the root of every rational process lies an irrational one; that reason, from a scientific point of view, is itself a natural product; and that the whole material on which it works is due to causes, physical, physiological, and social, which it neither creates nor controls, we shall (as I showed just now) be driven in mere self-defence to hold that, behind these non-rational forces, and above them, guiding them by slow degrees, and, as it were, with difficulty, to a rational issue, stands that Supreme Reason in whom we must thus believe, if we are to believe in anything.'' [11] He also says, ''For they worship One Who is no remote contriver of a universe to whose ills He is indifferent. If they suffer, did He not on their account suffer also? If suffering falls not always on the most guilty, was He not innocent? Shall they cry aloud that the world is ill-designed for their convenience, when He for their sakes subjected Himself to its conditions? It is true that beliefs like these do not in any narrow sense resolve our doubts nor provide us with explanations. But they give us something better than many explanations. For they minister, or rather the Reality behind them ministers, to one of our deepest ethical needs;

[11] *The Mind of Arthur James Balfour,* selected and arranged by Wilfrid M. Short, pp. 355-56.

to a need which, far from showing signs of diminu-
tion, seems to grow with the growth of civilisation,
and to touch us ever more keenly as the hardness of
an earlier time dissolves away." [12]

The exponent and the origin of such theoretical
understanding and faith is the Bible itself. Speaking
of the increasing knowledge which the modern world
has of the history of the Jewish people and of the
Roman Empire at the time of the beginning of the
Christian Church, Balfour says, "These researches
make it far more a living record of the Revelation of
God to mankind than it ever was or ever could be
to those who, from the nature of the case, had no adequate conception of the circumstances under which
that Revelation occurred, or the peoples to whom it
was revealed. And I most truly think that not only
is the Bible now, what it has always been to the
unlearned, a source of consolation, of hope, of instruction, but it is to those who are more learned
—but not probably nearer the kingdom of heaven—
it is to them augmented in interest, and not dimin-
ished, a more valuable source of spiritual life now
than it could ever have been in the precritical
days." [13]

Yet, in addition to the Bible, Balfour expressly
declares that ecclesiastical organization and organizations are necessary and inevitable in the Christianity of the present time. He says, "I have for myself

[12] *Ibid.*, p. 368.   [13] *Ibid.*, p. 67.

to face the fact, and I do face it, that Christendom is and must remain ecclesiastically divided, that the Churches into which it is divided are necessary for the spiritual welfare of the world, and that what we have to do is to be able to see, beyond the separate organisation to which we all belong, the greater whole of which we are all members.'' [14]

Of his own personal faith there is a record remaining, written by Lady Frances Balfour, which is more profoundly significant than any confession which I have found of his own making. For, she declares, that for a mind and heart and character of the type which he incarnated, it was only a great spiritual belief which could have provided a foundation and an inspiring force. He valued the sacramental observances and the worth of prayer. '' 'I like to hear anyone is praying for me,' he said heartily once when I told him how prevailing prayer was constantly being offered for him. In life's fretful way, when quarrels arose, in public and private life, his own attitude was always Christian. . . . He was no professor of vain words, but whenever a thing of good report came in his way one saw how his spirit rejoiced in it. Example is more than precept, and in a world that mourns him as a dearly beloved brother every one who knew him must feel today that he was a great follower of the one perfect Pattern of all mankind.'' [15]

[14] *Ibid.,* p. 76.
[15] *The British Weekly,* March 27, 1930, p. 551.

For the purpose of this personal study it is proper to say that one of the most important of all the works of Balfour was his endeavor in behalf of education. The subject of education of every sort in England has called forth debate formal and informal for hundreds of years. In the endeavor progress has been made, but it has been a progress quite akin to the method of progress in political and civil liberty. It has been marked by deviousness, slowness, regressiveness, recriminations personal, political, ecclesiastical. Lack of efficient organization and administration, lack of good teaching have been permanent characteristics. Of Balfour's contribution to the great endeavor for reconstruction and improvement the *Times* said editorially, ''These changes all spring from Balfour's philosophic conception of the unity of all education and his singular administrative and statesmanlike ability, which, with the suavity of complete conviction, managed by the sheer effort of personality to place the Acts of 1899 and 1902 and 1903 on the Statute-book. Balfour stood above politics in this matter of education. He appealed to the reasonableness of political thinkers and administrators, and his reward is that at the present time we have the best educational machinery in the world, and should have after the next twenty years that educated democracy which he longed for. Balfour lifted education out of the range of party politics, and it is the duty of succeeding statesmen, of whatever political complexion, to keep it free of party. This will be his best memorial." [16]

In the traditional neglect of education as a progressive force, such commendation has the worth of prophecy well fulfilled. The fulfillment becomes more and most significant when the fierce opposition to the Educational Bills of 1895-6-7 is considered. His triumph was the consummation of educational labors of a century and the new birth of unending progress.

If Balfour belonged to the last decades of the nineteenth and the first decade of the twentieth century in respect to progressive educational policies, he belonged to the Victorian decades in respect to literary tastes. Indeed it might be said that he belonged to the pre-Victorian age. For with the makers of the literature of the mid-decades of the nineteenth century he had small sympathy. Wordsworth and Shelley were dearer to him than Tennyson and Browning. Miss Austen was also to him more appealing than either Thackeray or Dickens. Carlyle was a voice, and only a voice, loud and rather empty, and John Henry Newman was unimpressive. Books were indeed to him what Bacon says of them: "Some books are to be tasted, others to be swallowed, and some few to be chewed and digested."

I began this interpretation of Balfour with an al-

[16] The London *Times* Educational Supplement, March 29, 1930, p. 143.

lusion to his intellectual gifts and powers.[17] As I draw the interpretation to a close I ask myself, what were the weaknesses, the faults, the defects of this man? For to these defects and weaknesses neither the reader nor the writer is to be blind. The answer is awaiting my pen. The weakness is not found in the intellect in and of itself. It does lie in the relation which the intellect bears to other personal forces and gifts. The solidity of the intellect exists in disproportion to the weight of the emotions. The intellectual perceptions were more sensitive than the feelings, and the judgment more weighty than the affec-

---

[17] *Punch* for March 26, 1930, just a week after Balfour's death, printed these verses by "O. S.":

Not the desire of fame—he cared for none,
  Who better loved the Muses' shadowed glades—
Drew him to face the arena's dust and sun
  And the clash of ringing blades.

To put his knightly honour to the proof,
  This was the call that made his destiny clear—
Service that claimed a mind serene, aloof,
  And a heart too great for fear.

No triumph moved his spirit's inward calm;
  Lightly he met defeat and paid the cost,
Content that other hands should bear the palm
  So the game were clearly lost.

Noble of manners, touched with nothing base,
  He, when his bright lance laid a rival low,
"Forbore his own advantage"; such the grace
  That has passed and left no foe.

And we, whose wondering pride the charm confessed
  Of that fine courtesy of speech and thought,
We bring the tribute, where he lies at rest,
  Of a love he won unsought.

tions. The thinking power mastered the feelings. The intellectual overcame the emotional. The feelings were not lacking. They were present in quite as great a force or warmth as they are found in most men; yet the intellect was so much greater, its rationalizing processes so much more constructive, the gifts of the mind so much richer than are found in most of us, that in him the lack of proportion, the lack of harmony, the want of proper co-working, resulted. He might be called a saunterer, but rather an emotional than an intellectual one. This lack of heart led to an apparent lack of conviction concerning certain of life's fundamental conditions. It created a seeming indifference, or possibly superciliousness. I am told by one who was present at a conference of the leaders, military and political, held in March, 1918, that a dispatch came in saying that the Germans had a free way to the Channel ports. Balfour was present in this conference. Hearing the statement, he said, ''How very annoying.'' Of course such a remark made in some conditions may be called self-poise. But it is open to the charge of either indifference or superciliousness.

The dominance of the intellectual forces finds special evidence in his desire for knowledge. Pure science in its broadest as well as in its narrow relation meant to him far more than poetry, and applied science more than criticism. Of course philosophy in its largest connotation remained his chief interest. He once said, it is reported, ''I would rather be known as having added something to our knowledge of truth and nature than for anything else I could imagine.'' The Harvard motto of *Veritas* would have been a proper word to surround his coat of arms.

It is also apparent to some that Balfour lacked sympathy with, and some would say he even had a certain quiet contempt for, the average man. This impression probably arose, at least in part, from his keeping his heart to himself. He gave much, but he some way failed to give himself. The indifferent feeling served to make him a mere dialectician. It intimated without creating the cynic. A great debater in great causes, he believed in and represented the imponderables. But these imponderables were far more intellectual than emotional. He was a gentleman devoted to affairs philosophic, he was a metaphysician devoted to affairs human. He was the type of public servant and of the gentleman which English society creates and nourishes. A public committee, of which he was for several years chairman, at the conclusion of their common service presented to him a large and beautiful piece of plate, bearing this inscription of gratitude and appreciation: ''For his wisdom, fairness, and sweet reasonableness.'' The words are an epitome of his manhood and noble service.

The interpretation of Balfour suggests likenesses and contrasts with two of his great contemporaries and co-workers: Bryce and Morley.

Balfour was a statesman who chose philosophy as an avocation; Bryce was a humanist and an interpreter, to whom politics was a form of man's supreme interest and devotion; Morley was a critic to whom humanity was a subject of analysis, to whom great men like Gladstone and Burke were to be weighed in the balances of noble appreciation. Balfour's mind was deepest in its thinkings; Bryce's broadest in its knowledges and reflections; Morley's of the keenest cutting edge. Balfour's family was, as a family, the more distinguished; Bryce and Morley belonged to democracy. Balfour seemed to move in a world of his own making, though not selfishly; Bryce lived with and for men, an altruist; Morley ever seemed to be reflecting on great men and greater movements, trying to fathom their secrets. Each was more of a writer than a speaker. Balfour bestowed a favor graciously; Bryce rejoicingly; Morley freely. Balfour was more at home in the cabinet, Bryce in the world, Morley in the library. Bryce's face was probably the best known of any face in and to the whole world. Each was a moralist, an embodied conscience, and in each imagination was a part of the intellectual gift and equipment.

Balfour was to be honored; Morley to be admired; Bryce to be loved. No children carry forward their names: Balfour was unmarried; Bryce married late in life; Morley was a stepfather and dearly beloved. They each will live in the future development of the British Constitution and in the great human results which the last decades of the nineteenth and the first of the twentieth century transmit to the enduring future of humanity.

IV

WILLIAM HOWARD TAFT

BORN in Cincinnati, Sept. 15, 1857; died March 8, 1930. Received B.A., Yale, 1878 (2d in class of 121, salutatorian and class orator); LL.B., Cincinnati Law School, 1880, dividing 1st prize; LL.D., Yale, 1893; admitted to Ohio bar, 1880; practiced law at Cincinnati, 1883-87; assistant county solicitor of Hamilton Co., 1885-87; judge Superior Court, Cincinnati, 1887-90; solicitor-general of United States, 1890-92; U. S. circuit judge, 6th circuit, 1892-1900; professor and dean of law department, University of Cincinnati, 1896-1900; president of U. S. Philippine Commission, March 12, 1900-July 4, 1901; first civil governor of P. I., 1901-1904; sent to Rome by President Roosevelt, 1902, to confer with Pope Leo XIII concerning purchase of agricultural lands of religious orders in the P. I.; twice declined appointment from President Roosevelt as associate justice Supreme Court of U. S., 1903; Secretary of War in cabinet of President Roosevelt, 1904-1908; sent to Cuba by President Roosevelt to adjust insurrection, 1906, and acted as provisional governor; in March and April, 1907, visited Panama, Cuba and P. R., by direction of the President. Elected President Nov. 3, 1908; renominated for the Presidency, June, 1912; defeated in November election. Kent professor of law, Yale, 1913-21; appointed Chief Justice of the U. S., June 30, 1921.

Author: Popular Government, Its Essence, Its Permanence and Its Perils; Four Aspects of Civic Duty; The Anti-Trust Act and the Supreme Court; The United States and Peace.

IV

WILLIAM HOWARD TAFT

FRIEND, HUMORIST, PHILOSOPHER

WILLIAM HOWARD TAFT belies the ancient proverb of counting no man happy till his death. For though happy in death, he was also happy in life.

Taft was blessed with an education regular in its methods and rich in its content. His was an education complete, given under normal forms and best conditions. In it were found neither experiments nor short cuts. Educational experiments, rewarding as they may be in the ultimate improvement of the theories of education, are liable to be damaging to those who are experimented upon—the victims. Taft, preparing for college in the first-rate high schools of his native and historic city of Cincinnati, entered Yale College as a student in 1874. Yale was perhaps the college best fitted to educate a boy from Cincinnati, and especially a boy whose name was Taft. For his father had taken the A.B. degree at Yale in 1838, and to Yale he sent no less than five sons. Yale is indeed more akin to the spirit of the West than its companion historic college, Harvard. For Yale represents social democracy. It stands for a collective society and for coöperative action. It embodies a continuing and firm faith in religion. It speaks the conservative note. Its historic companion on the banks of the Charles represents literature and culture, individualism, professiveness, experimentation. In the year 1841 Professor Kingsley of New Haven wrote to his colleague, Professor Silliman, ''I am not bigoted in my attachment to old plans of study; nor am I disposed to be caught with every novelty. Let them at Cambridge try experiments, and we will try to profit by them. They are better able to experiment than we are.'' [1] If Harvard stood, as it still stands, for independence and for criticism, given as well as received, Yale has stood, and still stands, for uniformity. If Harvard has been interpreted as especially a Massachusetts and New England college, Yale has stood for the West. Young Yales have been founded in many a Western state. Western Reserve College at Hudson even modeled its dormitories after the dormitories at New Haven. New colleges of the West filled their faculties with Yale graduates. It was, therefore, normal, natural, inevitable that William Howard Taft should become a student at Yale. It may be also added that the continuity of tradition which Yale embodied was needed in the new West. The democracy of Yale, too, fitted into the democratic spirit of Taft himself. In Yale's class of 1878 Taft was graduated

[1] *Life of Benjamin Silliman,* by George P. Fisher, Vol. I, p. 401.

as second scholar,[2] as his brother Peter was the first.

While Taft was pursuing his undergraduate course at Yale from 1874 to 1878, another American with whom he was to have relations most important, both intimate and remote, was a student at Harvard from 1876 to 1880, Theodore Roosevelt. Roosevelt was pursuing studies quite unlike the conservative curriculum of Taft. "Just one-half of Roosevelt's total elective work was devoted to natural history, almost a third to modern languages, but not a single [elective] hour did he give to Latin or Greek, not a single [elective] hour to English composition or history."[3] In a class of one hundred and sixty-one members, Roosevelt's rank was twenty-first. In a word, Roosevelt's studies represented a progressive or a scientific course, Taft's the conservative and classical. It is worthy to note that in three successive years, 1878, 1879, 1880, three successive and more outstanding Presidents of the United States received successively degrees from three of the most outstanding of American colleges. Wilson at Princeton in the year 1879 at once unites and divides Taft of Yale, and Roosevelt of Harvard.

[2] The early standard of scholastic grades was 4 or 400. 400 was the highest, or perfect. In the eighth decade of the last century any grade over 300 was, as Provost Charles Seymour writes me, absolutely first-class. Taft's records for the three terms of the Freshman year were 361, 362, 353. His grades of the three terms of the Sophomore year were 350, 339, 325. His grades for the three terms of the Junior year were 335, 339, 352. His average grade for the whole Senior year was 338.5, and the four-year average was 347.

[3] *Theodore Roosevelt as an Undergraduate.* By Donald Wilhelm, p. 26.

The contrasts in education of Taft and Roosevelt are intimations of the contrasts which belong to the later part of their political careers.

The normal and regular course of Taft's education was followed by a life also quite as normal and regular in its enlarging opportunities for public service. Each of these advancing opportunities seemed to await only the conclusion of the preceding. The record is indeed significant and impressive. From early practice of the law for five years, Taft was presently called to serve on the bench of the courts of his city and county. This service continued for eleven years. He also was professor and dean of the Cincinnati Law School. He was appointed Solicitor-General of the United States at the age of thirty-three. He became president of the Philippine Commission, and was made the first civil head of the government in the Philippines. He also served as Secretary of War. He was hardly more than thirty years out of college when he was elected President. His defeat for a second term for the Presidency was followed by his service as Kent Professor of Law at Yale. In 1921 he was appointed Chief Justice of the Supreme Court, and between these many and diverse offices, he also served the people in chairmanships and on commissions also diverse and numerous.

For Taft, as for two of his greater predecessors in the office of President, opportunities awaited as his powers increased. To Lincoln and to Grant there was offered a single opportunity. Into it each was prepared to

enter. For Taft the opportunities were the less significant as they were more numerous than the single
door which opened to Lincoln and to Grant. But the
members of this informal and diversely constituted
triumvirate were alike in one fundamental element:
they each sought to know and to do his duty. To know
and to do one's duty is the characteristic element of
the great ones of our English race. It belongs no less
to Robert Gould Shaw of the 54th Massachusetts
than to Nelson, sixty years before, at Trafalgar. Of
the offices offered to Taft, one, a service in the Philippines, he did not wish to accept, but, as he said to a
friend of mine, "What can I do? The President has
asked me to go." He obeyed, as he ever willingly
obeyed, the imperative. Whether certain offices were
attractive or repulsive, whether they were to be made
objects of ambition or of avoidance, was a consideration secondary in his sense of proportional values.

The maintenance of the sense of proportional
values was constructively aided by his sense of humor.
Examples of this happy resource will occur to the
reader. Let me refer to a single instance of which I
was both auditor and spectator. The occasion was a
great meeting in Cleveland in behalf of the cause of
peace. Taft was the chief speaker. In the course of
his address he referred to the refusal of the Senate
in his administration to ratify certain treaties which
had been negotiated. "But," he added, "in our disappointment we comforted ourselves with the assurance that a future Senate might ratify them, for

through the forth-coming elections the Senate might
be changed. But," he went on to say, and in advance
of the remark one could hear the prophetic chuckle,
"they didn't change the Senate. They changed me." *
Speaking of the defeat of his party and of himself in
the Election of 1912, he said he had retired from the
Presidency with the full consent of the American
people!

This sense of humor was one with his great-hearted-
ness. The emotional gift was at least as constructive
as his intellectual power. For if wit is a note of the
intellect, humor is of the heart. There was in him no
revengefulness, bickerings, backbitings of any sort.
One could not think of his heart, as one could not

* In a course of lectures given at Yale in 1913, on popular
government, he speaks of these treaties as follows: "But the
treaties were defeated. Sometimes I have been very much
disappointed, because I thought that their defeat was a retro-
grade step. Here we had two countries willing to go into a
very comprehensive peace treaty with us of general arbitration, and after they were made, the Senate defeated the plan.
If those nations could afford to make such treaties, why
couldn't we do so? Have we any interests that could be
prejudicially affected by such treaties more important to us
than their interests could be to them? Is not the real objec-
tion to be found in the feeling on the part of many Senators
that they are only in favor of arbitration when we can win
and not when we may lose? That is not sincere support of
the principle of arbitration.

"Still I think the making of the general arbitration treaties
and the discussion of them before the people have been useful, and that sometime in the future some other Executive
may have the good fortune to negotiate another such treaty
and to find a Senate not so sensitive as to its prerogative."
*Popular Government, Its Essence, Its Permanence, and Its
Perils.* By William Howard Taft, pp. 265-66.

think of his body, as having any type of smallness.
He was, indeed, capable of great indignations. But if
his friends knew of them, they also knew of his power
which restrained their expression. A big sense of
friendliness, and friendliness of a most informal nature and manner, clothed him as a large garment.
His friendliness created friendliness. Once I heard
him say that when he was in the Philippines, discouraged, more or less heartbroken over difficulties that seemed insurmountable, a message came
to him from his classmates, assembled in their commencement anniversary at Yale—"Bill, we are with
you."

In this friendliness, both as a formative cause and
as a happy consequence, was his sense of the boy. In
a way Taft never grew up. He was always a boy.
Fun was constructive. Playfulness belonged to him
no less as a grandfather than as a grandson. The
ermine might disguise his boyishness, but it also revealed it. His real kindness and graciousness gave
him a right to use his boyishness, as his power gave
him the right to have it, and as his essential dignity
preserved him from abusing it.

These qualities and elements lying in different zones
and of different proportional values were united in a
character which seems to me to deserve the adjective
comprehensive. Early in his career comprehensiveness became a characteristic, impressive and significant. In fact as early as the year 1901 Theodore
Roosevelt wrote, saying, "A year ago a man of wide

acquaintance both with American public life and American public men, remarked that the first Governor of the Philippines ought to combine the qualities which would make a first-class President of the United States with the qualities which would make a first-class Chief Justice of the United States, and that the only man he knew who possessed all these qualities was Judge William H. Taft of Ohio.'' [5] Such testimony given at the time had and still has rich meanings. It bears one ahead a dozen years—to the epoch of a personal crisis and division.

The comprehensiveness of Taft's character was especially manifest in his service to and through the government. His statesmanship represented service judicial, executive, and also as a party leader.

For Taft was what is called a party man. He believed in the party as a method of government in a democratic republic. The party was not an end of government, but was simply a means, method, force, for carrying on government. For in an address given to the students of Yale in 1913, he said, ''Popular government is impossible without parties. If you have 15,000,000 voters, and every voter is going to have a different view, or every voter differs from every other voter on something, and so they do not agree politically on anything, you will have a chaos that will result in simple negation. In a proper system of party government, the members of each party must agree on certain main doctrines in respect to governmental

[5] *The Outlook,* August, 1901.

policy and yield their views on the less important ones, in order that they may have united action, and in order that these main and controlling doctrines, when the party is successful at the election and controls the Government, may furnish the guide for governmental action. But parties can not be organized and can not give expression to their views without having leaders, captains, lieutenants and file leaders, without taking the advice of those leaders, and without being influenced by their leadership.'' * Despite the value of the party as a method of carrying on a democratic government, he yet believed that the interests of the two great parties in the American government were more or less identical. This identity would relate primarily to the fundamental concerns of the state. It might not relate to the minor interests. In a matter as constructive as the control of the Philippine Islands he said, as early as the year 1906, ''It is supposed that if the Democratic party comes into power it will give up the islands and turn them over to the control of the people who inhabit them. I venture to predict— although prediction is dangerous—that the Democratic party, should it come into power, would not assume this responsibility, but would proceed on practically the same lines as have been followed hitherto. Such a result would be desirable, because then it would be shown that both political parties were in favor of the policy which has been instituted, and that

* *Popular Government, Its Essence, Its Permanence, and Its Perils.* By W. H. Taft, pp. 29-30.

the people of our country would unite in a great and successful effort for the benefit of humanity." [7]

This breadth of understanding is also illustrated in his interpretation of the relative values of the conservative and of the progressive wings of the Republican party. While serving as Kent Professor of Law at Yale in the year 1913, he said, "Those of us who are thus unjustly classed [as reactionaries] must be content to be so until vindicated by the event. But we must fight for our principles and maintain them without fear, because unless we do, as I verily believe, our form of representative democracy will[8] be destroyed and its power to aid and maintain the happiness of the individual will cease.

"There is nothing to show that all legitimate governmental purposes sought by the so-called Progressives may not be promoted and brought about under the representative system. Admitting that it may be somewhat more slow in its results, it will insure wiser action in detail because of greater deliberation. Great reforms should not be brought about overnight. They need time. They should be marked by careful consideration." [8]

Yet perhaps the comprehensiveness of the character and statesmanship of Taft are most clearly illustrated in the weight of his argument and of the urgency of his appeal that America should enter the League of

[7] *Four Aspects of Civic Duty.* By William Howard Taft, pp. 88-89.
[8] *Popular Government, Its Essence, Its Permanence and Its Perils.* By W. H. Taft, pp. 37-38.

Nations. The argument and the appeal offer inspiring and conclusive evidence of the breadth of his understanding, of the depth of his feeling, and of the power of his will and conscience. To this League, he gave heartiest and constant support. In season and out of season, for the four years between 1915 and 1919, he labored to achieve his great purpose. With President Wilson and the executives and legislators, and before popular gatherings, he argued and he pleaded for America's entrance. The methods followed, as well as the goal of achievement, proved the comprehensiveness of his judgment as well as the fullness of the sincerity of his zeal.

In further evidence and illustration of the comprehensiveness of his understanding, as well as of the kindness of his heart, let me quote what his successor, Chief Justice Hughes, said of him before the Supreme Court on the first of June of the year 1931:

The Chief Justice said that "Mr. Taft, from the time he became solicitor general at the age of 33, until his death, exemplified the varied undertakings of grave responsibility, the finest type of public servant and enjoyed an increasing general esteem, until, in the closing years, after the wounds of political strife had been healed and the victories of a magnanimous spirit had been acclaimed, he was enriched beyond any man of his time with the wealth of a universal affection.

"He carried with him an invincible armor of kindliness against which the shafts of opponents had proved harmless. With him, service in the temple of justice was not an austere performance with the ill-grace of an unnatural aloofness, but a necessary human endeavor, with the dignity of lofty purpose, pursued with a benignity and an affection for his fellows which made his presence in that temple a constant benediction.'' [9]

Of course religion represents a broader field than democratic statesmanship, as infinity in both time and space is greater than the finite. The note of comprehensiveness is made most impressive in the evidence provided by his religious faith. Taft was an adherent of the most liberal of Protestant churches, the Unitarian. To the first act of the Apostles' Creed he could give assent—''I believe in God the Father Almighty.'' At the altar of the Unitarian church he paid his vows. The last rites were observed in the very church at which he had been for years a devout worshiper, and of which he was a constant supporter.

[9] Report in New York *Times,* June 2, 1931.

V

WALTER HINES PAGE

Born Cary, N. C., August 15, 1855; died December 22, 1918; student Randolph-Macon College, Virginia, 1872-76; fellow at Johns Hopkins, 1876-78. Editor of The Forum, 1890-95; literary adviser of Houghton Mifflin & Co., 1895-99; editor of The Atlantic Monthly, 1898-99, The World's Work, 1900-13; ambassador extraordinary and plenipotentiary to Great Britain, 1913-1918. Member of firm of Doubleday, Page & Co., publishers, 1899-1913. Trustee Gen. Edn. Board.

Author: The Rebuilding of Old Commonwealths; A Publisher's Confession; The Southerner.

V

WALTER HINES PAGE

AMBASSADOR, EDITOR, PATRIOT

THE word humanity in noun, verb, adjective, adverb, original in form, or derived, shortened or lengthened, takes on no less than a dozen meanings and relationships. It is, therefore, a word of the broadest, deepest, as well as most diverse, connotations. In many forms the word belongs to Walter Hines Page. For Page, born in North Carolina, lived and worked in New York and Boston; born in the country, he was urban by association and service; born in America, he became a world personality. A political democrat he was also, and more, a social democrat; a social democrat he was a great gentleman; a great gentleman he was also at home with all sorts and conditions of men. A man of silence and of solitude, in his friends he found his larger and largest self. For companionship and for conversation he had a deep and constant craving. Presidents, kings, governors of states, prime ministers, chancellors, were his friends, yet with the humblest he was at home. A maker of great magazines, he was also a publisher of books; a student at small colleges, he received degrees from outstanding universities; a philosopher, he was also an administrator; a joyous lover and helper of his kind, he spent

his last years in scenes and associations of deepest
sadness; a man of vision, he was also a master of detail; of great place and power, he was humble; robust,
he was gracious without condescension; warm of
heart, he was free from irrational sentimentalism; devoted to simple duty, he looked out on life with a
"Lucretian evenness" of mind; strong and valiant,
he had deep sympathy with the weak and the suffering; eager to help the feeble, if worthy, he had indignation for the dishonest and the mean. Walter Hines
Page was a humanist in all the meanings of the great
word.

Preparing at one time in his youth to be a
Unitarian minister, his career was devoted to literature in at least two forms, and he died as an ambassador of the American Republic to the British
Empire.

My first relation with this man of diverse and deep
relationships was as a contributor to the magazine of
which he was editor. The *Forum* was the means and
the method of our friendship. Page's idea of the
function of a monthly magazine was indicated in his
own words: "The magazine in the United States is the
best instrument that has yet been invented or developed or discovered for affecting public opinion in our
democracy. It gives the only way in which serious
men can continuously reach the whole reading public.
No newspaper goes many hundred miles from home.
Every newspaper is, therefore, dominantly local. Few
newspapers live longer than a day or a few days at

most. But the magazines reach practically the whole reading people, and the better of them have a life of at least a month, and many copies are preserved and read much longer. A serious man, therefore, is now put quickly within reach of everybody in the United States—everybody who reads. And this is not only a great fact, but it is a new fact in the world—that the magazine is of universal circulation."[1] Page held that a great editorship is a great trusteeship. "I hold a place in trust : it is not mine to use for my own personal ends nor for my personal friends. So at least I regard the editorship of the *Forum*."[2]

Page's service on and through the *Forum* was at once constructive in aim and form and optimistic in tone and atmosphere. No name, however great, was allowed to interfere with this constructive purpose and method. This comprehensive aim and atmosphere ruled. It overruled in even declining contributions from the more outstanding of editors and authors. He cared much for the contribution, he cared little for the contributor. For papers which were not constructive, or which failed to be optimistic, thoroughly hopeful in their tone, he had an editorial negative. To Mr. Godkin of the *Nation* and *Evening Post,* he wrote, reinforcing his declining to use an article, "Wherever you make application to our own conditions or tasks, you make the difficulties (as we think) so much greater than

[1] *The Training of an American.* The Earlier Life and Letters of Walter H. Page, 1855-1913. By Burton J. Hendrick, pp. 204-5.
[2] *Ibid.,* p. 219.

they are and give the whole paper so hopeless a tone
that its publication would strike a false note for us.
. . . I regard it my duty to give all help possible—not
shutting my eyes to faults and dangers, but not laying
too much emphasis on the difficulties: they are ob-
vious.'' [3]

Page wished to make the *Forum* his contribution to
human betterment. He sought to arouse the interest
of the independent thinkers and publicists. Yet certain changes in the ownership and resulting control of
the magazine resulted in his resignation. His resignation from the *Forum* was almost contemporaneous
with the receiving of an invitation to the editorship
of the *Atlantic Monthly*.

The qualities and the forces which contributed to
the making of the *Forum* a dominant influence in
American life were manifest in the *Atlantic* editorship of brief years, ending in 1899, and also in the
subsequent founding of the *World's Work*. Page's
successor in 1899 in the editorship of the *Atlantic* was
Bliss Perry. Years after Page resigned the *Atlantic*
editorship, Perry wrote him saying, ''I often sit here
. . . in leisure quarters of an hour, and wonder by
what extraordinary talent you rescued this magazine
from perdition. No one who has not seen something
of its inside history can appreciate how great a debt
the *Atlantic* owes to you for breathing into it the
breath of life. If it had not been for your impatient
energy in getting the magazine out of the ruts, the

[3] *Ibid.*, p. 215.

grass would be growing over its grave to-day.'' [4]
Page himself also said, "If I can find people with eyes
in the front of their heads and with daring enough,
who have anything to say, of course the magazine will
become such a power as it never was. The conditions
all exist—except the men. I have no more doubt that
a real man, if one were to rise in American literature,
would be hailed with such joy as men feel only when
a deliverer comes—of course the mere conventional-
ities and cowardices and provincial tempers all count
for nothing. I care less than nothing about them. I
live chiefly on the hope that the day will come before
I die when I may silently point to some national, sane
utterance and say 'That is it!'—beside which the little
gliding, mincing things that we now endure for lack
of bigger will be utterly forgotten—and instantane-
ously.'' [5] The tone of this quotation is exactly of the
intent of a remark which Page once made to me, "If
only I could know what people would be thinking of
three months from this time, what an editor I could
be!" He also confirmed the significance of the optimistic prophecy by saying once to me, "I have had a
thousand editorial comments upon an article I have
published in the *Forum*."

A similar purpose moved him in the founding of
the *World's Work* by the firm of which he was a member. The business side of the work of publication
made an appeal to him similar to that of the editorial.
His place in the quartette consisting of Doubleday,

[4] *Ibid.*, p. 234.   [5] *Ibid.*, p. 236.

McClure, John Finley and himself, which sought to reconstruct the fallen or falling firm of Harper and Brothers, was succeeded by the formation of the firm "Doubleday, Page and Co." The work of a publisher was united with the work of an editor. Of both these elements he wrote in saying, "My wish and aim . . . is to become a helpful partner of some of the men and women of my generation who can, by their writings, lay the great democracy that we all serve under obligations to them for a new impulse. By serving them I, too, serve my country and my time. And when I say that this is my aim and wish, I could say with equal truth that it is the aim and wish of every other real publisher. Of downright quacks in the publishing world, there are not many. But there are incompetents a-plenty and a fair share of adventurers. We shall both—authors and publishers—get the proper cue if we regard the swarming eager democracy all about us as a mass of constantly rising men and women, ambitious to grow, with the same higher impulses that we feel in our best moods; and if we interpret our duty as the high privilege of ministering to these higher impulses and not to their lower senses, without commercialism on one side and without academicism on the other, men among men, worthy among the worthy, we may make our calling under such a conception a calling that leads." [6]

High as were his purposes, constructive as were his methods, precious as were the results of his editor-

[6] *Ibid.,* p. 354.

ships and partnerships, yet this service was not to
prove to be the most efficient or the most enduring of
Page's life, methods and achievements. The final years
were to be consummations as well as finalities. These
conditions and forces were destined to make him a
partner in relationships and forces in a prolonged
crisis of the nations. Of these consummating years
Page had a far narrower vision than had the nations
themselves who were to be the participants in the
Great War. These years were years of many relationships, yet for my present purpose, be it emphasized,
they were years which gave to him a special association with two men. In the sixteen years preceding the
election of 1912, Page saw in Woodrow Wilson a
future President of the United States. The judgment
of these years was based upon a relationship to Wilson which began early in the career of each. This relationship was constantly surrounded by, or con-
structed of, an atmosphere of deep admiration, of
sturdy loyalty, and of high hopefulness. In the
months that passed between the election of 1912 and
the inauguration of 1913, Page was often named for
membership in the Cabinet either for the Department
of the Interior, or for the Department of Agriculture.
For neither portfolio was he ultimately selected. But
he was appointed to a place which proved to be far
more important than either, the Ambassadorship to
England.

The comparison of Page with a preceding minister
at the Court of St. James, Charles Francis Adams, is

evident and indeed almost compelling. For in the critical months previous to Lincoln's inauguration in 1861, Adams was often mentioned for a place in the Cabinet. The place most frequently associated with the name of the great Massachusetts son and statesman was the Secretaryship of State. Adams was not made Secretary of State, but he was made minister to the Court of St. James. For both Adams and Page the English mission proved to be quite as essential and useful as any Cabinet portfolio: it was a Secretaryship of State for the British Empire, or, some would add, for the nations of the world.

The bracketing of Adams and Page in the English mission suggests certain comparisons and certain contrasts. In origin and environment Adams was a Massachusetts man, son and grandson of a President; Page was of North Carolina, of honorable but not distinguished ancestry. Adams was a Harvard graduate; Page was a student of North Carolina country colleges. Adams was one with the best citizenship of Quincy, of Boston, of Massachusetts, of New England; Page was one with "the forgotten man" of the South. Adam's mind, like his body, was stout, strong, sturdy; Page's mind was enthusiastic, upreaching, and was a first-rate co-working force. The character of Adams was the resultant of two generations of striving and achievement (Henry Adams once said to me that his great-grandfather, John, was the ablest of the family); Page had to make his own way through life, but he also was an inspiring leader.

Adams was an Adams, and he knew, felt, and showed it; Page was humble. Adams was courtly, discreet, restrained, conservative; Page was direct, informal, simple, his heart suffusing the intellect. One thinks of Adams as sober-minded; one thinks of Page as bristling with fun. Adams was self-centered; Page, sympathetic and altruistic. Adams was the gentleman, cultivated and disciplined; Page, the man natural.

These contrasts, both fundamental and superficial, were surrounded by, and in part founded upon, likenesses. Each was a thorough American, though Page was accused (and unjustly) of Anglophobia. Both Adams and Page believed in and embodied intellectual orderliness. Each was gifted with a wisdom which recalls Burke's great definition. Each, after his own type, was a gentleman. Each was an optimistic interpreter of a national, bi-national, and international future, a future which, be it said, at times was dark and ominous. Each had robustness and ruggedness, Adams of the cultured Massachusetts Puritan type; Page of Lincoln and of Lincoln's commonwealth,— his face having, it is said, certain resemblances to the martyred President's. Each was gifted with independence of judgment, and each embodied duty incarnated. Adams was his own counselor; Page was frank and free in his utterance. In both writing and talk Adams touched life deeply; Page broadly. Adams seemed to love the past, Page was devoted to the future. Each recognized the value of religion as a constituent part of life and character, and each was intensely loyal to the American tradition. Page once said to me, "There is nothing in life but religion."

The government and the people to whom each was accredited were quite as unlike in their attitude to America as were the upbringing and character of the diplomats themselves. Adams met a government which was sympathetic with the Confederate cause, and a people whose mood was of allegiance to the North. Adams wrote to his son of his name under date of July 31, 1863, saying, "The London Times last Monday graciously allowed the people of England to believe that Vicksburg had actually fallen. The notion that General Lee was in possession of Washington and Baltimore is not quite so strong as it was, but I am not sure that it has been dissipated yet by any positive denial in that press. There was a general sense of the happening of some lamentable disaster here, the nature and extent of which had not been fully defined. The clearest evidence of this was found in the stock market, where a panic took place among the holders of the rebel loan. It fell from three per cent discount to seventeen, and has not stopped yet. I should not be surprised if some bankruptcies were to follow. People here must pay something for their pro-slavery sympathies. What a pity that the sum of their losses could not have been applied to the emancipation of the slaves! In that case England would have maintained her character for philanthropy, which has gone down, as it is, quite as far and as fast as the rebel loan.'' [7]

On the contrary, Page was accredited to a nation engaged in a life struggle, and which in its heart of hearts desired the help of the United States. Each, moreover, was concerned with such affairs as rights of neutrals, contraband, blockades,—matters of the utmost perplexity and provocative of irritation which easily would have led through antagonisms to war. Each, furthermore, was gifted with the supreme virtue of grace and patience, and each, be it said, finally won. The mission of Adams was continued and brought to the highest degree of triumph by the Geneva award which Adams himself conducted. The ambassadorship of Page was concluded only by his death, the death of a martyr to the world's freedom.

In Page's term as Ambassador his chief relation was not, as it normally would have been, with the Secretary of State, but with Wilson himself. As I have already intimated, this relation, beginning early in their careers in 1881, continued till Page's death. It began with high hopefulness. The succeeding forty years were distinguished by risings and fallings of the tides of friendship, of intimacy, of most important coöperativeness. The great volumes of Hendrick give a definite and complete interpretation. From them I quote liberally. At the time of the Lusitania disaster Page wrote to House, saying, ''I cannot express my

[7] *A Cycle of Adams Letters 1861-1865.* Edited by Worthington Chauncey Ford. Vol. II, pp. 65-66.

admiration of the President's management, so far at least, of his colossal task of leading us right. He has shown his supreme wisdom up to this point and I have the profoundest confidence in his judgment. But I hope he doesn't fool himself about the future; I'm sure he doesn't. I see no possible way for us to keep out, because I know the ignorance and falseness of the German leaders. They'll drown or kill more Americans—on the sea and in America.''[8] In the year 1918 Page wrote to Polk, under date of March 22nd, ''The most interesting thing going on in the world to-day—a thing that in History will transcend the war and be reckoned its greatest gain—is the high leadership of the President in formulating the struggle, in putting its aims high, and in taking the democratic lead in the world, a lead that will make the world over—and in taking the democratic lead of the English-speaking folk. Next most impressive to that is to watch the British response to that lead. Already they have doubled the number of their voters, and even more important definite steps in Democracy will be taken. My aim—and it's the only way to save the world—is to lead the British in this direction. They are the most easily teachable people in our way of thinking and of doing.''[9] And also, ''It's about time we were saving them from this bloody Thing that we call Europe, for our sake and for theirs.

[8] *The Life and Letters of Walter H. Page,* by Burton J. Hendrick, Vol. II, p. 16.
[9] *Ibid.,* pp. 361-362.

"The bloody Thing will get us all if we don't fight our level best; and it's only by *our* help that we'll be saved. That clearly gives us the leadership. Everybody sees that. Everybody acknowledges it. The President authoritatively speaks it—speaks leadership on a higher level than it was ever spoken before to the whole world." [10] But the confidence which was thus expressed was yet becoming somewhat dimmed. For in September of 1915 Page wrote to House saying, *"But I tell you with all solemnity that British opinion and the British Government have absolutely lost their respect for us and their former high estimate of the President. And that former respect is gone for good unless he acts now very quickly.*[10a] They will pay nothing more than formal and polite attention to anything we may hereafter say. This is not resentful. They don't particularly care for us to get into the war. Their feeling (I mean among our best old friends) is not resentful. It is simply sorrowful. They had the highest respect for our people and our President. The Germans defy us; we sit in silence. They conclude here that we'll submit to anything from anybody. We'll write strong notes—nothing more." [11] A little later Page wrote to the President himself, under date of October 5th, saying, "The high esteem in which our Government was held when the first Lusitania note to Germany was sent seems all changed to indifference or pity—not hatred or hostility, but a sort of hopeless and sad pity. That ship was sunk just five months

[10] *Ibid.,* p. 362. [10a] The italics are Page's. [11] *Ibid.,* p. 37.

ago; the German Government (or its Ambassador) is yet holding conversations about the principle involved, making 'concessions' and promises for the future, and so far we have done nothing to hold the Germans to accountability." [12] Personal criticism presently emerges. In the year 1916, after a visit to Washington, Page writes in a memorandum concerning Wilson, "It is very hard to understand why so intellectual a man doesn't have notable men about him. It's the college professor's village habit, I dare say. But it's a great misfortune. This is one way in which Mr. Wilson shuts out the world and lives too much alone, feeding only on knowledge and subjects that he has already acquired and not getting new views or fresh suggestions from men and women." [13] "What an unspeakably lamentable loss of opportunity! This is the more remarkable and lamentable because the President is a charming personality, an uncommonly good talker, a man who could easily make personal friends of all the world. He does his own thinking, untouched by other men's ideas. He receives nothing from the outside. His domestic life is spent with his own, nobody else, except House occasionally. His contact with his own Cabinet is a business man's contact with his business associates and kind—at his office." [14] "The influence of this lone-hand way of playing the game extends very far. The members of the Cabinet do not seem to have the habit of frankness with one another. Each lives and works in a water-tight compart-

[12] *Ibid.*, p. 41.   [13] *Ibid.*, p. 173.   [14] *Ibid.*, p. 174.

ment.''[15] ''There is a great lesson in this lamentable failure of the President really to lead the Nation. The United States stands for democracy and free opinion as it stands for nothing else and as no other nation stands for it. Now when democracy and free opinion are at stake as they have not before been, we take a 'neutral' stand—we throw away our very birthright. We may talk of 'humanity' as we like: we have missed the largest chance that ever came to help the large cause that brought us into being as a Nation.''[16] The breach suffered a still further widening. At the close of his visit to Washington, in 1916, Hendrick writes of the final interview, saying, ''Mr. Wilson at this interview did not impress his Ambassador as a perverse character, but as an extremely pathetic one. Page came away with no vexation or anger, but with a real feeling for a much suffering and a much perplexed statesman. The fact that the President's life was so solitary, and that he seemed to be so completely out of touch with men and with the living thoughts of the world, appealed strongly to Page's sympathies.''[17] The simple fact was that the intense absorption of Wilson in himself was manifest in the vagaries of official action and of personal bearing and conduct.

Various phrases of the President's utterances and various phases of the President's silences had the deepest personal meaning for Page. ''Peace without victory'' was almost a personal blow, as well as an

[15] *Ibid.*, p. 174.   [16] *Ibid.*, p. 178.   [17] *Ibid.*, p. 188.

international blunder. On the first of April of the year 1917, the Ambassador made a list of the blunders of the President for the preceding two and one-half years. His first error was in his interpretation of neutrality. His second error was the judgment that he could play the part of a great peacemaker. "He shut himself up with these two ideas and engaged in what he called 'thought.' The air currents of the world never ventilated his mind.

"This inactive position he has kept as long as public sentiment permitted. He seems no longer to regard himself nor to speak as a leader—only as the mouthpiece of public opinion after opinion has run over him.

"He has not breathed a spirit into the people: he has encouraged them to supineness. He is *not* a leader, but rather a stubborn phrasemaker." [18] Page's interpretation of Wilson as late as March, 1918, made to his son Arthur, was that "The Great White Chief is at bottom pacifist, has always been so and is so now. Of course I do not mean a pacifist at any price, certainly not a cowardly pacifist." [19] The anti-British mood of Wilson was a constant pain to Page. Wilson once said, "that he seriously questioned the desirability of drawing the two countries any more closely together than they already were." [20] Page wrote to his son Arthur in May, 1918, saying, "It's mere common sense, mere prudence, the mere instinct of safety to keep close to Great Britain, to

[18] *Ibid.*, p. 223.   [19] *Ibid.*, p. 336.
[20] *Ibid.*, p. 346.

have a decent respect for the good qualities of these people and of this government.'' [21]

The drifting continued. The breach widened. Page had a gift for friendship; Wilson seems not to have been thus endowed. The experience of Wilson as President of Princeton, the antagonisms which either he created or allowed to be promoted are evidence. The antagonisms arising from the wish to abolish certain clubs, and regarding the location of the building or buildings of the Graduate School may have been only occasions, but they were at least occasions for antagonisms over which even death has not thrown the mantle either of forgiveness or of forgetfulness.

Page lies buried beneath the sod of the State to which he gave his lifelong love and his best devotion. He worked for North Carolina; and unto ultimate triumph.[22] He served also his whole country at all times, and all countries in their crises. His life was a noble and consistent battle for the common humanity of which he was a part.

[21] *Ibid.*, p. 385.

[22] "In 1897 Walter Page summed up the educational tragedy of 'Bourbonism' in the single phrase, 'The Forgotten Man.' At that time, twenty-six per cent of the white population of North Carolina above ten years of age was illiterate! Public education had not then become an interest of the average person; the traditions of education as a luxury and a privilege of the rich and the well-born still lingered in the mind of the common man. In 1900, three years after Page coined his phrase, North Carolina spent a trifle more than $1,000,000 on her public schools, and for a like sum valued the entire public school property of the state; twenty-five years later she spent $34,000,000 on public education and valued her public school property at $70,000,000."—*The American Historical Review*, October, 1930, p. 61.

VI

THOMAS WENTWORTH HIGGINSON

BORN of Puritan stock in Cambridge, Mass., December 22, 1823; died May 9, 1911. Graduated from Harvard in 1841. He was a schoolmaster for two years, a student of theology at the Harvard Divinity School, and pastor of the First Religious Society (Unitarian) of Newburyport, Mass., and of the Free Church at Worcester. He was so ardent an abolitionist that he felt moved to resign his first pulpit. In the Civil War he was captain in the 51st Massachusetts Volunteers; colonel of the first South Carolina Volunteers, the first regiment recruited from former slaves for the Federal Service; was retired in 1864 because of a wound received earlier. Afterward, his life was spent chiefly at Newport, R. I., and at Cambridge, devoted to writing and to helping on good causes.

Author: Outdoor Papers; Malbone: An Oldport Romance; Army Life in a Black Regiment; Common Sense About Women; Life of Margaret Fuller Ossoli; Women and Men; Travellers and Outlaws; The Afternoon Landscape; Life of Francis Higginson; Henry Wadsworth Longfellow; John Greenleaf Whittier; Lowell Institute Lectures; and many other books.

VI

THOMAS WENTWORTH HIGGINSON

SOLDIER OF HUMANITY

THE thirty years between 1831 and 1861 form the most constructive generation of American history. In the earlier year the American Anti-Slavery Society was organized. In the latter began the Civil War. The Civil War was a result to which the preceding years, some would say inevitably, led. It was the age of new thought and of new thoughts, of visions, of come-outerisms, of know-nothingism, of Millerism, and of revelations. It was the age of newness. It was a repetition of Virgil's fourth Eclogue:

"Now come the world's last days, the age foretold
By Cumæ's prophetess in sacred song.

*　　*　　*　　*　　*

The iron race of mortals shall away,
And o'er this earth a golden people reign." [1]

It was the new and dawning age of faith, it was the age both of discontent, and of reconstruction. It was

[1] *The Georgics and Eclogues of Virgil,* translated by Theodore C. Williams, p. 138.

111

the age of new impulses demanding fresh organization. It was an age, as Emerson wrote of the Chardon Street Convention, composed of "Madmen, madwomen, men with beards, Dunkers, Muggletonians, Come-outers, Groaners, Agrarians, Seventh-day Baptists, Quakers, Abolitionists, Calvinists, Unitarians and Philosophers."[2] Yet, while it was the generation of revolutions and of reconstructions, it was also an age of achievement in literature. In history it was the age of Parkman, of Prescott, of Motley, of Bancroft, and of Palfrey. In poetry it was the age of Lowell, of Longfellow, of Whittier, and of Holmes. In romance it was, following the time of Irving and of Cooper, the age of Hawthorne. In the philosophic essay it was above all the age of Emerson. In preaching it was the age of Channing, of Parker, of the earlier Storrs, of Bushnell, and of Beecher. It was the lyceum age of Wendell Phillips.

The life of Thomas Wentworth Higginson began a few years before the beginning of this generation. It was lived through this generation, and its second half came to its end fifty years after the close of the generation. It was a life long in its length of years, covering almost four score and ten. It was a life rich in its environment of personalities, unique in its experiences and noble in its diverse achievements.

Higginson's was above all else a life and career given to emancipation; his was a liberalizing service.

[2] *Lectures and Biographical Sketches,* by Ralph Waldo Emerson, p. 374.

It sought to give rights for wrongs, freedom for limitation, opportunity for enslavement, and breadth for narrowness. It tried to create cubical relations. Higginson sought to do away with inequality by lifting the lower up to the level of the higher and of the highest. To the unprivileged he wanted to give endowment, and to the oppressed freedom. In his idealism he was what Shaftesbury, the seventh earl, was to England of the same period. The leading motives of his life in early years he wrote were, "The love of personal liberty, of religious freedom, and of the equality of the sexes." [3]

The earlier of Higginson's endeavors for emancipation was for the freedom of the negro slaves. Though not sympathetic with certain of their extreme methods, he was yet a co-worker with William Lloyd Garrison, and with Wendell Phillips. At the time that the Fugitive Slave Act was passed and was being applied, he wrote to George William Curtis, saying, "Remember that to us, Anti-Slavery is a matter of deadly earnest, which costs us our reputations to-day, and may cost us our lives to-morrow." [4] He was a supporter of the underground railroad. He participated in the Anthony Burns riot. John Brown awakened his deepest enthusiasm. His loyalty to the cause of the negro has its most lasting memorial in his being Colonel of the First Slave Regiment mustered into

[3] *Thomas Wentworth Higginson—The Story of His Life,* by Mary Thacher Higginson, p. 7.
[4] *Ibid.,* p. 142.

service. The 54th Massachusetts, Colonel Shaw's regiment, followed Colonel Higginson's. As he was about to assume command, he wrote, "The first man who organizes and commands a successful black regiment will perform the most important Service in the history of the war. . . . To say that I would rather do it than anything else in the world is to say little; it is such a masterpiece of felicitous opportunity that all casualties of life or death appear trivial in connexion with it." [5] In the introduction of his history of the Black Regiment he wrote, "It was a vast experiment of indirect philanthropy, and one on which the result of the war and the destiny of the negro race might rest; and this was enough to tax all one's powers. I had been an abolitionist too long, and had known and loved John Brown too well, not to feel a thrill of joy at last on finding myself in the position where he only wished to be." [6] In the conclusion of the essay he wrote, "The peculiar privilege of associating with an outcast race, of training it to defend its rights, and to perform its duties, this was our especial need. The vacillating policy of the Government sometimes filled other officers with doubt and shame; until the negro had justice, they were but defending liberty with one hand and crushing it with the other. From this inconsistency we were free. Whatever the Government did, we at least were working in the

[5] *Ibid.*, p. 215.
[6] *Army Life in a Black Regiment,* by Thomas Wentworth Higginson, p. 4.

right direction. If this was not recognized on our side of the lines, we knew that it was admitted on the other. Fighting with ropes round our necks, denied the ordinary courtesies of war till we ourselves compelled their concession, we could at least turn this outlawry into a compliment. We had touched the pivot of the war. Whether this vast and dusky mass should prove the weakness of the nation or its strength, must depend in great measure, we knew, upon our efforts. Till the blacks were armed, there was no guaranty of their freedom. It was their demeanor under arms that shamed the nation into recognizing them as men.'' [7]

From this service in the war, Colonel Higginson was mustered out by reason of a severe wound. In all the following years he was known as Colonel Higginson.

If the cause of the freedom of the slave was Higginson's most outstanding and thrilling of his endeavors for human liberty, it was not the only example, for he was essentially a reformer and protestant. His life, his speech, his writing, his diverse services, were a constant indictment against human wrong, injustice, limitation. Early did he enlist in the cause of women's rights. His regular and long-continued contributions to the *Woman's Journal* gave weight and dignity to that aggressive paper. He wrote and spoke much on temperance and total abstinence. An early apostle of prison reform, he was a

[7] *Ibid.,* pp. 266-67.

helper of that helpless outcast, the discharged
prisoner. He was a worthy co-worker in this field
with President Hayes. Causes as diverse as political
mugwumpism and simplified spelling commanded his
loyalty. He was an unflagging and loyal public servant. Early in life he wrote, "An aesthetic life—how
beautiful—but the life of a Reformer, a People's
Guide 'battling for the right'—glorious, but, Oh how
hard!" [8] Near the close of his life he wrote, "Personally I should like to live to see international arbitration secured, civil service reform completed, free
trade established; to find the legal and educational
rights of the two sexes equalized; to know that all
cities are as honestly governed as that in which I
dwell; to see natural monopolies owned by the public, not in private hands; to see drunkenness extir-
pated; to live under absolute as well as nominal religious freedom; to perceive American literature to
be thoroughly emancipated from that habit of colonial
deference which still hampers it." [9]

To these many diverse and lifelong movements
Higginson brought qualities which reformers do not
usually possess or contribute. He brought the heri-
tages of culture, the disciplines of many unique experiences, friendships of good and great women and
men, and the urbanities of the best society. These
elements were united in and supported by a sense of

[8] *Thomas Wentworth Higginson—The Story of His Life*, by
Mary Thacher Higginson, p. 71.
[9] *Cheerful Yesterdays*, by Thomas Wentworth Higginson,
p. 363.

aggressive yet restrained forcefulness. He was a great
gentleman; but the gentleman wore shoulder straps,
which, if concealed, were still there.

Yet the life of the reformer was not inconsistent
with a life of friendships. Indeed the reformer's life
which Higginson lived helped to create and to continue friendships. His friendships were of the best
of his generation. His books bear abundant illustrations of the precious personal relationships, many
and diverse. His interpretations of these friendships
are full of charm, both of commendation and of criticism. At the age of thirty-four, and still serving as
a minister of a church in Worcester, near the middle
of the century, he wrote of several of his friends,
saying:—"Mr. *Emerson* is bounteous and gracious, but
thin, dry, angular, in intercourse as in person. *Garrison* is the only solid moral reality I have ever seen
incarnate, the only man who *would do to tie to,* as
they say out West; and he is fresher and firmer every
day, but wanting in intellectual culture and variety.
Wendell Phillips is always graceful and gay, but in-
wardly sad, under that bright surface. *Whittier* is
the simplest and truest of men, beautiful at home,
but without fluency of expression, and with rather
an excess of restraint. *Thoreau* is pure and wonderfully learned in nature's things and deeply wise, and
yet tedious in his monologues and cross-questionings.
Theodore Parker is as wonderfully learned in books,
and as much given to monologue, though very agreeable and various it is, still egotistical, dogmatic, bitter

often, and showing marked intellectual limitations. Mr. *Alcott* is an innocent charlatan, full of inspired absurdities and deep strokes, maunders about nature, and when outdoors has neither eyes, ears, nor limbs. *Lowell* is infinitely entertaining, but childishly egotistical and monopolizing.'' [10] But later of Emerson he said, ''From Emerson, I differ, . . . in temperament, attitude, and many conclusions; but in spite of this I know of no author whose writings seem to me so densely crowded with absolute truth, and so graceful in beauty; though there is never any artistic wholeness in his Essays; they are a series of exquisite sentences; and yet more than this I value for you that noble calmness, gentleness, courage, and freedom; and that pure air and unflinching moral heroism which make him the very strongest teacher for the moral nature that this generation has given.'' [11]

Of Charles Sumner on an epochal day he wrote: ''On the day before Charles Sumner's funeral it seemed that Boston, too, had but one voice within her walls, and that it came from the mute form reposing in the Doric Hall of the State House. Emerson has said

'The silent organ loudest chants
Its master's requiem,'

and never was there an appeal more potent than

[10] *Letters and Journals of Thomas Wentworth Higginson, 1846-1906,* edited by Mary T. Higginson, pp. 93-94.
[11] *Ibid.,* pp. 105-6.

came that day from the very speechlessness of that noble organ, the voice of Charles Sumner.

Standing amid that crowd at the State House, it was impossible not to ask one's self: 'Can this be Boston? The city whose bells toll for Sumner—is it the same city that fired one hundred guns for the passage of the Fugitive Slave Law?' " [12]

For Wendell Phillips likewise he had at once warm appreciation and just discrimination:—"With all his faults, his inconsistencies, his impetuous words, and his unreasoning prejudices, Wendell Phillips belonged to the heroic type. Whether we regard him mainly as an orator, or as a participant in important events, it is certain that no history of the United States will ever be likely to omit him. It is rarely that any great moral agitation bequeaths to posterity more than two or three names; the English slave-trade abolition has left only Clarkson and Wilberforce in memory; the great Corn Law contest, only Cobden and Bright. The American anti-slavery movement will probably embalm the names of Garrison, Phillips, and John Brown." [13]

Of Longfellow likewise he wrote in a comparative interpretation:—"It will perhaps be found, as time goes on, that the greatest service rendered by Longfellow—beyond all personal awakening or stimulus exerted on his readers—was that of being the first

[12] *Contemporaries,* by Thomas Wentworth Higginson, pp. 280-81.
[13] *Ibid.,* pp. 278-79.

conspicuous representative, in an eminently practical and hard-working community, of the literary life. One of a circle of superior men, he was the only one who stood for that life purely and supremely, and thus vindicated its national importance. Among his predecessors, Irving had lived chiefly in Europe, and Bryant in a newspaper office. Among his immediate friends, Holmes stood for exact science, Lowell and Whittier for reform, Sumner for statesmanship, Emerson for spiritual and mystic values; even the shy Hawthorne for public functions at home and abroad. Here was a man whose single word, sent forth from his quiet study, reached more hearts in distant nations than any of these, and was speedily reproduced in the far-off languages of the world. Considered merely as an antidote to materialism, such a life was of incalculable value. Looking at him, the reign of the purely materialistic, however much aided by organizing genius, was plainly self-limited; the modest career of Longfellow outshone it in the world's arena. Should that reign henceforth grow never so potent, the best offset to its most arrogant claims will be found, for years to come, in the memory of his name."[14]

The friendships of Higginson, broad as they were with men, were also broad with women. Among the friends were Lucy Stone, Julia Ward Howe, Emily Dickinson, Helen Hunt Jackson, and Lydia Maria

[14] *Henry Wadsworth Longfellow*, by Thomas Wentworth Higginson, pp. 294-95.

Child. His reverence for women is intimated in an interpretation, given in his essay on the "Greek goddesses," of Hestia. Hestia "represents woman as queen of home. Houses are her invention. No separate temple is built to her, for every hearth is her altar; no special sacrifices are offered, for she has the first share of every sacrifice. Every time the household meets before the hearth, she is named, and the meal becomes thereby an act of worship." [15]

Of Lucy Stone he writes that she is "Queen of us all . . . and delights the whole country from Maine to Kentucky; she is a household word down here on the Penobscot, after one visit a year ago. You have no idea of the eloquence and power which have been developed in her; she is one of the great Providences of History." [16]

Of Lydia Maria Child, whose name with the fast-going decades rapidly fades, he says, "She was placed where there was as yet no exacting literary standard; she wrote better than most of her contemporaries, and well enough for her public. She did not, therefore, win that intellectual immortality which only the very best writers command, and which few Americans have attained. But she won a meed which she would value more highly,—that warmth of sympathy, that mingled gratitude of intellect and heart which men

[15] *Atlantic Essays,* by Thomas Wentworth Higginson, p. 283.
[16] *Letters and Journals of T. W. Higginson,* edited by M. T. Higginson, p. 59.

give to those who have faithfully served their day and generation." [17]

Of Helen Hunt Jackson he says, "To those who knew her best she was a person quite unique and utterly inexhaustible; and though her remoteness of residence during the last ten years had separated her from the society of many of her earlier friends, there is not one of them who did not feel the world deeply impoverished by her going out of it. She did not belong to a class; she left behind her no second; and neither memory nor fancy can restore her as she was, or fully reproduce, even for those who knew her best, that ardent and joyous personality." [18]

Yet, while one thinks of Higginson as a political and a social protestant and as a great friend, one is also to remember that he was primarily the writer. He was essayist, historian, biographer, poet.

In the citation which was used in conferring the degree of LL.D. upon Higginson at the Harvard commencement of 1898, a degree which could fittingly have been given much earlier, President Eliot said, "minister, teacher, early Abolitionist in theory, and in practice, Colonel of the First South Carolina Colored Volunteers in the Civil War, historian and man of letters." [19] "Man of letters" is the formal and most comprehensive term. Early came the impulse to

[17] *Contemporaries*, by Thomas Wentworth Higginson, p. 141.
[18] *Ibid.*, pp. 165-66.
[19] *The Harvard Graduates' Magazine*, September, 1898, p. 49.

write, and the impulse continued for a longer period than with any one of his contemporaries. It manifested itself in subjects most diverse. In all this diversity of theme, two qualities are constructive. They are, as he himself confesses, fineness and fire. These two elements are characteristic. It is, however, rather fineness than fire that dominates. The common remark that the style is the man is also quite as true when reversed, the man is the style. Fineness of thinking, fineness of feeling, fineness of appreciation, ever seem to me to belong to him, and therefore to form, or to give at least atmosphere to, his writing. This fineness belongs to his interpretation of his contemporaries, to his interpretation of historic periods, and also to his appreciation of nature. Fire belongs more to his understanding of movements. When he confesses that he has "some want of copiousness and fertility which may give a tinge of thinness to what I write," [20] I find myself not at all sympathetic. Yet I do feel a certain "thinness" which seems to spring from writing under mere "inspiration" at the "golden moment." In this inspiration I do not feel the concentrated laboriousness, conscious or unconscious, which belongs to the great and the enduring works.

The fact is that Higginson, though a hard worker, was a hard worker in many fields. If he had concentrated his interests and brought his many and diverse

[20] *Thomas Wentworth Higginson—The Story of His Life*, by Mary Thacher Higginson, p. 274.

activities to a single point, literature would have been
more deeply enriched, enriched indeed as it has been
by his many and miscellaneous contributions. At the
age of nineteen he said, ''My great intellectual difficulty has been having too many irons in the fire.'' [21]
After his death his wife wrote, confirming the early
self-judgment. Such a condition is not exceptional.
In the very midst of his career Longfellow confessed,
''I find no time to write. I find more and more the
little things of life shut out the great. Innumerable
interruptions—letters of application for this and for
that; endless importunities of foreigners for help
here and help there—fret the day and consume it.'' [22]

It may also be said that one cause of Higginson's
desultoriness may lie in his not having the sustaining
and controlling power of a regular vocation. The
demands of a professorship were to Lowell, for instance, the force which gave form and substance and
a certain concentration to his essays and poems. It
would have been well if Higginson had been thus
confined. The brook needs the limitations of banks
for getting power. The wandering stream becomes
thin, and lacks directness and force.

Yet even despite this dissipation of interest and of
activity, Higginson's contributions as a man of letters have, I believe, enduring qualities. His hymns
and poems possess noble lyric and devotional ele-

[21] *Ibid.*, p. 47.
[22] *Henry Wadsworth Longfellow,* by Thomas Wentworth
Higginson, p. 187.

ments. The best hymn writers of his generation were
adherents of the Unitarian faith. The names of Oliver
Wendell Holmes, of Hosmer, of Gannett, of Samuel
Longfellow, are the most eminent. To this small num-
ber Higginson belongs. His hymn, *Pantheism and
Theism,* deserves to be sung with Holmes' *Lord of
All Being, Throned Afar:*

> "No human eyes Thy face may see,
> No human thought Thy form may know;
> But all creation dwells in Thee,
> And Thy great life through all doth flow!
>
> And yet, O strange and wondrous thought!
> Thou art a God who hearest prayer,
> And every heart with sorrow fraught
> To seek Thy present aid may dare." [23]

The whole volume of poems, *The Afternoon Landscape,* dedicated to "James Russell Lowell, schoolmate and fellow townsman," is not unworthy of the
personal and neighborly association. Of the verses of
one *Decoration Day* I quite two and two only:

> "Youth and beauty, dauntless will,
> Dreams that life could ne'er fulfil,
> Here lie buried; here in peace
> Wrongs and woes have found release.
>
> Turning from my comrades' eyes,
> Kneeling where a woman lies,
> I strew lilies on the grave
> Of the bravest of the brave." [24]

[23] *The Afternoon Landscape,* by Thomas Wentworth Higginson, p. 75.
[24] *Ibid.,* p. 25.

But more characteristic than the poems and hymns, and more enduring than the essays and novels, is the appeal which his biographies make. They are, as a whole, his most important achievement in letters. For they embody those elements which that prince of biographers, William Roscoe Thayer, interprets as of essential worth. They incarnate the constructive element of human sympathy, they are real. They also possess the supreme gift or achievement, felicity of style. They describe, moreover, men and women who lived and wrought in his own atmosphere. Their times were his years; their feelings his experiences; their struggles his battles; their achievements his victories; and their purposes his ideals. In biography as in painting the one who makes the portrait is quite as important as the man of whom the portrait is made. Thayer intimates that "four-fifths depends on the biographer." [25] It is necessary for each to see and understand alike. Higginson writes of his *Contemporaries*. He interprets in the *Harvard Memorial Biographies*, which he in part wrote and in part edited, the men who gave their all in the struggle in which he rather hoped he might lose his own life. The *Cheerful Yesterdays* he had himself lived. His *Army Life in a Black Regiment* was his life and career. His biographies are essentially autobiographies. We see, hear, understand, feel him. As he writes of Whittier or of Wendell Phillips he is essentially writing of himself. One can hardly forbear be-

[25] *The Art of Biography*, by William Roscoe Thayer, p. 139.

lieving that novel and essay, too, are personal interpretations. *Malbone* is a picture of Newport. *Old
Cambridge* is his home, earliest and latest. His *Hints
on Writing and Speech Making* grew out of his long
continued and fruitful experiences. Chapters in the
Atlantic Essays, as "A Plea for Culture," are a bugle
call of hope and achievement; and other chapters, like
"Ought Women to Learn the Alphabet?" teem with
wit as well as with wisdom of a very personal sort.
The translations of Epictetus bear evidence that his
interpretations grew out of the richest soil of his own
disciplined thinking. The understanding which he
gave to the great causes had for their standards of
measurement the eternal principles of thought, of
morals, which were the elements of his own manhood.
In fact, as I read these twenty-five volumes, I am
surprised, and yet not surprised, at their essentially
autobiographic impression and impressiveness.

Worthy as were Higginson's writings, commanding as were his unique services in war, useful as
were his manifold achievements as a reformer, constant and constructive as was his usefulness as a citizen, I ever feel as I read his writings, and as I felt
as I talked with him, that he himself was far greater
than anything he attempted or achieved. For his was
a full character, a rich nature, a strong and complete
manhood. He embodied the fulfillment of Christ's purpose—a more abundant life. That abundance became
almost a superabundance. That superabundance began early to be made conscious to himself. He was

"constantly sensible of the superabundance of beauty
and good in the universe, a thought which is never
for an instant out of my mind, and in view of which
I cannot conceive of being overcome by anything." [26]
He felt that his one great possession in life was "this
sunny vigor of nature and unfailing animal spirits,
which have carried me buoyantly over everything so
far, and which I am sure I inherited from you. And
many as are my other causes of gratitude, this seems
the greatest." [27] On his seventieth birthday, too, his
wife acknowledges, "the different eras through which
he had passed made him feel as if he had lived several
lives." [28] To each of these lives he gave his most
vital self, and each of them in turn ministered unto
his enduring vitality.

In this fullness of life both as cause and result were
several vital and vitalizing elements. Among them
was his dominant courage. The courage was of every
sort: military, civil, social. Fear seemed to have no
part in his make-up. Happiness, too, belonged to him,
both as a birthright and as an acquisition. At the
age of fifty-seven he writes, "I have what would have
seemed to me reputation and wealth from the stand-
point of my early years; I have also a singular health
of body and youthfulness of mind; even the fire of
passion and adventure is I fear unabated in me; but
in the anchorage of my own home I am guaranteed

[26] *Thomas Wentworth Higginson—The Story of His Life,*
by Mary Thacher Higginson, p. 85.
[27] *Ibid.,* p. 125.   [28] *Ibid.,* p. 381.

from danger. . . . My imagination is as active as
ever, and my literary faculty; they are only checked
by the multiplicity of cares and interests that come
with advancing years." [29]

Optimism, too, belonged to him quite as thoroughly
as did courage and the gift of happiness. His interpretations of history and of individuals teem with
the belief in the best. He declares, "Lamentations,
doubts, discouragements, all are wasted things." [30]
His thought and feeling for America and the future
are well united with his ethical optimism, and are as
warm and keen as Browning's.

In this value of courage, of happiness, and of optimism, his love for men was most constructive. As
a young man, while contemplating the choice of a
calling, he wrote, "I crave action . . . unbounded
action. I love men passionately, I feel intensely their
sufferings and short-comings and yearn to make
all men brothers . . . to help them to strive and
conquer." [31] This human passion endured to the
end.

The love for men was united with, and yet distinct from, his love of nature. While suffering from
the death of a little daughter, and at the close of a
summer in New Hampshire, he writes, "The old love
of nature seems to have come back and the sorrow

[29] *Ibid.*, p. 300.
[30] *Atlantic Essays,* by Thomas Wentworth Higginson, p.
22.
[31] *Thomas Wentworth Higginson—The Story of His Life,*
by Mary Thacher Higginson, p. 69.

which threatened to overshadow us has been mercifully soothed. I have neither 'looked before nor after nor pined for what is not.' '' [32] And years after this sorrow, near the beginning of summer, he says, ''Began thoroughly to enjoy the primitive forest feeling. Felt that conscious happiness which Thoreau describes—every little pine needle seeming to stretch toward me. There was a feeling as of late summer in the air and the crickets' incessant chirp seemed saturated with happiness. It was enough simply to live and look round on the trees I love.'' [33]

Higginson's love of man was the mother of a great quality and force which lay in him and which he gave to others, inspiration. A talk with him lifted the spirit, enlarged the mind, quickened the heart, strengthened the will, purified the conscience. For he was altruistic. He entered into the feeling and understood the thought of friends. Even for antagonists he had a just and kind appreciation. He sought to occupy their point of view, and to see with their eyes. In the deepest and largest relationships he possessed the gift of sympathy, both intellectual and emotional. This inspiration, begun and manifesting itself in personal leadership, has illustration in the fact that forty years after he retired from his command of the black regiment, his old associates declared at a reunion, ''Your influence remained with us, a constraint from what is unworthy, and an incentive

[32] *Ibid.*, p. 296.   [33] *Ibid.*, p. 372.

to what is high. We cannot say that through these
many years we have been faithful to the standard;
but we may say that in its presence it has been easier
to be noble and harder to be mean." [34]

Higginson's life was not a circle. It did not move
in the same round and at the same level. It was a
spiral. As it went round it went up. "One thing,
however, I must remember. I cannot live a past experience over again. Life is a spiral, not a circle. If
I try for an instant to reproduce a past experience,
except in a higher form, I shall *fail*." [35]

From youth to age and from age to age Higginson
faced the deathless future with both wit and faith.
Once speaking with some degree of doubt of the advantage of a future life, he met the opposing intimation with the remark, "But I should have to meet so
many people who bore me!" [36] Yet with the wit of
discrimination and of justice was united the firm and
lasting faith of the disciple. In the very midst of his
career he said, "So far as any personal plans of my
own are concerned, I am absolutely free and could I
leave M—— out of view could die to-morrow with no
feeling but of a happy confidence in the Eternal
Laws, not unmingled with a sweet curiosity." [37] His
remark reminds one of the remark of Charles Kings-

[34] *Ibid.*, p. 252.
[35] *Letters and Journals of Thomas Wentworth Higginson,
1846-1906.* Edited by Mary T. Higginson, p. 348.
[36] *Thomas Wentworth Higginson—The Story of His Life,*
by Mary Thacher Higginson, pp. 379-80.
[37] *Ibid.*, p. 212.

ley, that he looked forward to the day of his death
with profound curiosity.

At the time of his death in 1911, a Harvard undergraduate whom he befriended wrote a sonnet in his
memory. That the writer was and is my son, Francis
Wendell Butler-Thwing, shall not prevent me from
copying the verses :—

First of thy country's sons in thought and deed
  Who mingled, stern and faithful, with thy peers
  And fought for nobler life in changing years
As thou didst serve thy nation in her need—
Today, merged in thy largeness, thoughtful, freed
  From narrow aims and petty, low-born fears
  We come in wond'ring grief and solemn tears
To pay thy memory a brave man's meed.

Soldier and priest! Friend of the great and good,
—Whose long life-battle, nobly fought, is done,
Ah! would that we might stand as thou hast stood
And, scarred in strife of years, grow like to thee,
Worthy the gifts thy toil and thought have won,
Thy peers in strength and Christ-like courtesy!

VII

WILLIAM ROSCOE THAYER

BORN Boston, Jan. 16, 1859; died Cambridge, Sept. 7, 1923; fitted for college under tutor in Europe; A.B., Harvard, 1881, A.M., 1886; assistant editor of Philadelphia Evening Bulletin, 1882-85; founder and editor Harvard Graduates' Magazine, 1892-1915; overseer, Harvard University, 1913-1919, 1920-1923. Delegate of Harvard College and American Historical Association to International Hist. Congress, Rome, 1903, and to Italian Hist. Congress, Milan, 1906; president Harvard Chapter of Phi Beta Kappa, 1920.

Author: Confessions of Hermes; Hesper; The Best Elizabethan Plays; The Dawn of Italian Independence; Poems, New and Old; History and Customs of Harvard University; Throne-Makers; A Short History of Venice; Italica; Life and Times of Cavour; Life and Letters of John Hay; Germany vs. Civilization; Letters of John Holmes (edited); George Washington; Theodore Roosevelt—An Intimate Biography; Out of Their Own Mouths (introduction); Collapse of Superman, and other volumes. Awarded gold medal for biography, National Institute of Arts and Letters, 1918.

VII

WILLIAM ROSCOE THAYER

BIOGRAPHER, POET, VALIANT SOUL

My friendship with Thayer was a late harvest. It began with our first personal talk at a meeting of the Harvard Clubs in Detroit in the middle nineties. Earlier, however, I had written for the *Harvard Graduates' Magazine,* of which he was the founder, and which he edited for twenty-three years. This personal touch naturally and speedily created friendship. Friendship ripened into intimacy. We soon found ourselves calling each other by our first names.

For Thayer was a most friendly man. He did not wear his heart upon his sleeve, where hearts never ought to be worn, but keeping his heart in its proper place, its pulse-beats of affection were strong and regular. These tokens of affection became also on occasion signs of love, and of detestation and of hate as well as of love. In fact, out of his emotional nature grew not a few of his great forces and qualities. Friendly, his friends were found among the best men of his generation. Charles Eliot Norton, James Russell Lowell, Charles Francis Adams, Albert Bushnell

Hart, Worthington C. Ford, Theodore Roosevelt, Henry Osborn Taylor, James Ford Rhodes, H. Nelson Gay of Rome, are among the names which immediately spring to the lips. These friendships become yet more significant when contrasted with the sense of indignation and of enmity of which he was capable. The depths of his feeling against what he considered base movements and against those who worked in such movements were easily stirred. The Great War provided illustrations, impressive and sad. In volume, in talk personal and in speech public, his polemic indignations flowed forth in tossing floods. These tempests become possibly more significant as one knows of the beautiful companionship and happiness which came into full flower and fruitage in his home. To wife, of distinguished ancestry, and to daughter he gave of his deepest and highest, and from them received like precious offerings.

His home for the largest share of his life was in the midst of homes in their workings and personal qualities quite like his own. That home stood near one end of the street bearing the philosophic name of Berkeley. Opposite it was the home of Basil King, the novelist. At the other end was the house built for and occupied by John Fiske, and now belonging to Wambaugh of the Harvard Law School. Near by was the home of the international interpreter, Kuno Francke. Not far off, too, was the home of Longfellow; and on the other side of Brattle Street, was the simple, severe, and historic house, Elmwood. His simple

house with its addition of a room built for his library and his workshop stood, and still stands, in
the very midst of holy and beautiful associations. It
was a fitting environment.

In it all was Thayer. His personality was dominant
and constructive. Most formative, too, among all his
forces and qualities was imagination. Thayer is chiefly
known as a biographer, but early and late he felt that
he was first a poet. In the year 1907 he wrote, "You
remind me—what in my heart of hearts I have always
felt—that I ought to have devoted all my energy to
Poetry. I made a struggle for it, but the combination
of ill health and lack of means drove me back to
prose."[1] His first book was a book of poems published in 1884, and as early as 1905 he had published
three volumes of verse. As late as the year 1917 he
wrote to John J. Chapman, saying, "For the fact at
the bottom of my heart is that poetry is my deepest
interest."[2] He sang:

> "I walked with poets in my youth,
>   Because the world they drew
> Was beautiful and glorious
>   Beyond the world I knew.
>
> The poets are my comrades still,
>   But dearer than in youth,
> For now I know that they alone
>   Picture the world of truth."[3]

[1] *Letters of William Roscoe Thayer.* Edited by Charles
Downer Hazen, p. 137.
[2] *Ibid.,* p. 304.
[3] *Poems New and Old,* by William Roscoe Thayer, p. 104.

This mind, creative in forms and forces of imagination, and made vital by emotion, was a mind disciplined by study and also richly stored. Such a combination of discipline and of intellectual wealth is unique. He read much and widely, both *multum* and *multa*. Italian was, of course, almost as much a vernacular as English. Massachusetts and Italy were alike his countries, Cambridge and Rome his homes, Berkeley Street and Piazza di Spagna his thoroughfares. The shelves of his library intimated his intellectual and literary riches. The historians of Italy, like Ferrero, came to his door. Scholars, like the Trevelyans, were his correspondents. No knowledge of a literary type and character was foreign to him. Without the universal learning of Acton, he yet devoted his treasures to more useful applications than did the learned Englishman. Yet this knowledge was not held for imposition upon friends. In his prodigal outpourings, the full floods were held in by good taste and by gracious considerations. He was neither a Samuel Johnson nor a Macaulay.

His power native, disciplined, enriched, was largely devoted to the writing of history and biography, and the field was rather biographical than historical. Yet, even his Italian histories were also biographical, and his Italian and American biographies touching epochs, crises, movements, were also histories. For history is largely a study of men comparatively interpreted. His *Life and Times of Cavour* and his *Dawn of Italian Independence* illustrate the double truth. The *Dawn*

gives background for the *Cavour,* and the *Cavour,*
carrying in its very title the temporal and national
environment of the hero, brought up to the zenith
the meaning of the *Dawn.*

To his biographical writing Thayer bore what he
says, in his Page lectures at the University of Virginia, the biographer ought to bear, several principles
or interpretations. Among them was a deep sense of
humanness or even of humaneness. Sympathy is an
"indispensable qualification" as is a unique sensitiveness. "In truth, the ideal biographer is one who is
so sensitive to his subject's qualities that he, better
than any one else, perceives them." [4] With these
elements of humanness, sympathy, and sensitiveness is
to be joined an appreciation of reality—"In writing
history or biography the first aim should be to tell
the story as nearly as possible as the actors or hero
underwent it." [5] In all such writing the biographer
is to be the artist. "A work of art, a true book or
painting, a statue or temple, does not exist ready-
made, needing only to be discovered by some fortunate
finder. The work of art is a creation, and it can never
come into being without the transmuting agency of
the artist." [6] The biographer is also to be possessed
of a method which may properly be called scientific.
This method in recent years has exerted a structural
influence over biographical writing. The year of 1859
in which was published the *Origin of Species* is the

[4] *The Art of Biography,* William Roscoe Thayer, p. 70.
[5] *Ibid.,* p. 46.   [6] *Ibid.,* p. 95.

year, too, in which Macaulay died. It is a sort of a biographical epoch. The biographer, moreover, is to observe the Greek law of proportion.

In this very personal sketch it is fitting and indeed necessary to intimate how fully Thayer followed his own interpretation of the functions of the biographer. The great Cavour best illustrates and embodies his principles. The other three biographies of Hay, of Roosevelt, and of Washington, furnish further illustration, although less adequately. For the Hay was more of a formal interpretation, written with the aid and full approbation of the family; the Roosevelt was a personal tribute to a loving and loved friend; and the Washington was almost a postscript to his writing, as it was to his life. Toward the close Thayer said to me, ''I wish to write a life of either Lincoln or Washington.'' Washington was the choice, but the result was, as he knew it would be, only an outline and synopsis. In the two volumes of Cavour he has united his own name and service with the triumphs of one of the greatest political creators of the nineteenth century. In the other biographies there is also a union, but the union is far less significant.

In all his writing one does not forget his editorship. As I have intimated already, he was the founder of the *Harvard Graduates' Magazine,* and for twenty-three years he was its great editor. The quarterly was devoted largely to the forces and conditions which constitute Harvard University, and to the careers of

its graduates. But it was also a magazine for articles
on the great subject of education, greatly interpreted.
It was on the whole the best of all the magazines of its
type. Of his life and work as editor he wrote to his
friend Barrett Wendell, ''In heaven, how pleasant an
editor's life must be! No obituaries, no political ties,
no book reviews, no advertisements. Every angel will
know by intuition what books to read. Athletics won't
exist. On the whole—perhaps there won't be any
need of editors in heaven—and that may be why so
few of them here qualify themselves to go there.'' [7]

But my testimony concerning my friend is far less
concerned with him as a great biographer and historian than with him in his essential manhood. In
this manhood there were, it seems to me, at least four
elements constructive. They were courage, wit, humility, reverence.

Thayer's life was smitten not far from the beginning of its active career by a nervous collapse. The
first breakdown began in 1896, and lasted either
directly or indirectly for more than a decade. ''For
four or five years he was able to do nothing that involved any concentration or continuity of effort. With
great difficulty and self-distrust the *Harvard Graduates' Magazine,* so auspiciously begun, was kept going and the sense that he was accomplishing something had a considerable therapeutic value, relieving

[7] *Letters of William Roscoe Thayer.* Edited by Charles
Downer Hazen, p. 160.

for a few moments at least, now and then, the deep melancholia of these days, a melancholia diversified at times by twinges of hysteria.''[8] But even in this long period he continued to work on the *Cavour,* for the writing of which the preceding years of study had so well fitted him. He has told me of his writing not a few of these great pages while lying on the lounge suffering intensely, hardly knowing what he was writing.

Twenty years later, following the recovery from the general collapse, his right eye failed him. In his diary he writes, July 25, 1915, ''Sunday morning, on going downstairs, everything looked black. I found that my right eye was mostly blind. Monday Dr. Williams said this was due to retinal hemorrhages. (Aug. 18th) Dr. Williams says there is little likelihood that I shall ever recover use of my right eye. The left is still intact. So there is something less than half a chance that I shall not become totally blind,''[9] and again, ''The clot in the retina doesn't budge. I am allowed to write or read three times a day, for half an hour at a time. This is like coming to the surface for a breathing spell, after being half-drowned.''[10] The editor of his letters, Professor Charles Downer Hazen, to whose rich volume I am in the greatest debt, says, ''There was no complaint from Thayer. He faced the situation quietly, firmly, stoically. But the conditions of his life were permanently altered for the worse, his work henceforth was impeded and curtailed. But it

[8] *Ibid.,* p. 90.   [9] *Ibid.,* pp. 251-252.   [10] *Ibid.,* p. 252.

did not cease. Adjusting himself, as best he could, to the new and unfavorable circumstances, he carried on." [11]

Often did Thayer speak to me of the constant peril of total blindness. He also wrote to his friend and my friend, Walter Hines Page, in 1904, of his general limitations, saying, "You who have strength to work so splendidly, can never understand—I hope you never may—what it means to go through eight or nine years of eclipse, say rather of hell, unable to fulfil the ordinary duties of life, much less to try to achieve work to which you have devoted years of preparation. It isn't being taught by Fate that your aims and plans are of no importance that is hard to bear; it is being forced to live in a state of dry rot, and to be perpetually tantalized with the desire to do, when the power to do is denied." [12]

Thayer's composure under his nervous breakdowns, his acceptance of the limitations of his eyesight provide glorious illustration of his intellectual courage and moral heroism.

With this unconscious sense of bravery is allied his humor and his wit. The gift is heard in his talk, the gift sparkles in his letters. For instance, in the very midst of the Great War and of his consequent deep depression he writes a charming sketch to his friend and his wife's friend, Mrs. Michael Foster, saying. "A new vocation seems to beckon me, and I have prepared the following card for the papers:

[11] *Ibid.*, p. 252.   [12] *Ibid.*, p. 104.

BREAKFASTING A SPECIALTY

A Gentleman of Parts is open to engagements at breakfast, formal or cosey. A good mixer; very discreet; speaks his mother tongue and several languages; has traveled extensively; has the chameleon's faculty of taking the color of the opinion of those round him; bristles with anecdotes; a judicious provider of chestnuts and *marrons glacés,* which he has collected on three continents; possesses a keen sense of humor, which he discreetly veils from those who have none; EXCELS AS A LISTENER—the highest quality in a conversationalist; equally good at head-to-heads, square parties, and breakfast banquets. *Being on a diet, consumes few victuals.* Terms moderate, on application; vary with the difficulty and dulness of his commensals. His presence suffices to set the seal of fashion on any job-lot gathering, and to shed lustre on any group of aristocratic boneheads." [13]

In the year 1921 he writes to his friend and my friend, Henry Osborn Taylor, saying, "I shall have ceased to read any books on this side of the Great Divide, and shall either know much more or nothing about the mystery which we call Life. I wish that I could feel sure that the Future has in store for me, if I reach the cherubic state, a long, long, afternoon with Leonardo da Vinci seated on a dry and comfortable cloud." [14]

The heroism and gleesomeness of this life sprang

[13] *Ibid.,* p. 285.   [14] *Ibid.,* p. 405.

out of a character which was also gifted with a sense of humility. His was the humility of greatness. The *Cavour* is recognized as one of the great biographies, and as certain of a lasting place in literature as any biography can be. Yet of its earlier stages he says to his friend and co-worker Gay, "I have been going over my recent chapters with unalloyed disappointment. They won't do. The entire work won't do. I have tackled a subject which no living historian— tho' you rolled Goldwin Smith and John Morley into one—could be equal to. Except that I don't approve of 'retiring under fire,' I would abandon history and devote the rest of my life to writing short poems, short stories, and a *journal intime, à la* Pepys, to be printed in the next century, or never. But there's the seductive Cavour, who knows very well that I can't escape from his spell until I have written 'Finis' to his story or 'R. I. P.' is carved on my 'broken column.' I dread not only making a mess of the history, but of turning out one of those desiccated historical cusses whom I have held up all my life as a warning." [15] He also writes to his friend, Mrs. Foster, saying, "Fate decreed that I should not fly, but plod, and often only crawl. Still, I hope that at least the outlines of Cavour's greatness and allure will be found in the book. The subject surpasses every other in the nineteenth century." [16] He also confesses to him who became his biographer, Professor Hazen: "I am very distrustful of my ability to achieve the

[15] *Ibid.,* p. 174.　　　　　[16] *Ibid.,* p. 186.

results which I see ought to be achieved; and I am more conscious of my shortcomings and of my handicap from half-blindness than of any mastery: and so I shall remain humble, in spite of your splendid 'reward of merit.' " [17] To his fellow historian John T. Morse, Jr., in the year 1919, he writes, "I have reached the age when I am more than ever impressed—often staggered—by my own shortcomings, and correspondingly amazed by the excellence of the Masters, who seem to increase in worth with the passing of time." [18] Such humility is indeed the humility of greatness.

With Thayer's courage, wit, humility, there was united a noble sense of reverence. He had a vision of the highest. His support was found in the deepest forces. He was filled with the desire for the broadest understanding. With him the imponderables weighed. Devotion and devoutness rested upon him as a garment. Life was to him sacred. Its duties commanded consecration. Among his papers after the end were found lines entitled *My Prayer*. They were written in the year 1905, at a time when the call to be brave was upon him:

> "I ask not that the blows be spar'd;
>   I would endure, or die:
> I only ask that what my soul has dar'd
>   My flesh may not deny." [19]

Such in bare outline and feeble interpretation was my dear friend, William Roscoe Thayer. In many

[17] *Ibid.*, p. 377.　　[18] *Ibid.*, p. 378.　　[19] *Ibid.*, p. 410.

respects his was an ideal life. To his sister Mabel, in 1889, he wrote, ''At least I see that the ideal life is that in which the balance, between thinking and action, is kept level: unfortunately most of us tip too much to one side or to the other.'' [20] In April, 1918, after interpreting his controversial and polemical life of the war years, he wrote to me, saying, ''I hate controversy. . . . My dream, on the contrary, is to have a year or two after polemics are over, to write some lectures on Biography, and, still more, to spend much time in reading. That dream is based, of course, on the premise that I still have a makeshift for one eye.'' [21] The writing of the lectures on biography, (beyond the Page lectures), and the spending of much time in reading, were not privileges given him in the wished-for fullness. His work, however, was completed. His task was done. That task, early conceived, in great vision, pursued under peculiar stress and strain, was one not wholly unworthy of a Tacitus. The result in biographical literature is lasting.

This very personal sketch I wish to end with the closing lines of Tennyson's ''Ulysses,'' which Hazen says ''seemed to run through his mind as a constant undertone.'' [22]

.   ''Come, my friends,
'Tis not too late to seek a newer world.
Push off, and sitting well in order smite
The sounding furrows; for my purpose holds
To sail beyond the sunset, and the paths

[20] *Ibid.*, p. 67.   [21] *Ibid.*, p. 327.   [22] *Ibid.*, p. 419.

Of all the western stars, until I die.
It may be that the gulfs will wash us down:
It may be we shall touch the Happy Isles,
And see the great Achilles, whom we knew.
Tho' much is taken, much abides; and tho'
We are not now that strength which in old days
Moved earth and heaven; that which we are, we are;
One equal temper of heroic hearts,
Made weak by time and fate, but strong in will
To strive, to seek, to find, and not to yield.''

VIII

WILLIAM EVERETT

BORN October 10, 1839, at Watertown, Mass.; died February 15, 1910. After studying in the Cambridge High School and the Boston Latin School, in 1855 he entered Harvard College, graduating in 1859. At the age of twenty he entered Trinity College, Cambridge, England, becoming B.A. in 1863. He received the degree of LL.B. from Harvard in 1865 after studying at the Law School two years. He was admitted to the Massachusetts Bar in 1866. Appointed Latin tutor at Harvard in 1870, he became assistant professor of Latin in 1873. This place he resigned in 1876. Licensed to preach by the Boston Association of Unitarian Ministers in 1873. In 1878 appointed Master of Adams Academy at Quincy. This office he held for fifteen years, until August, 1893. He entered the House of Representatives in the same year of 1893. This service followed and preceded also a vigorous interest in Federal and local politics. In 1897, on the death of his lifelong friend, William Royall Tyler, he was recalled to the Mastership of the Academy.

Author: On the Cam; College Essays; School Sermons; Hesione, or Europe Unchained (poem); Patriotism (oration); Changing Base; Double Play; Thine, Not Mine; Italian Poets Since Dante; Peace or War.

VIII

WILLIAM EVERETT

STUDENT, TEACHER, INDIVIDUALIST

THE life of William Everett was tragic, his career pathetic. That life and career were full of contrasts, fundamental and superficial. Born to the purple, he wore both the scholar's scarlet gown and the buffoon's cap; educated at both Cambridges, he incarnated the weaknesses and strengths of each; precocious, reciting the *Odes* of Horace, passages from Aristophanes, and telling the length of the principal rivers of the world at the age of six, he yet remained in many ways an untrained boy for three score years and ten. He was a student of the law, but he never practiced; a preacher but he never was installed in a church; a politician having many marks of a statesman, he commanded, for a brief time only, the loyalty of his Massachusetts' constituency; a teacher at Harvard, he failed to receive a full professorship; the head of a New England academy which, bearing an historic name, had at one time given promise of becoming historic itself, he saw it languish into a day school; a Phi Beta Kappa poet, his verses lack sustained

151

imagination; admired and loved, he was also pitied and scorned; capable of high devotion to friends, he was also the victim of his own indifference and contempt; calm and self-controlled, he was the subject of strange outbursts of language and of furious conduct, often ending in an hysteria of tears; called by his cousin Henry Adams, in *Letters,* a "nuisance," he was also described as "grand"; possessing broad interpretations of historic epochs and events, and endowed with visions of high duty, he was also meticulous; vigorous and determined, he was not free from fickleness, petulancies, and pettinesses; inheriting a great name, he demanded a respect for it which went beyond the merit of his own methods and manners; called in the family "Willy" or "Willie" (both spellings were used by his father), he came to be commonly known in the Harvard yard as "Piggy"; kin of historic families, he lived a lonely life, and died almost, if not quite, alone.

Evidences and illustrations of these contrasts and contradictions abound. The members of his own family have given to me not a few. Some of these incidents indeed are too intimate to be printed.

These contrasts and contradictions begin early. A member of the family tells of him as a boy, rushing in from school, "muddy and wet from the street, leap into the middle of a white bed, making strange sounds and screaming with hysterical laughter at the mild reproof of the housekeeper, 'O Mr. Willy dear, your

boots dear.' " . . . "He had such unreasoning atti-
tudes about people; he disliked Phillips Brooks, and
always repeated that he preached excellent Unitarian
sermons." . . . "He was painfully aware of what
people thought of him. I was chiding him once for
not accepting some social function, and he answered
quite pathetically, 'My dear, when I come into a
room, I hear people say, O here is that odd Dr. Everett, and I can't stand it.' " . . . "He once said to a
near relative, 'You are the three things I object to
most, the Episcopal Church, a Southerner, and you
married into the Navy.' "

Paul Frothingham's life of his father, Edward
Everett, offers some intimations, and a chapter in
Later Years of the Saturday Club, 1870-1920, by
Archibald Cary Coolidge gives facts and inferences.
Many letters of Everett entrusted to me bear proof of
the contrasted elements of his character and of his individualistic interpretations of men, of books, of events,
and of movements. These criticisms, even though full
of contrasts, are yet usually given in a tone of severity.
They bear sunshine and also thunder and lightning.
In writing of the performance of the *Œdipus Tyran-
nus* in the year 1894 he says, "I thought Riddle's
conception all wrong, and his performance detestable;
I thought Paine's music impertinent, in every sense
of the word, inappropriate and obtrusive, Osgood's
solo being especially offensive; I thought that with
the exception of Curtis Guild—and perhaps Gardner
Lane—Riddle's false theories dominated and ruined

the otherwise good actors, like Norman and Opdyke." [1]
Everett's epithets bite and his verbs sting like a
hornet. In letters as well as in speech, controversies
easily arose, and his controversies were liable to be
marked by asperities. These controversies frequently
concern things that for the time being were small, as
the spelling of words and the correction of proof
sheets. "According to Webster," as support for pro-
nunciation or spelling, awakened his special venom.
In one letter his comment is "bah." Matters that
now seem quite atomic were debated with the weight
which belongs to constitutional questions. To address
him as "Professor," a form of approach which I once
heard a classmate use, was liable to provoke sallies of
rebuke for the free-speaking, well-intending, offending
student.

Special antagonisms divided the Adams family
from him. Mrs. Charles Francis Adams, Senior, was a
sister of his mother. ". . . it seemed to have been a
kind of Adams pastime to abuse Uncle Will among
themselves. . . ."

These contrasts were found also in his work and life
as a principal. One of his students tells me, "I was
a rather poor Latin scholar, and I remember one day
in class I did something wrong, and he took the
pointer which he had in his hand and broke it over
the back of a chair again and again, and said—'There,
I'd like to break it that way over your back!'

[1] Letter from William Everett, 21 February, 1894, written
in Washington to Mr. William R. Thayer.

"Another day I stood outside the door without a hat on, and he said, pounding one hand on the other —'. . . you little fool you, you deserve to die on that very spot.' "

For certain men too in particular he seemed to have contempt. Senator Hoar he calls the most disagreeable man of his generation. Henry Cabot Lodge quickens special derision. A simple literary problem about Leopardi makes him furious. A type of Italian philosophy is outrageous. Yet at times he writes with moral sublimity and discrimination, as when he says, "If Browning's 'Lost Leader' is unjust to Wordsworth—as I believe it is not—or if Whittier's 'Ichabod' is unjust to Webster—as I believe it is—it seems to me the literary critic should consider the injustice as well as the passion, the vividness, and the pathos. Poetry is a part of duty—there's fine old morality for you." [2] He describes Mary Magdalene as one of "the sweetest and holiest characters in the New Testament." [3] It is also proved that Everett has a kind heart and humble spirit when he writes to William Roscoe Thayer saying, "I thank you very sincerely for your renewed approbation. Without mock modesty, the thing is not all I meant to make it. A very little added and pruned would have made it much nearer my ideal. I experience the common difficulty in getting at my subject. A schoolmaster has habitually to explain so much before he moves ahead, that

[2] *Ibid.*, from Quincy, June, 1904.
[3] Letter from Quincy, May, 1904.

he finds it difficult to avoid long winded poems.'' [4]
The same spirit is likewise breathed in the verses
which he read at the Harvard Phi Beta Kappa dinner
in 1895 to Holmes, Winthrop, and Judge E. R. Hoar.
I quote the three concluding stanzas.

''Holmes, Winthrop, Hoar! through man's appointed
    time
  Full in our sight they trod the grand review;
So let our record swell their passing chime,
  To friendship, honor, duty, Harvard, true.

Past beyond strife, beyond mean cavil past,
  Our country's sky gives every star its sphere;
Since from such rays our horoscope is cast,
  Their light be ours, to guide, to warn, to cheer.

The old must fall; we elders take our turn;
  Youth presses manhood; each their losses know;
Pass, brothers, pass the torch; where'er it burn,
  Responsive sparks in heroes' ashes glow.'' [5]

Everett, entering the older Cambridge at the
age of twenty, had Henry Sidgwick as a tutor. The
tutor was only a year older than the student. In
Sidgwick's *Memoir* we have evidences of the better
and best side of Everett. To his sister Sidgwick writes
soon after the beginning of the association. ''I have
got a young American [W. Everett] reading with me
—a very nice fellow. . . . He has let me into a thing or
two about America.'' [6] Three years later, in 1862, he

[4] *Ibid.,* 4 August, 1900.
[5] *The Harvard Graduates' Magazine,* IV (1895-1896), p. 18.
I also have the manuscript of the whole poem.
[6] *Henry Sidgwick—A Memoir,* p. 44.

writes, "The Society, of course flourishes. [W.] Everett is the only new member. It was a very good election in my opinion. I have had much most interesting talk with him. He has considerable interest in Metaphysics, though his mind is primarily rhetorical. His declamation in chapel was a wonder.[7] The old Dons, to my surprise, were enraptured, Whewell especially."[8] In turn, Everett came to write of his tutor. He says, "I entered Trinity the day I was twenty years old [Sidgwick himself being twenty-one], and almost immediately made arrangements for being his private pupil, the first, I think, he ever had. From that day to this he has occupied a position in my life absolutely unlike any other man's. To say that I admired his talents and enjoyed his company is what so many can say that it tells nothing personal; but he always understood me. I never needed to explain anything. . . . And every time I met him—alas! so sadly rare in all these forty years—was as if we never parted."[9] I may add that I have a copy of Everett's Lowell Lectures *On the Cam* which was given to Sidgwick by Everett himself. It bears this inscription: "Henry Sidgwick with the author's best love. Sept. 27, 1865."

As a partial and yet unique interpretation of the Cambridge years, I want to insert an extract from

---

[7] "The prize declamations were by old custom recited in chapel; W. Everett's striking oration, on Arctic Explorers, was long remembered for its eloquence and effective delivery." *Ibid.*, p. 80, footnote.

[8] *Ibid.*, p. 80.   [9] *Ibid.*, p. 313.

Everett's address on the character of Webster. This
address is included in a thin and rare volume, entitled
*College Essays Delivered in Trinity College, Cam-
bridge,* February 22 and December 16, 1862. It
is not unfitting for special as well as for general reasons to quote what a son of Edward Everett
says to an English academic congregation in the midst
of a dark period of the Civil War. "For higher even
than the glorious gift of eloquence was his heavenly
spirit of patriotism and allegiance to duty; and for
this America honors him. She thanks God in this her
darkest hour that sons were born to her who loved
their country and controlled her counsels well. She
knows their blood has not yet perished. Her hosts now
call for valiant and skilful generals: the voice of the
orator is hushed, the pen of the statesman is still.
But when the strife is over, when peace and union
have returned, as return they shall, she knows that
the old blood will rise again, and a new generation
unite once more the jarring passions and quell the
mad feuds: and for the lessons which such will learn,
must learn, from the life and works of Daniel Webster, is she grateful. If such are hers, she asks for no
others; not for her sculptors, whose breathing mar-
bles are the delight of far countries; not for her
philosophers, who are tracking the finger of the Creator through the mazes of Orion and Hercules; not
even for her eloquent orators and profound jurists;
but for her whole-souled patriots who careless of their
own fame have given their lives to guide aright their

country." [10] (Thirty years after, in the House of Representatives, Everett also made a speech on Webster. It was a rhetorically splendid footnote to the Cambridge eulogy.)

The study of the causes that led to the origin and growth of a character so unique, uniting extraordinary and contradictory forces and weaknesses, belongs rather to the psychologist or psychiatrist than to the layman. Yet I do venture to make two intimations. The first cause is found in the commonplace phrase, Everett was born so. The father's temperament, at once self-ward and generous, and his mother's permanent invalidism gave to him a constitution precocious, highly organized, its diverse parts and functions ill-coördinated. He himself reports that "he heard sounds at a key or two higher than did other people. I have often wondered, supposing this to be true, if the fact that voices and other noises were shriller to him than to the rest of us might not help to explain his ever ready irascibility." [11]

A second influence in the formation of this unique manhood lies in what I venture to call his homelessness. A father was once conferring with Principal Stearns of Phillips Academy, Andover, regarding the ill conduct of his son. The father was affirming in a tone of complacency that he had done everything for

[10] *College Essays Delivered in Trinity College, Cambridge,* by William Everett, p. 38.
[11] *Later Years of the Saturday Club, 1870-1920.* M. A. De Wolfe Howe, Ed. (chapter by Archibald Cary Coolidge), p. 362.

the boy and had given everything to the boy, but that the boy had not proved worthy. "No," said Mr. Stearns, "you have not given to your son everything. You have not given him the most important thing—a home." It would not be just to say that William Everett never had a home. It would be just to say that many of the precious elements of a home were lacking. It might be just to say that he did not have a home because he had so many homes. His mother, as I have intimated, was an invalid, and finally died in her invalidism when he was about twenty years old. As an infant of eight months, he was with the family taken to Europe. It was more than five years before he returned. In four of these years his father was the American minister in London. Returning in 1845, Edward Everett was almost immediately made president of Harvard College. His term of office was brief. Its three years were full of troubles, troubles, too, of many kinds. He left the office in disgust. In 1852 he was made Secretary of State, and while holding this office he was elected Senator. In the first twenty years of William Everett's life, therefore, years in which a boy most needs a home, Boston, London, the two Cambridges, Washington, were the places or homes of his homelessness. He was indeed a peripatetic. Besides this constant changefulness, his father, resigning his seat in the Senate in 1854, felt himself to be a failure in life, the victim of defeats. Such a mood in a father and distressing illness in the mother were not conditions to make a home for a boy who was nervous, sensitive, highly organized. In illustration of this homelessness a member of the family writes me, saying, "During the Everetts' stay at London they lived in a gloomy, vast house in Grosvenor Square; the hall was a dark rising tunnel, pierced on the stairs by oval-topped niches, with no statues; there must have been several of these. My Mother (who was much too old to act so), Uncle Ned, and Uncle Sid would each step into a niche, about the time 'little Willy' was coming up to bed, and as that poor infant came along through that terrifying dark, the others would plunge out on him with gruesome noises and say *'Do you see the eyes of a lull?'* He would run screaming to Ruah and it would be hours before he could be calmed. No wonder his nerves were shattered. And what kind of a man could my grandfather have been to have permitted such actions on the part of children as old as the others. Those fiends of older children put him through fearful tests; one that my Mother thought showed great cleverness on their part was carefully prepared weeks ahead. They made a list the signs on all the shops on each side of the Strand and as they drove along 'Willie' read them. Mama said some he could not pronounce, he was such a baby. They turned and he read the signs on the other side of the street. He was a rival of Macaulay in naming the Popes backward. When they got home he repeated both sides without missing one name. I asked how they could be so cruel and my mother said they were fed up with the child, that they were sick to death of the everlasting showing off and endless quoting his sayings and extolling his brains. Natural, but that showed total lack of judgment on his Father's part.''

It is, therefore, in his original nature and in his homelessness that I find the causes of the uniqueness of his character and of the contrasts and contradictions of his manhood. A boy who begins life a bundle of precocities and of nerves and whose early life is marked by homelessness and an environment of changing conditions is pretty certain finally to possess oddities, quips, crankinesses, and wiles of every sort. Like many a youth of much different social standing and conditions, William Everett did not have a fair chance.

Yet despite all contrasts in conduct, despite every inconsistency in character, despite the uniting of the tragic and comic in his career, despite the contradictions superficial and fundamental, there still remain in William Everett forces and elements solid, substantial, and rich in the noblest parts of manhood. I venture to name four, the intellectual, the ethical, the diversely human, uniting both the intellectual and the ethical, and also, in a comprehensive interpretation, the individualistic.

Everett's intellect was alert and keen, apprehensive of individual facts, discriminating, scholarly, intense in its working, broad in its knowledges, rather classical than scientific, inquisitive and acquisitive. It did not have the accurately arranged linguistic stores which enriched his colleagues, Goodwin and Lane.

Neither did it have the logical power of another associate, Bowen. It was interrogative, like that of his cousin and for a time his colleague, Henry Adams, grasping of facts, eager to know, appreciative. Everett's was an intellect lying close to his emotions. So intimate in fact was the association that at times the feelings leaped over into the intellectual domain and seemed to prevent the proper working of the intellectual forces.

Everett was also a man of essential good will. If he had contempts, and he had them plentifully and painfully, he had also, and more, loyalties. His deepest and lasting loyalty was to his father. The concluding paragraph of the Introduction to his Lowell Lectures given in 1865 is, "As I finish these lines, the last written of this book, a feeling of irresistible sadness comes over me, which no one will reprehend. I went to Cambridge with the counsel, the help, the blessing of one to whom, under heaven, I owe all that makes my life worth living. I passed nearly four years of exile in the light of home thoughts where he was the central sun. I delivered these lectures on my return with his constant encouragement and favor; and now that I make my first start on the path he chose for his own, I can only sigh for the presence which would have excused all errors, doubled all efforts, and supplied all needs, and which is taken from me, from his country, forever." [12] A similar

[12] *On the Cam,* Lectures on the University of Cambridge in England, by William Everett. Introduction, pp. xiv-xv.

loyalty was in kind felt to his friends and co-workers. His Latin poem to Lane voices his feeling. The dedication of *On the Cam* to President Walker of Harvard College is convincing illustration: "My constant model of Christian eloquence and academic culture, and the beloved friend of two former holders of the same honorable position, whose example was my best instruction in college, and whose memory is among my choicest treasures." [13] Everett's were the ethical virtues and verities, even if he lacked the ethical graces. He had no subterfuges, no private meannesses. He was frank, too frank often beyond courtesy, seeking to be just even if unjust, generous with his means to the consequent lessening finally of his own property. "He spent $10,000 for a portrait of Peter Chardon Brooks and $20,000 for a statue of his father. And after his death there were found mountains of bills for household expenses," writes a relative to me. He was kind in heart, even if his words at times seemed thoughtless and even cruel. Happy, be it also added, were many of his experiences. Of one form or cause of his happiness in the older Cambridge he writes with deepest appreciation. "But I know by the joyful contests, the happy encounters of four years, the mornings and afternoons of hard strife, succeeded by the noon recess of hasty comparisons, and the long, merry evening of conviviality, that the dearest friends are the closest rivals, and the happiest hours are in the snatches of competi-

[13] *Ibid.*, Dedication.

tion.''[14] His years in England were without doubt the happiest of his whole life.

Uniting both the intellectual and the ethical and other elements and qualities, Everett was an orator and poet, an interpreter and a teacher. As an orator his power was seen and heard in the pulpit, in the House of Representatives, and in lectures. Samuel McCall of Massachusetts, who entered the House with Everett, declared after no less than seventeen years of membership, "Dr. Everett was as brilliant an orator as I have served with in the House. He had extraordinary animation and a faultless style of expression. The single Congress in which he served had also Bryan, Cockran, and Wilson as members. I think that as an orator he would compare with any one of them.''[15]

In the year 1902 he wrote me, saying, ". . . my correspondents . . . write to me in a tone of most respectful good will, and yet wholly ignore the fact that I was in Congress. Yet my service in the House of Representatives was the only one I ever performed that bore any reference to my real ambition; the only one that was not, from my point of view, a mere accident, rendered on account of connection with other people. I don't say I made much of a statesman, and I know I made a very poor politician; but those things I always meant to be, and a teacher I have

[14] *Ibid.*, p. 89.
[15] *Later Years of the Saturday Club, 1870-1920,* by M. A. De Wolfe Howe, Ed., p. 363.

happened to be." In another letter he also refers
with evident happiness to his service in Congress.
Is it not therefore probable that his "real ambition"
was political?

Everett's Lowell Lectures, *On the Cam,* have many
passages of moving qualities. I quote, however, only
one. It is taken from the concluding lecture. This
quotation should be prefaced with the remark that the
address was given in the closing months of the Civil
War. "Fellow citizens, there is a work, a mighty
work for the united action of England and America.
Let all the orators of both countries come forward to
repeat the glorious destiny awaiting either one of
them. Let them count over every tender memory, and
every brilliant hope known to either, let them pile
up the colossal structure of their towering climaxes
to enshrine the lesson of national duty,—let them recount every state or every colony acknowledging the
sway of either, from the Mackenzie River to Norfolk
Island, from the mouth of the Columbia round east-
ward to the China Sea, over which either country is
bound to diffuse her national blessings,—and their
united eloquence will not realize a tithe of the glories
that await the action of the united nations. What
power on earth can resist two such mighty energies,
leading to some future Chattanooga of liberty the
whole vast army of the Saxon name, in one unbroken
charge along the entire line, circling the flanks, right
and left at once, breasting the heights, crushing
through the rifle-pits, and thundering down the

farther slope on the scattering rabble of darkness?" [16]
The whole passage seems to have the thrill which
Whewell felt in hearing Everett in a declamation six
years before. His cousin, Henry Adams, writes, however, in the year 1871, of a possible article for the
North American, which Everett might submit to him
as editor: "I shudder at the prospect of having to cut
out all his fine writing." [17]

Everett was also a poet. Few examples remain.
But several of the few have both weight and charm.
I quote the last stanza from a "Song for Cambridge"
which closes the Lowell Lecture on "The Great Men
of Cambridge since 1688":

> "O take our greeting! from the sons
>   Of those that left thee for the wild!
> Still in our veins the current runs
>   That kindled then each pious child.
>   And still for all thy triumphs past,
>   In all thy strife to come,
>   God's love and grace on thee be cast,
>   Our fathers' honored home!" [18]

Everett's poetry did not improve with the increasing
years. If it did not lose its versification, it lost its
imagination. The Phi Beta Kappa verses which I
already have quoted could have been put into prose
almost as well as into verse. In his poetry he was
rather an interpreter than the poet, the maker. But

[16] *On the Cam,* by William Everett, pp. 379-380.
[17] *Letters of Henry Adams, 1858-1891.* Edited by Worthington Chauncey Ford, p. 209.
[18] *On the Cam,* by William Everett, p. 291.

he saw life largely even if he did not see it sanely. For Everett was also an interpreter. In both prose and in verse he tried to make the reader and hearer understand, and to understand with justice and appreciation.

Above every other of his special elements and forces, Everett had the gift of teaching. He was himself filled with the highest appreciation of the worth of the teacher. The worth of the teacher he unfolds in a memorial sermon on his "cherished pupil" who "for thirty years he loved as a brother"—William Royall Tyler. At the time of his death, at the age of forty-five, Tyler was the master of Adams Academy. Everett's interpretation is that a teacher is to be "full of authority, of truth, of knowledge, of wisdom, of gentleness, of sympathy, of patience, of courage, of justice, of honor." [19] These qualities, no less than ten in number, Everett infers from the character of Jesus Christ, whom he calls the "great teacher."

Everett himself possessed at least two of the fundamental forces of a great teacher—a knowledge of the subject taught and a sense of life. His knowledge of Latin, the special subject of his teaching, was not that of Lane or of Greenough. He could not have written a formal Latin grammar. But his knowledge of the language was broad and exact as far as it went. It was devoted rather to the literary than to the lin-

[19] *The Great Teacher,* by W. Everett (A sermon delivered in the Stone Temple, Quincy, Massachusetts, December 12, 1897, in commemoration of the life and services of W. R. Tyler), p. 12.

guistic or to the philological side. It was a comparative knowledge and full of spirit. It was set with happy and apt allusions to English literature. From his teaching of the *Odes* of Horace one got lessons in English composition of precious worth. Moreover, all his teaching was touched by a sense of life. Horace was made to sing of his friends, of thrilling loves and of springtime, in appreciating beauty. Everett's touch caused Livy to breathe, and to speak in his heavy, compact, slow-moving paragraphs. Such vital teaching of the Latin classics was of priceless worth to the Harvard Freshmen of fifty and more years ago. His interest, too, in vital teaching is proved by his vigorous volumes of stories for boys.

In his service as teacher and as master Everett was also a preacher. He was a preacher under conditions at once hard and easy. To preach to boys is a task trying for the typical minister. For the minister is liable not to see with the boy's eyes, or to feel with the boy's heart, or to appreciate as the boy appreciates. But if the preacher does see, feel, and appreciate as do the boys, the privileges of such a preacher are priceless. Everett was one of the few happy preachers to boys. His little volume of school sermons is evidence and proof. For they are short, never exceeding twenty minutes' delivery and often not fifteen. They are in part *extempore,* and even if written they seem to be *extempore.* They are filled with a feeling of love for his young hearers. "My dear boys," "My own dear boys" is, without patronizing, a common form

of address. The themes are such as boys delight in.
Among them are ''Thoughtfulness a Duty,'' ''Energy,'' ''Friendship,'' ''Strength.'' In the list are
found six sermons on Christ: ''Christ a Light,''
''Christ the Lifter,'' ''Christ an Example,'' ''Christ's
Self-Denial,'' ''Christ Our Master,'' ''Christ the Son
of God.'' They are thus filled with thoughtfulness,
aimed at direct points—and they are eloquent. I wish
I could quote several paragraphs in illustration. I
must be content with only one: ''Gird up the loins of
your mind, fight the good fight of faith, run with
patience the race set before you. If your strong body
goes with a weak will,—if your strong passions silence
a feeble conscience,—if your smart brain conquers a
fainting honor,—if your keen wit crushes a faltering
faith,—spring to your feet; lift up your voice to God
in prayer; for the sake of truth, of duty, of love,
brace every power you have got to trample that base
strength, which is weakness. Call out that tender,
humble, confiding weakness which is really strength.
Acknowledge, as we all have to do, how feeble we are
at our best,—how utterly at the mercy of disease, of
passion,—how much we need our friends, our Master,
our God.'' [20]

In conclusion, and in sum, I wish to say that William Everett ever seems to me to be a mighty individualist. Such an interpretation may not be an explanation of the man, but I wish to set it down as a

[20] *School Sermons,* by W. Everett (Preached to the boys at
Adams Academy, Quincy, Massachusetts), p. 186.

fact. He was himself. He was rigidly apart, he was indeed unlike other men. Unlike his comrades in childhood and youth, he continued to be unlike all of his contemporaries of each generation. In his pervading and prevailing individualism he seemed to find contentment. In the concluding paragraph of his fourth Lowell Lecture *On the Cam* he says, "But it is from the last element in her system of study,—the element of individual action, that each student shall choose his own course for himself, and carry it out by himself,—that Cambridge derives her peculiar strength and power. It is by this that her student obtains a sense of personal duty in his work that nothing else can give. There is no compulsion on him; no task-work. Silently are the doors of the mother's temple thrown open; if he will, he may enter, and take his place with the initiated. If, therefore, he choose to enter, rather than remain with the jesting throng without, it is for his honor and his conscience to carry out the noble work he has undertaken. If he fail aright to gain the mystic secret,—if, when the heavens are about to open, and the revelation of the tender goddess to descend, he mar the ceremony with words or acts of ill-omen,—when the minister thrusts him from the temple, he will see the sad faces of the worshippers turned to him, saying plainer than words, 'Thou thyself would'st have it so.' " [21] The individualism of his English college and university entered

[21] *On the Cam, Lectures on the University of Cambridge in England,* by W. Everett, pp. 127-28.

into his own unique character, possessing and ruling it.

As I read over what I have written, I find a grateful quickening of my relation to Everett. It was a relation made up of affection, of admiration, and of pity. His loyalties and his generosities called out one's love. His unique abilities and his achievements commanded admiration. The failures and the thwartings of his career, largely though not entirely of his own making, his personal sorrows, his lack of the sense of proportional values, his misunderstood, his unnecessary, enmities quicken a lasting pity. Both a smile and a tear for William Everett.

IX
TALCOTT WILLIAMS

BORN at Abeih, Turkey, July 20, 1849; died January 24, 1928, in New York City. A.B., Amherst, 1873, A.M., 1883; Hon. A.M., University of Pennsylvania, 1891; L.H.D., Amherst, 1896, Western Reserve University, 1897; LL.D., University of Pennsylvania, 1895, Hobart, 1899, Western Reserve, 1909; Litt.D., University of Rochester, 1902; on staff of New York World, 1873-77; Washington correspondent for New York Sun, and San Francisco Chronicle, 1877-79; editorial writer for Springfield Republican, 1879-81, Philadelphia Press, 1881-1912; dean, Pulitzer School of Journalism of Columbia University, 1912-19; Emeritus 1919-28.

Author: Turkey, a Problem of Today; The Newspaper Man; associate editor of the New International Encyclopædia.

TALCOTT WILLIAMS

MAN OF MANY KNOWLEDGES

My friendship with Talcott Williams was of early origin, and of late growth. I knew him at Phillips Academy, Andover, in 1868 and 1869 as a younger schoolmate knows an elder, but if he knew me at all it was only as an upper-classman knows a junior. After he graduated, in 1869, our paths divided. He went to Amherst, and on graduation in 1873 began his great career as a journalist. His first service was on the *New York World,* then under the brilliant editorship of Manton Marble. Our relations, however, were resumed in the middle of the last decade of the last century. At that time he was in the midst of his outstanding editorial service on the *Philadelphia Press.* Some common academic duty brought us together. He became Talcott to me, and I, Charles to him.

Talcott knew more about more subjects than any man I ever met. He was willing, with diffidence, to acknowledge the variety and fullness of his information. To a remark of my wife regarding his knowledges, he replied: "Philadelphia street car conductors, you know, have to carry Two Dollars in change. Two Dollars serves their needs. A small amount of knowledge of any subject fills my immediate needs.'' Yet the thoroughness of his knowledge was greater than its variety intimates. It was *multum* as well as *multa*. Such intellectual acquaintances and avariciousness ran in the blood of the family. It was also developed by his own vocation and avocations.

For Talcott was a son of an American missionary, William Frederic Williams, who went to Turkey in 1849. His service, beginning at Beirut, was continued at Mardin, Northern Mesopotamia, for thirteen years, till his death at Mardin in 1871. Talcott's boyhood memories concerned Mardin; in his last years he wanted to return there.

His uncle was S. Wells Williams, who went to Canton as early as 1833. For forty years he was devoted to affairs in China, and in 1874 he crowned his diverse labors by the publication of *The Syllabic Dictionary of the Chinese Language*, a monumental work and apparently of lasting worth. In the last ten years of his life he was Professor of Chinese in Yale.

Out of such stock came Talcott Williams. He was born on the slope of the Lebanon Mountains. His early environment was an old civilization. His father was his first, and most formative, teacher. He has told me of the comradeship which his father gave to him. His playmates were Arab, Turkish, and Syrian boys. His knowledge of these three languages and

of conditions in these three lands began early, and
it was never forgotten. The homes in Philadelphia
and New York bore visible evidence. Manuscripts
and plaques, marble slabs, many types of archæologi-
cal research and discovery were witnesses of, and
ministers to, the vast diversity of his interests.

His writings, moreover, were both a cause and result of his learning. His service on the *Philadelphia
Press,* largely as editorial writer from 1881 to 1912,
contributed to this breadth of knowledge. He once
said to me, "I have written more than is contained
in the 'Encyclopædia Britannica.' " It was a modest
statement. On subjects of all sorts he wrote: political, educational, financial, commercial, social, literary,
æsthetic, religious.

This diverse and broad knowledge was an essential
part of his character. It was almost a living and
breathing force. He held it, not as a selfish treasure,
but as a trustee, and in a most altruistic spirit. For
Talcott was a very friendly man. If in New York or
Philadelphia one more learned could be found,
surely no man more friendly was seen or felt. He
was interested in people just as people, he loved human beings as human beings. His interest in, and
love for them, was in some part at least, quickened
by their uniqueness, their remoteness from the home
base, and by their distresses. Seldom did one dine at
his home without finding a Turkish woman, or a
professor of a Near East college, or a Syrian youth
also as a guest. His wife's guest book was a world

compendium. His mood toward his friends, and they were of course numberless, was a beautiful emotional, intellectual response and appreciation, and a desire to help them in their many quests and diverse needs. His mind teemed with suggestions. As my *Guides, Philosophers, and Friends* was passing through the press, he spoke to me of the advantage of prefacing each sketch with a page of biographical data. The addition was at once made. Yet his intimations were free from patronizingness. In his love, as in his learning, he was prodigal. His love went out unto all sorts of strange characters, and into all sorts of remote places, but its holiest radiance shone in his own home.

In this friendliness were joined together two characteristics, by nature opposed, but which, united, helped to form the beauty and holiness of Talcott's character—humility and pride. I should call Talcott a humble man. He measured himself not with other men, but with the infinite standards. He thought far more of what he ought to do or could do than of what he had done. His vision rested rather on opportunities to be entered than on the service he had already given. His humility was remote from a spirit of humiliation. It was far from abasement. If it showed itself in modesty of manner, as it did, it was at heart sincere, genuine, real. But with this sense of insufficiency, normal in great souls, was joined a sense of pride. This pride was fundamental. It was the essence of respect for one's self. It belonged to the

origins of manhood. It meant a keen appreciation of
responsibilities. It was integral to his being, it stood
for a relationship between his divine master and himself. It represented an altar at which he was the
single priest. It embodied the dignities, the civilities,
the sanctities of individual being. It was so strong
and so true that it could not show itself ostenta-
tiously. It had no need of assumptions: it was of
royal birth. This union of humility and of pride was
normal and most necessary to Talcott. Humility
without pride is in peril of becoming humiliation and
abasement. Pride without humility is in like peril
of becoming ostentation, pomposity, and a spectacle.

Such a union of opposing qualities helped to create
in Talcott a constant openness of mind. Advancing
years, and he was in his seventy-ninth when he died,
did not diminish at all his avidity for knowledge or
the liveliness of his interests. His face was ever toward the sunrise. His anticipations were structural.
Waiting for surprises was natural. Every new
caller might be a messenger from some celestial para-
dise, or even purgatory. His constant progress from
the smaller place to the larger, from reporter to editorial writer, from editorial writer to the directorship
of a school of journalism, illustrates his enlarging responsiveness. The rise has its origin and moving force
in the glorious essence of expectation. The better and
the best were to him yet to be. He embodied Browning's glorious optimism. This openness of mind was,
in a sense, a door, swinging both ways. Out of it

came suggestions for improvement in method, and for enrichment of content in some service, and for broader inclusiveness of well-doing. Every meeting of the senators of Phi Beta Kappa was waiting for intimations of better ways of doing yet better things. In this breadth was embraced a willingness to receive and to consider every suggestion made regarding any piece of work yet to be done. His mind went out to other minds, and other minds were welcomed into his own treasure house.

Having richer meaning for his own personal character than any other force or element was his religion. Talcott was essentially and fundamentally religious. Such he was by birthright, early environment, and education. By heritage and by personal choice he was a Christian. His was a faith intelligent, rational, and also emotional. Its psychological elements were held in proper proportion and relation. His faith, based on evidence, was bathed in feeling, intimated itself in noble conduct, and ever went forth into good deeds. It was as remote from intellectual autocracy as it was from pietism. The intellectual verities were closely joined to the ethical severities. For his life was no Roman holiday, but a condition for noble service and for hardest striving. He worked as if he were ever in his great taskmaster's eye. He heard the oracles of God as if they were commandments, and he obeyed them soberly, reverently, gratefully. He focused his attention on the great things. Dissipation on the trivial was foreign to his nature.

His religion helped to form his whole character, and the resulting character in turn helped to constitute his faith.

This faith was of a broad type; many scriptures, I believe, were to him holy, but different scriptures differed in their degree of holiness. The Christian Bible was far more revealing of God and authoritative than the Koran. If he knew the Buddhistic philosophy, he knew also, and better, the Gospel of St. John. If indeed he did accept the first part of the first verses of the Epistle to the Hebrews, "God, who at sundry times and in divers manners spake in time past unto the fathers by the prophets," he also accepted the conclusion, "hath in these last days spoken unto us by His Son, whom he hath appointed heir of all things, by whom also he made the worlds." As has been said by one of his associates of the School of Journalism, Professor Roscoe C. E. Brown, "He could be at the same time a vestryman of an Episcopal Church in one town and an officer of a Congregational Church in another." [1] In Jesus he found the summation of the articles of his creed, and the consummation of life's purposes and forces.

Talcott's religion was not a personal affair only. It went out from him almost as an institutional power, guide, and creator. More than once he has told me of the administration of the sacrament of com-

[1] "Dr. Talcott Williams," an address delivered at the annual service of the School of Journalism at St. Paul's Chapel, Columbia University, May 16, 1928, by Roscoe C. E. Brown, Litt.D., Professor of Journalism.

munion at the time of the opening of the School of Journalism at Columbia, and of the continuance of the celebration at the beginning of each annual session. He knew and felt that, quickened by the religious impulse and atmosphere, the great undertaking, both for teachers and for students, would reach a nobler level of achievement. He believed, and he labored in the belief, that all American and all world institutions should be founded on religious principles and developed through religious motives and other religious forces and conditions. This belief touched his interpretation of life with its numberless numbers of interests and of omnipotent forces. A soldier of humanity, he fought with a sword bathed in heaven. Yet, be it said, his was not the life of a recluse, of a pious monk, or of a devoted and remote suppliant. He lived with men. A happy comrade he was, exulting in, and contributing to, the jollity of every occasion. A fraternity man in college, the Alpha Delta Phi, a fraternity man he continued to be to the last. If he felt that the springs of his life, as should be the springs of the life of every man, were in God, he also knew that the restoring waters should flow through the human pastures, making them green, beautiful, fruitful. To thousands he was a dear and great friend. Thousands found in him the best elements of friendship. To me as one of the thousands he gave of his best. I loved Talcott.

X

HENRY THEOPHILUS FINCK

BORN Bethel, Mo., Sept. 22, 1854; died October 1, 1926; A.B., Harvard, 1876; resident graduate, Cambridge, 1877-78, student of sociology; received Harris fellowship and studied psychology at Berlin, Heidelberg, Vienna, 1878-81. Musical critic and general editorial writer, The Nation, New York Evening Post, from 1881.

Author: Romantic Love and Personal Beauty, 1887; Chopin, and Other Musical Essays, 1889; Pacific Coast Scenic Tours, 1890; Spain and Morocco, 1891; Wagner and His Works, 1893; Lotos Time in Japan, 1898; Pictorial Wagner, 1899; Anton Seidl, 1899; Primitive Love and Love Stories, 1899; Songs and Song Writers, 1900; Fifty Mastersongs, 1902; Fifty Schubert Songs, 1903; Grieg and His Music, 1909; Fifty Grieg Songs, 1909; Success in Music and How It Is Won, 1909; Massenet and His Operas, 1910; Food and Flavor, 1913; Richard Strauss, 1917; Gardening with Brains, 1922; Girth Control, 1923; Musical Progress, 1923.

X

HENRY THEOPHILUS FINCK

FRIEND, PHILOSOPHER, MUSICAL CRITIC

IT would be hard to find a friend to whom I offer more or greater contrasts than to Henry Finck. He was of German stock, I of Anglo-Saxon; he was born in Missouri, I in Maine; he came to Harvard from the Pacific Northwest, Oregon, I from the Atlantic Northeast, Maine; his early religious training was of the German type, mine of the orthodox Congregational; he was a great interpreter of music; I am liable to get the sonatas of Beethoven mixed up with the operas of Wagner. But we had one element in common: our love for philosophic studies. Yet with him these studies took on constantly and finally an artistic relationship, with me they became directed toward theology and academic administration. Early in college we became close friends. Fifty years after our graduation, it became my duty to commit ashes to ashes, dust to dust.

Henry's life itself contained contrasts: the contrast of a long, consistently followed vocation and of several minor, yet important, avocations. For forty-three

185

years he was a musical critic of the New York *Evening Post,* and devoted to writing books on Wagner and Grieg. He also wrote books on themes as diverse as anthropology, horticulture, and personal health.

Henry's foundation for his musical interpretation and judgment was laid in philosophy. Beginning with such a foundation, he was able to build a superstructure, beautiful, impressive, apparently lasting. He had as his teachers William James, George Herbert Palmer, and Francis Bowen. Of Bowen, the head of the department and the least known of the trio, Finck says: "Bowen was as belated and reactionary in philosophy as Agassiz was in science. I shared hardly any of his convictions, yet I revered and adored him and he liked me." [1] Under such personal tuition he came to the works of Fichte and Schelling; but he regarded their books as "words, words, words." Yet in Kant he found much, very much, besides verbosity and a bad style. Schopenhauer and Hartmann also made rich and fresh contributions. At graduation he took highest honors in philosophy.

Among the outstanding personalities of the Harvard faculty of the eighth decade of the last century were Charles Eliot Norton and John K. Paine. With both Norton and Paine, Henry was personally more intimate than with the formal philosophers. Of Norton, he writes: "Charles Eliot Norton was one of the Harvard professors to whom I look back with the

[1] *My Adventures in the Golden Age of Music,* by Henry T. Finck, p. 99.

warmest gratitude for benefits received," [2] and "I kept in touch with Norton after leaving college. The following letter dated March 6, 1877, is printed here because it illustrates his kind interest in his pupils: 'I was pleased to receive a few days since your letter from Munich, and your account of Wagner's 'The Mastersingers.' I put your article at once into Mr. Godkin's hands, and am glad to say that it will appear this week (or next week) in the *Nation*. I read it with much interest and thought it was well done.' " [3]

But the relationship with Paine became more and most intimate. "My friendship with Paine is one of the most agreeable chapters in the story of my life. He was a most kind and companionable man." [4]

Philosophy and æsthetics represent responsiveness in the learner as well as scholarship and wisdom in the teacher. Henry was born a genius in music. Of his genius I cannot give better evidence than that which he himself offers, writing of his first experience with Chopin. "One day, in Boston, I saw, at Ditson's, a collection of his nocturnes in a bright red paper cover. A glance showed me—for I could hear music with my eyes—that here was something rich and strange that would enchant me.

"It was a red-letter day in my musical life. That night, when everything was quiet in the college yard, I went into our basement music room, placed the nocturnes on the piano with feverish haste and began

[2] *Ibid.*, p. 71.   [3] *Ibid.*, p. 72.   [4] *Ibid.*, p. 80.

to play. It was like an opium dream, a vision of strange, thrilling, voluptuous delights. With the sole exception of Schubert's songs, no German music had ever so enchanted me as these melancholy Polish strains.

"Hour after hour passed. I played through the whole collection and then some of the pieces over and over again. Tears of joy often dimmed my eyes so that I could not see the printed page." [5]

Building on such philosophic, æsthetic, and personal foundations, Henry continued generation after generation to make wisest and most edifying interpretations of the works and workers in the great field of music.

Yet, for my present personal purpose, Henry as a man, and as a friend (and the human qualities, of course, are also most constructive in all technical work) is far more vital than his professional genius and service.

The one element, comprehensive and fundamental, which seems to me to constitute and to control Henry, was his simplicity of character. He was free from all complexities, intellectual or ethical. In every mood and attitude he was honest; in every method, genuine; in every act, sincere and direct. As such his life began and as such it continued to be and ended. He was innocent in the best and noblest sense. The look of his face in college days is proof, and his face seen in his last illness, as I saw it, adds evi-

[5] *Ibid.*, p. 77.

dence. It was as free from wrinkles in his seventieth
year as in his seventeenth. No face known to me
changed so little in fifty years. Childlikeness in look
and demeanor was characteristic at the end as it was
in the beginning, a characteristic, be it added, which
belongs to many great souls.

Consistent with his simplicity, were his enthusiasms.
He had a keen responsiveness to thrills. His confidence and faith in his friends was colored by noble
emotion. This emotion was manifest in richest service for his friends, and especially for his friends
when in distress. His interpretations of musicians
abound in the superlatives. In their death his heart
seemed to break. He writes of himself and of his
wife as "crying like babies" over the death of Seidl.
A childlike impulsiveness was very manifest in all
relations to his dearest ones.

Closely akin to his simplicity and enthusiasm were
his courage and frankness. This courage and frankness were both moral and intellectual. He was a de-
fender of good men, and a champion of worthy causes.
Any apparent injustice stirred his soul. To his
friends he was loyal, to himself he was loyal, but
he could condemn himself as well as his antagonists.
"My attacks" he says, "were sometimes unreasonably
severe," [6] and he writes, too, of his "ridiculous sav-
agery." [6] He also writes of Godkin, his chief, as
"curbing my fierceness." [7] He once speaks of himself,
saying "I was a fool." [8] Under a figure he gives his

[6] *Ibid.*, p. 191. [7] *Ibid.*, p. 253. [8] *Ibid.*, p. 286.

idea of the perfect musical critic—"He should don his armor and fight fiercely for what he thinks the best and most important things in art." [9]

Henry's courage and frankness were especially intimated in his wit and humor. Despite the fact that the first and most moving examples of wit and humor are found in the oral utterance, yet there is a secondary worth belonging to the written. As he himself says, jokes are more interesting than serious matters. His chief, Villard, says of him, "If Henry Finck had turned professor instead of critic he would undoubtedly have been the Fliegende Blätter kind, he would at times absentmindedly have put his umbrella to bed and himself in the hall clothes-closet." [10] One of his reviewers writes of his witticisms as having a longer life than the judgments of many of his coördinate critics of other journals. Henry even fell into the pit of making puns, and of puns his own are apt to be based on things rather fundamental. The title of one of his books, *Girth Control*, illustrates.

As I have already suggested, a fundamental part of Henry's character lies in his capacity for friendships. Such a capacity sprang from and was joined with his simplicity, his courage, and his enthusiasms. He was a most friendly man. His friendliness was felt in deeds as well as in moods. His relations to Paderewski and Kreisler are proof. His wise plans for the boy Hofmann illustrates his feeling. "When he made his first American tour he was, as I have

[9] *Ibid.*, p. 254.   [10] *Ibid.*, p. 269.

said, only eleven years old. I soon noticed alarming indications that he was being overworked, so I started an agitation for saving his genius to the world. A wealthy music lover offered the funds for enabling him to retire a few years for the sake of his health. He became a pupil of Rubinstein, and when he returned to the stage he was a robust young man as well as a great artist.'' [11] His intimacy with Woodberry also gives evidence. But with his capacities for friendships went along also an equal capacity for enmities. His enmities were products indeed of his impulsiveness. These enmities were not deep, unless the enemy was at bottom bad, deceptive, corrupt, corrupting. In his enthusiasm, he writes, ''There were days during the war when, if I could have done so, I would have eagerly touched a button that would have exterminated every man in the German Empire. Yet that did not make me turn my back on the music of the Germans.'' [12] In a semi-jocose vein he also writes of pansies, and of his feeling toward a certain type of them. ''Pansies are like humans. Some are overbig and loud and commonplace and vulgar—I positively *hate* them.'' [13] I am sure that his feeling for his enemies was a good deal like his feeling for the ''overbig'' pansies, free from all maliciousness. Therefore, his enemies, if he have any still left, admire, honor, and like him.

As I began I intimated that with his great vocation

[11] *Ibid.*, p. 305.   [12] *Ibid.*, p. 389.
[13] *Gardening with Brains*, p. 162.

Henry had several avocations. Most of us are happy
enough if we have a single avocation to run by the
side of our chief calling. Henry had several side-paths.
Perhaps his study of the origin and development of
certain characteristics of the human race represents
his chief minor calling. In his researches in this field
he came to a conclusion. He believed he was the
"originator of the theory that romantic love is a modern sentiment unknown to savages and the ancient
civilized nations." [14] It is a conclusion which in its
essence still has great weight with the anthropologists.

In his autobiography, happily called *My Adventures in the Golden Age of Music*, Henry frequently
writes of his good luck. The best fortune which ever
befell him, as he himself knew and recognized, was
his marriage. For, his meeting Abbie Cushman was
not only a case of love at first sight and first hearing,
but also a case of love of infinite relationship. Sal-
lust's remark of similarity of tastes being a basis of
friendship applies also even more strongly to fundamental family relations. For Abbie and Henry were
one in all matters of musical interpretation. She
many a time has taken his place as critic in important undertakings. A justifiable substitution it all
was. As Villard in happy praise has intimated, "he
has palmed off some of his able wife's music criticism
as his own." [15]

[14] *Who's Who in America,* 1926-27, p. 704.
[15] *My Adventures in the Golden Age of Music,* p. 269.

XI
FRANCIS EDWARD CLARK

BORN Aylmer, P. Q., of N. E. parentage, Sept. 12, 1851; died May 25, 1927, Newton, Mass. Orphaned at seven, and adopted by his uncle, Rev. E. W. Clark, and assumed his name; graduated from Dartmouth, 1873; Andover Theological Seminary, 3 years. Became pastor of Williston Church, Portland, Maine, which from a small mission he built up into a large Congregational church; founded, Feb., 1881, the Society of Christian Endeavor; pastor of Phillips Church, South Boston, 1883-87; devoted his life to the Christian Endeavor work, as president of the United Society, editor of The Christian Endeavor World; traveled around the world five times in interest of the work.

Author: Our Vacations; Life of William E. Harwood, Portland, Me.; The Church and the Young People; Our Business Boys; Looking Out on Life; Danger Signals; Young People's Prayer Meetings; Ways and Means; Christian Endeavor Saints; Our Journey Around the World; The Mossback Correspondence; Fellow Travelers; The Everlasting Arms; The Great Secret; World-Wide Endeavor; Old Lanterns for New Paths; A New Way Around an Old World; Training the Church of the Future; Christian Endeavor Manual; The Continent of Opportunity; Similes and Figures from Alexander Maclaren; Old Homes of New Americans; The Holy Land of Asia Minor; In Christ's Own Country; The Charm of Scandinavia (with Sydney A. Clark); Our Italian Fellow Citizens; The Gospel of Out-of-Doors; Memories of Many Men in Many Lands. Also of many other books, together with leaflets, addresses, sermons, etc.

FRANCIS EDWARD CLARK

A BISHOP, HAVING THE WORLD AS HIS DIOCESE

THE anthropologists, both learned and unlearned, have long debated and will long continue to debate, whether heredity or environment makes the larger contribution to the constitution and development of the individual. It is a good question to debate, for it embraces the deepest interests of humanity. It is a question, too, to which, in our present knowledge, no exact answer can be given.

In the life and career of him whom I have long called, and shall ever think of as, Frank Clark, were found evidences concerning the value of both heredity and environment. For Frank was the son of a minister, the father dying at the son's age of three years. His mother, a student of Mary Lyon, was a teacher. The head also of a home, her devotion to her family and to her school was of the deepest meaning. At his age, however, of seven she too died. Committed to the care of her brother, Frank was brought up in the home of one who was a Congregational minister. He gave up the family name of Symmes, adopting the name of his uncle and foster father. Both his ancestry and his environment represent the noblest traditions and elements of the best Canadian and American homes. The environment was worthy of the origins. It stood for the neighborhood and the neighborliness of simplicity, for moral atmospheres, and for the historical and personal influences of the Christian family. It stood also for steady intellectual progressiveness. This progressiveness was represented in an historic New England Academy—Kimball Union—at Meriden, New Hampshire, in Dartmouth College, and in Andover Theological Seminary.

In Dartmouth College, for the four years between 1869 and 1873, Clark got an education which formed the constructive elements of character. His course of study was like the course found in most New England colleges in the seventh and eighth decades of the last century. In the Freshman year Greek, Latin, and mathematics were its only or chief subjects. In the Sophomore year Latin and mathematics were continued, and two modern languages, French and German, and "natural history" were added. In the Junior year Latin was continued, and Greek reappeared. Some seven other subjects were included in that curriculum. Among them were physics, international law, rhetoric, and logic, and what were called "evidences," together with the two sciences of astronomy and botany. The Senior year manifested a similar medley. Subjects bearing the names of metaphysics, English, chemistry, analytical chemistry,

Butler's Analogy, political economy, and geology were his studies. The whole course seems to lack a centre, direction, and guidance. But out of its diversities Clark after all got an education. His graduation proved that he ranked seventh in his class. He also was educated, like the typical student, somewhat by every other college student. Whatever may be the worth or lack of worth of the college teacher of the earlier time, the boys educated each other. But Clark was also educated, in part at least, by the president. For the president, Asa Dodge Smith, Clark had known previous to his coming to college. The acquaintanceship deepened in the college years. Of him Clark writes in his autobiography, "His kindness was continued throughout all my college course, and on one occasion at least, he talked with me very seriously about entering the ministry, and, before the interview was ended, dropped upon his knees and prayed that I might be led to give my life to such service. I am glad that his prayer was answered, and that he preached the sermon when I was ordained and installed as pastor of Williston Church, in Portland, Maine. This was one of the very last acts of his life, for he was soon after taken ill, and within a few months went to his great reward.

"To think of a president of our great colleges of to-day praying with an individual student that he might be led into the ministry! Well I am afraid, that to some it might savor of the impossible, I hope not of the ludicrous. I am convinced, however, that

there would be more graduates from our universities
in the ministry to-day if there were more Asa D.
Smiths in the presidential chairs, though I admit that
Dartmouth has had greater presidents in these later
years." [1]

Clark's chief interest outside of his studies was
found in journalism. His son, Eugene, wrote me not
long before his early and lamented death saying, "He
was, in fact, quite undecided up to the end of his
senior year as to whether he would go into the ministry or into journalistic work. He was an editor of
The Dartmouth and apparently a very active editor
during his last two years and as a senior was one of
a group of students who founded and edited a very
creditable journal known as *The Anvil* which, however, succumbed after the graduation of those responsible for its beginnings. He was also an enthusiastic
member of Psi Upsilon and active in all its affairs
and naturally one of the leaders in the religious life
of the college." [2]

From Dartmouth College Clark, like so many other
Dartmouth men of the middle decades of the last
century, entered Andover Theological Seminary. In
this seminary, as in the college, Clark found that the
greatest influence formative of his career was personal. Edwards A. Park, professor of theology, was
one of the great teachers of his time. But the influ-

[1] *Memories of Many Men in Many Lands,* by Francis E.
Clark, p. 45.
[2] Personal letter from Professor Eugene F. Clark, December 31st, 1929.

ence of Park was, on the whole, more personal than scholastic or philosophical. He writes, "Of all the teachers whom I have ever known, perhaps I might say of all the men I have ever known, Professor Edwards A. Park was the most pre-eminent in his personality. It was no task to take his lectures. Students looked forward to them as to a rare treat, as they would to a lyceum lecture by John B. Gough or some other brilliant light of the lyceum platform. Professor Park's logic was unanswerable if we accepted his premises, as most of us did without hesitation, and every lecture was lighted up by a rare humor, which never seemed to lose its edge as do the oft-repeated humorous interludes of many teachers." [3]

Andover was recognized as the chief seminary of the Congregational Churches, but to it came members of other communions. Among such ecclesiastical foreigners were William Lawrence, who became Bishop of Massachusetts, and also John Cotton Brooks, the younger brother of Phillips Brooks, who was a roommate of Clark. Of John Brooks, Clark writes, "In his seminary days he was a fellow of infinite jest and high spirits, and he could never settle down for a 'go' at the Hebrew lexicon or grammar without first throwing all the sofa pillows in the room at my head." [4]

Upon his graduation at Andover in 1876 Clark be-

[3] *Memories of Many Men in Many Lands,* by Francis E. Clark, p. 58.
[4] *Ibid.,* p. 58.

came immediately the minister of a new Congregational church in that most urban of all small cities, Portland, in the State of Maine. The most outstanding result of this ministry was the organizing of what has become known as the Young Peoples Society of Christian Endeavor.

For many years before the eighth decade of the nineteenth century the Protestant churches of the United States had been devoting themselves with special activity to the religious interest of the so-called young people. Organizations of many kinds and under diverse methods had been formed to interest boys and girls, young men and women in the church, and to promote their Christian culture. Such societies, however, had usually proved to be ineffective and of a short life. No one of them "seemed to accomplish the desired result of training up a company of devoted, earnest young people, outspoken among their companions in their acknowledgment of Christ's claim and ready to work for Him along all practical and systematic lines." [5] The Young Peoples Society of Christian Endeavor, however, was an "*out-and-out* Christian society. The pastor had become tired of half-way measures for training his young people, and while he doubted the efficacy of the new plans, he decided that they were well worth trying." [6]

The result of the foundation of this Society in the Portland church and in other churches in the following years added evidence to the truth of the great

[5] *Ibid.*, p. 78.   [6] *Ibid.*, p. 81.

interpretation that a summons to a hard duty quickens loyalty, arouses enthusiasm, and creates persistence and staying power in a devoted membership. The work thus begun in one small and new church in a small city was the origin and spring of a world-wide and moving tide of power and of influence. The movement spread to other churches and to other denominations than the Congregational. It moved forth to all parts of the world. It grew and it has come to fill the earth as the water fills the sea. The following figures are most significant, furnished by the central office:

Country	No. of Societies
North America:	
Alaska	75
Baffin Land	1
Canada	1,015
Cuba	30
Labrador	20
Mexico	200
Newfoundland	15
United States	55,700
Total	57,056
Central America:	
Canal Zone	6
Costa Rica	6
Guatemala	5
Panama	8
Total	25
South America:	
Argentina	10
Bolivia	10
Brazil	40

Country	No. of Societies
Chile	15
Colombia	15
Ecuador	8
Paraguay	10
Peru	18
Uruguay	15
Venezuela	35
Total	176
Europe:	
Austria	10
Belgium	18
Bulgaria	10
Czechoslovakia	25
Danzig	10
Denmark	20
Estonia	21
Finland	60
France	30
Germany	3,176
Gibraltar	1
Great Britain and Ireland	9,038

Country	No. of Societies	Country	No. of Societies
Europe (*Cont.*):		Baluchistan	3
Greece	25	Burma	276
Holland	7	Ceylon	80
Hungary	35	China	2,865
Italy	10	India	2,000
Jugoslavia	15	Japan	400
Latvia	20	Korea	300
Lithuania	5	Laos	30
Norway	10	Palestine	15
Poland	172	Persia	8
Portugal	30	Siam	20
Roumania	20	Syria	20
Russia	20	Turkey	30
Spain	50		
Sweden	20	Total	6,088
Switzerland	65		
Transylvania	10	Australasia:	
Volhynia	5	Australia	2,393
		New Zealand	80
Total 12,938		Tasmania	50
Africa:		Total	2,523
British Guiana	15		
Congoland	2	Islands:	
Egypt	215	Barbados	15
Gold Coast	1	Bermuda	5
Liberia	10	Borneo	6
Sierra Leone	3	Caroline Islands	6
		Ellice Islands	8
		Falkland Islands	8
South Africa:		Faros Islands	20
English Union	100	Fiji Islands	10
Dutch Union	200	Formosa	15
Other Africa	200	Gilbert Islands	10
		Greenland	20
Total	756	Granada	5
		Guam	3
Asia:		Haiti (Dominican	
Afghanistan	5	Republic)	8
Arabia	6	Iceland	20
Armenia	30	Jamaica	20

Country	No. of Societies	Country	No. of Societies
Islands (*Cont.*):		Virgin Islands	10
Java	10	Hawaiian Islands ...	50
Loyalty Islands	10		
Madagascar	60	Total	551
Madeira Islands	10		
Marshall Islands	6	Summary by Continents:	
Mauritius	5	North America 57,056	
Mortlock Islands ...	8	Central America	25
New Guinea	20	South America	176
Philippine Islands ...	50	Europe 12,938	
Porto Rico	60	Africa	756
Samoa	25	Asia	6,088
Sumatra	10	Australasia	2,523
Tokalau Islands	10	Islands	551
Trinidad	8		
Upper Hebrides	20	Total 80,113	

The Young Peoples Society of Christian Endeavor is perhaps the most powerful of all the general influences and institutions of the church beginning in the last fifty years. Its growth I compare to the growth of the Society of Jesus, the Order of the Jesuits. This Order, founded in the year 1540, has come to have a distinct place in its church and in all parts of the world. Likewise the Society of Christian Endeavor, of many relationships, has gone forth, conquering for more than fifty years. In Clark, its founder, were incarnated noble constructive forces.

Among the chief of all these forces was Clark's breadth of intellectual vision, joined with a sense of aptness for immediate duties. He interpreted the social and religious order not only in single parts, but also in wholes. He saw the present not only as present in the here and the now, but also as united

in a sense of prophecy of the future. His understanding was of relations, as well as of individual
elements. His mind was a first-rate combination of
the philosopher's and of the administrator's. If his intellectual interpretations had been philosophical only,
his work would have perished before it was born, or
would have died a-borning. If he had possessed aptness and force for immediate duty only, his work
could not have lasted, and would have made no wide
appeal. Because Clark was both a prophet and a
pragmatist that work goes on with world power and
in world relations.

In this union of qualities and forces was also
found an instinct for coöperation. He easily worked
with all men, men like and men unlike himself. He
was ever ready to recognize himself as the responsible head of the Endeavor Society. He also recognized the truth that a service for, through, by men
demands co-working. Co-working without leadership
is in peril of ending in a mob. Co-working without
workers becomes a Hegelian schema. In Clark was
found a co-worker, a co-operator, laying emphasis on
both parts of the compound word. Therefore he
received a responsive coöperation from all associates.

In this gift of comprehensiveness, of understanding, and of partnership, the double elements of religion and of humanism were present and formative.
Clark was both fundamentally and superficially religious. He was also very human. If his uplook was
toward the divine, his outlook was human. If his

standards were set by his interpretation of God, his service was devoted to man. His society was named Christian; it also included the term people. In the science of theology he had small interest. In the art of theology as a personal endeavor his thought and feeling were deep and broad. Yet he knew that art without a science is in peril of being superficial and ephemeral, and that science without art is ineffective for many relations of man. Each unit made into a duet created and creates the God-ward impulse and the man-ward movement.

In Clark also existed a unique union of boldness and aggressiveness with humility. Bold aggressiveness in action is in danger of becoming personal haughtiness in character. Possibly, however, it might be said that aggressiveness is the result and not the cause of haughtiness. But, on the whole, I believe that the subjective element is rather a result than a cause of the exterior conduct. But in Clark no such process in either form emerged. For humility clothed him as a garment. He thought not of himself more highly than he ought to think. He thought indeed as Paul advised the Romans, "soberly." He measured himself against the higher standards. Therefore he was humble. Self-esteem belongs to those whose standards are low. Clark's humility, however, was as remote from self-abasement as was his aggressiveness from vaingloriousness. His was the middle course which gave self-contentment without self-conceit and bold aggressiveness without ruthlessness.

His was the livery of the Christian knight going
forth on a Christian crusade. He says, "I am particularly impressed in my devotional moments with
God's undeserved goodness in giving me my special
work in the world. Realizing my limitations of intellect and soul, I wonder that He called me to start,
and in some measure to develop, the work of the
Christian Endeavor society. I see hundreds of my
brother ministers more eloquent, more witty, more
gifted in many ways than I. Why were they not
chosen? Thousands of them were thinking along the
same lines of Christian nurture in the early eighties.
Why did He not give this honor to one of them?
Why was the little experiment in Williston Church
His chosen way of influencing millions in all lands
for good?" [7]

In the union of Clark's aggressiveness and humility are also felt both his native forcefulness and
his native fineness. These two qualities often seem
to be antithetical. Forcefulness in personal character
and conduct may have intimations of crudeness even
if not of coarseness. Fineness in personal character
and conduct is in peril of becoming a superfineness
which spells weakness and futility. In Clark forcefulness was strong without being crude, and fineness
was beautiful and fitting without feebleness.

In his devotion to his great cause, Clark constantly
showed himself to have a genius for friendship. The
devotion to the cause and the devotion to his friends

[7] *Ibid.*, p. 691.

were closely united. In his devotion to the cause he
made friends, and in his friendships the cause pros-
pered. For friendliness was his prevailing mood.
Without such a mood his general devotion would
have become resultless. With a common and mutual
love the co-workings spelled victory. Altruism was
natural to him. He loved people, and therefore people loved him. He felt with their hearts; he appreciated their angle of vision; he understood their difficulties; he entered into their spirit; he was moved
by their motives; he sympathized with their aims;
he was stimulated by their triumphs; and he was
heroic with them in their distresses and defeats.
Such friendliness, such sympathies, were both cause
and result of his devotion to his lifelong, world-wide
quest. To name his friends would be to name hundreds of the great men of the world. They were, as
he says of one, "kindliest, keenest, brainiest, bravest,
and most generous." [8]

Among the constructive elements, moreover, of
Clark's character, was optimism. If optimism was
not a constructive element, it was at least the atmosphere in which he lived and served. Every Christian
is, and must by logic be, an optimist. In Clark the
element, the mood, were both intellectual and emotional. It was a mood created by instinct and by
grace. It was also a conclusion based on evidence.
It was a belief founded in part on natural conditions.
It was also a conviction supported by practice.

[8] *Ibid.,* p. 180.

"Every night I like to recount the blessings and joys that have come to me during the day, though they are always too many to be counted." [9] Clark was not a disciple of Schopenhauer. He did not believe that this is the worst of all possible worlds, inhabited by the worst of all possible beings. He rather was a disciple of St. John and of St. Paul.

In all these diverse, comprehensive, and constructive elements there prevailed a mighty and wise leadership of a great cause. There are at least half a dozen factors which constitute personal leadership: first, a vision of the goal which it is desired to reach; second, an appreciation of the difficulties and of the aids for reaching this goal; third, the power to create and to quicken co-workers; fourth, untiring work on the part of the leader; fifth, losing one's self in the work itself; and sixth, on the other side, is to be found loyalty of co-workers to the leader. All these six conditions may possibly be summed up in the two words, personality and common sense. All these qualities were embodied in Clark. He saw the goal, the development of Christian character in the young men and women of the world. He also felt the difficulties of the quest: slothfulness, denominational antagonisms, geographical and racial separateness, personal jealousies, lack of money. Yet he had the power to create, to arouse, and to strengthen by word and by example a mighty army of co-laborers for the divine and for the human task. He was himself an untiring

[9] *Ibid.,* p. 691.

worker. His devotion was complete. He also had
the desire, and to a degree the power, to hide himself
in the movement. The cause was ever first, foremost.
Some leaders seem to inspire a special following to
themselves, a following in which they glory. Such
was Napoleon. Clark asked that the cause which he
led should be absolutely first. Clark did not inspire
so much loyalty to himself as a person: he lost himself in the cause. The cause was personified in him,
and it alone was to be recognized. If an institution
is the lengthened shadow of a man, and if a movement is indeed the lengthening shadow of a man, the
shadow lengthens as the movement proceeds.

Francis Clark was happy above most men, both in
his life and in his death. That life was long. He
died in his eighth decade, approaching the fourscore
limit. To great aggressive leaders a long period of
service seems almost necessary. The poets may die
young. Byron was in the thirty-sixth year, Shelley
in his thirtieth and Keats in his twenty-sixth. But if
Gladstone had died in his eighth decade several of
the noblest and most constructive elements and victories of that career would not have been achieved.
Clark lived to see the ship of his career sailing every
ocean, bearing precious treasures.

Clark was no less happy in building his life into
a movement which may be called institutional. He
was a founder. Bacon's interpretation of founders
belongs to him. Not only was he to lay corner stones,
but to him also was given the privilege of laying cap-

stones. His name, therefore, is to endure as long as the Young Peoples Society of Christian Endeavor endures, and that institution is sure to endure as long as there are young people, as long as there are a faith and a work which deserve to bear the name of Christian.

XII
BARRETT WENDELL

Born August 23, 1855, Boston; died February 8, 1921. A.B., Harvard, 1877. Engaged in teaching at Harvard from October, 1880: instructor in English, 1880-88, assistant professor, 1888-98, professor 1898-1917, professor emeritus, 1917; lecturer at the Sorbonne and French universities, 1904-05.

Author: The Duchess Emilia (novel); Rankell's Remains (novel); English Composition; Cotton Mather; Stelligeri and other Essays concerning America; William Shakespere, a Study in Elizabethan Literature; A Literary History of America; Raleigh in Guiana; Rosamond; A Christmas Masque; The Temper of the Seventeenth Century in English Literature (Clark Lectures given at Trinity College, Cambridge, England, 1902-03); History of Literature in America (with Chester N. Greenough); Liberty, Union, and Democracy—the National Ideals of America; The France of Today (1907); The Privileged Classes; The Mystery of Education; The Traditions of European Literature; and other volumes.

XII

BARRETT WENDELL

TEACHER, INDIVIDUALIST, A CONSERVATIVE ICONOCLAST

AMONG my friends are two who were primarily personalities: William Everett and Barrett Wendell. Wendell was an alluring teacher in our oldest college for more than a generation. He was the author of several books, some weighty and on weighty and diverse themes. He was a lecturer at the Sorbonne and at the English Cambridge. His whole life was fruitful. But above all that he achieved, Barrett Wendell was a personality. I have been trying to find out, through vital and grateful memories, and through his books, the secret of Wendell's character. It is probable I have failed in my quest. Yet I do venture at once to say that the fundamental and constructive element of that character was Life: the abundance, the fullness, the intensity of Life. Of course the reader may reply, saying, "That is no interpretation. It is only a common-place commonplace, for life belongs to each as a member of the race." True is the answer, of course; but it is the fullness, the abundance, the intensity of life, more

213

full, more abundant, more intense, which characterizes Barrett Wendell. His was a life which, as George
Herbert Palmer says of William James, "coruscates."
Even his oddities, eccentricities, and absurdities give
evidence of his supreme possession of the fundamental
principle—Life.

For Wendell was odd, eccentric, absurd; and,
furthermore, he knew that he was odd, eccentric, absurd. The process belonged to, or began with, the
body. In the year 1915 he writes to his daughter
Mary, saying, "For some time past I have been on
the edge of 'nervous prostration'—whatever that
may be." [1] Some would say that "nervous prostration" was a condition toward which he constantly
moved or in which he was constantly found. He also
declares that he is comically subject to purely physical fatigue. Seriously he writes to his dear friend
Stimson, from Geneva in 1905, "Throughout this most
arduous of my years, I have not had what you might
fairly call a well day. It takes me in the form of internal pain and such overpowering fatigue that, half
the time, I don't feel up to walking a block." [2] His
voice was a high staccato. He says, "My own style, in
print, pleases me as little as my own voice did when
for the first and only time I heard it from a phono-
graphic record." [3] His health, always infirm, became
yet more broken by a motor accident in 1916.

[1] *Barrett Wendell and His Letters,* by M. A. De Wolfe
Howe, p. 268.
[2] *Ibid.,* p. 167.   [3] *Ibid.,* p. 274.

These personal peculiarities and individualisms were both the cause and result of forces which ruled him quite as fully as William Everett's moods mastered him. For Wendell was the subject or victim of moods. The moods at times showed themselves in a temper which for a moment became his master. It is told that he kicked over the camera of a newspaper photographer who sought to invade the privacy of his home. At a football game in the Harvard stadium he smashed the hat of a spectator who interfered with his sight. He accomplished his purpose, and saved the conditions of a duel by exchange of cards and by his purchase of a new hat for the victim.

Wendell's sense of life was also manifest in ways far more normal and fundamental. These ways, diverse in character, seem to me to be well summed up in what may be called his desire to maintain the standards of life. These standards are to be applied to the family, to literature, to education, to society, and to the church. The family, as the most important of all social institutions, called out his deepest loyalty and reverence. Of his own family he was proud, and justly. He embodied and represented an ancestral and a personal conservatism. Portraits of his forefathers, painted by Copley, hung in the rooms of the beloved Portsmouth home. Literature, of course, was at once the tool with which he labored, the material in which he labored, the quickening force which inspired his labor, and the achievement of his labor. Whether he wrote seeking to do the impossible task of interpreting European literature of the later centuries of the middle ages, or trying to interpret American literature, it was the maintenance of the categories of truth, of justice and of thoroughness which moved his pen. In his biographical studies it was the same highest purpose of doing justly, even if not of loving mercy, which inspired him. Judged by not a few to be prejudiced in his intellectual processes and conclusions, permitting his emotions to rule his literary verdicts, yet few could be found who would depreciate the honesty of his intentions or the righteousness of his will. In education, as well as in literature and in the matter of the family, he held it to be his special duty to defend the fundamental, the lasting, the worthiest. His book, *English Composition for College,* and other studies, is an embodiment in itself of the principles and methods which he practiced and defended. Conservative, the education of the past as fitted to the environment of the present he upheld in method, in purpose, and in content. To maintain the standards of society, too, he felt a peculiar call. He would accept Cardinal Newman's definition of the gentleman, giving it both a narrower and a more intense meaning. If in principle he was a democrat, in taste and general walk and conversation he was an aristocrat. The evidences which some find of his snobbishness, and which he would be the last to deny, were also evidences of his loyalty to the standards which good breeding upholds. President Eliot, writing in the year 1901, said, "Wendell's fre-

quent discourse on the subject of birth and descent
seems snobbish in an American, and will cause many
people to underestimate his judgment and good
sense." [4] I am also sure that the standards of the
church were dear to his soul. The church invisible
was far more to him than the church visible. The loss
of faith he regarded as nothing less than a tragedy
to most men. In the midst of the Dantesque doubts
and uncertainties in which many thoughtful men
moved, he was guided by the light which lighteth
every man coming into the world, and he sought to
aid other spirits in the eternal quest for truth.

Wendell's sense of life was furthermore made manifest in his self-appreciations—appreciations which
often become self-depreciations. In the year 1910 he
writes to Senator Lodge, "What I have been able to
do in this world has seemed a very thin frill on the
edge of reality." [5] To his dear, lifelong friend,
Stimson, he writes, "To me, my whole life seems to
have been a bewildered effort to get ready to begin." [6]
A little later he writes, "I have a genius—if I have
a gleam of any such thing—for being honestly but
profoundly in the wrong." [7] To his friend, Sir Robert White-Thomson, he writes on the death of his
father, "He thought, and I believe rightly, that I
had not quite the robustness of temper which is demanded for success in the stress of American life" [8];

[4] *Charles W. Eliot,* by Henry James. Vol. II, p. 135.
[5] *Barrett Wendell and His Letters,* by M. A. De Wolfe
Howe, p. 206.
[6] *Ibid.,* p. 276.　　[7] *Ibid.,* p. 281.　　[8] *Ibid.,* p. 121.

and again, saying, "My occasional work as a man of
letters compels me now and then to publish my name.
But my actual life is so quiet, so remote from any
public activity, that any mention of me in the public
prints always seems a bit impertinent. It amounts to
troubling people with a name which, to most of them,
must stand for nothing else than the letters which
compose it." [9] Also, to his friend, Ralph Curtis, he
writes, not long before his death, saying, "I wallow
beyond my depth, you will doubtless have remarked
already. It has pleased the Lord to keep me from
where my splashings can do any harm. Of all inca-
pacities to run things, my own appears to me the
most limitless I have ever come across." [10] In a personal letter written to me in 1916, he says, "This
year I have felt rather shaky, a good part of the
time; and, whether my hand trembles or no, I fancy
my wits do."

I also want to quote a letter which Wendell wrote
to President Eliot at a time when it seemed not im-
probable that he might be denied a reappointment to
his chair in Harvard College. The letter is a most
honorable one both for the writer and for the one
to whom it is addressed. "I need not add, I hope,
fresh assurance that I am sincerely sensible of the
frank kindness and consideration you have shown me
throughout my eighteen years of service; and that,
should you decide my usefulness to the college ended
or waning, I shall cheerfully accept your decision as

* *Ibid.*, p. 141.   [10] *Ibid.*, p. 322.

thoughtfully made for what seem to you the best
interests of Harvard." [11]

The sense of glad and of sad humorous truthfulness which breathes through these extracts, and many
other paragraphs which could be given, oblige the
conclusion of a certain contradictoriness in Wendell's
nature. With honesty and with fearlessness did he
depreciate himself. The process was a measuring of
himself by the highest standards. Unconsciously he
put himself up against the pillars of what we call
the universe. He, therefore, was convinced that he
was indeed small, and his stature short. But also in
Wendell was a certain self-respect, high and noble.
This self-respect was most manifest. This self-ward
regard brooked no interference. His integrity was
positive and absolute. The sense of power dominated.
In this double mood of self-respect and of self-depre-
ciation Wendell did his work as a teacher and as a
writer. He came to his place as an instructor in Harvard College without the advantage or the disadvan-
tage of special and formal preparation. In a memoir
of his father, he writes of the conditions of the beginning of his long and fruitful service. "I had chanced
to meet in the street my college teacher of English,
Professor Adams Hill. We had hardly come across
each other since I graduated. He asked me what I
was doing. I told him that I was reading law. He
asked whether I liked it; I said no. And on his duly
inquiring what kind of job I should prefer, I am said

[11] *Charles W. Eliot*, by Henry James. Vol. II, pp. 78-79.

to have answered, 'Even yours.' Somehow the inci-
dent stuck in his memory. So early in October, finding himself in need of some one to read sophomore
themes, he proposed my name to President Eliot,
who was always fond of experiments with inexperi-
enced teachers. The result was a telegram, inviting
me to come on and discuss the matter. . . . The telegram decided my career; it also gratified my father
as indicating, for the first time, that somebody
thought me conceivably useful. Though I began
teaching at Harvard thus fortuitously and with no
notion of keeping it up long, and though more than
once I came near dropping the work, I was actually
on the rolls there as a teacher for thirty-seven years;
and a few months before my father died he was gratified by my promotion to a full professorship.'' [12]

The contrast between such a beginning of a great
career and the beginning of a career which is usually
represented by the mark of ''M.A.'' and ''Ph.D.'' is
rather fundamental in present academic history. But,
be it said, one method of preparation or the other
method of the lack of preparation, may have special
worth. The judgment of worth depends largely upon
the character of the student and teacher.

Wendell was a teacher of literature. Literature he
has defined as ''the lasting expression in words of
the meaning of life.'' [13] In teaching literature,

[12] *Barrett Wendell and His Letters,* by M. A. De Wolfe
Howe, pp. 37-38.
[13] *Literary History of America,* by Barrett Wendell, p. 2.

therefore, life was the tool, the material, the force, the conclusion, of his instruction. The life of the individual is to be adjusted to its environment, and the best method of making this adjustment he held was in and through education.

Wendell's purpose in teaching was, like the purpose of every great teacher, to make his students think. His aim was not to convey certain facts about literature, not even to make them scholars in literature, though this result might unconsciously emerge. Rather, his purpose was, first, to quicken reflection, to strengthen the intellect, and secondly, to inspire a thinking which might relate to literature as a form of life. He wished, further, to inspire his students to think things together, never in or into individual separateness. His wish was to secure a united synthesis, important as he knew discriminating analysis to be. He thus inspired his students to think comprehensively. His talks were tonics. He belonged, although so different from each of them, to the Harvard chapter of inspiring thinkers, which included William James, Henry Adams, and George Herbert Palmer.

He also belonged to another order of Harvard. Undoubtedly, as a member in his undergraduate years of Mr. Lowell's class in Dante, Wendell was not only a most appreciative student of poetry and of life, but also he was an unconscious student of methods of teaching. Mr. Lowell's methods in the classroom were as unlike ordinary methods as a table of loga-

rithms is unlike verses in the ''Commemoration Ode.''
These methods were signally marked by naturalness
of behavior and of freedom. Of these methods, Wendell has himself said, ''Here before us was a great
poem (Dante's)—a lasting expression of what human
life had meant to a human being, dead and gone
these five centuries. Let us try, as best we might, to
see what life had meant to this man; let us see what
relation his experience, great and small, bore to ours;
and, now and then, let us pause for a moment to
notice how wonderfully beautiful his expression of
this experience was. Let us read, as sympathetically
as we could make ourselves read, the words of one
who was as much a man as we, only vastly greater
in his knowledge of wisdom and beauty. That was
the spirit of Mr. Lowell's teaching. It opened to some
of us a new world.'' [14] Such was the teaching of
Wendell, solid, personal, realistic, free, suggestive, of
unusual depths, heights, horizons. For reverent students the method, the conditions, the results, have received much acclaim. But also his academic interpretations, manner, manners, and mannerisms, have
been made the subject of caricature, and of fun of
many sorts. Unfortunate indeed is the college which
lacks characters. Wendell, as I have intimated, was
a character. His high voice, his apparent affectations,
his affirmations and repartees, his general manner so
often interpreted, even if falsely, as ''English,'' made

[14] *Barrett Wendell and His Letters,* by M. A. De Wolfe
Howe, p. 28.

this strong eccentric man the target of ridicule and of mimicry. Perhaps these conditions added to, rather than subtracted from, the worth and lasting impressiveness of his teaching. His teacher and his colleague, Professor Francis J. Child, affectionately called "Stubby," was also made, though in a less degree, the object of the happy and loving comment of undergraduates.

The contrasts in Wendell's nature, manifest in his college lectures, were also characteristic of him as a man. An editorial writer in the *Harvard Alumni Bulletin* has said, "He was absurd, cynical, caustic, and disposed to more or less wilful exaggeration. At the same time he was kind, honest, magnanimous, and lovable. Some of his qualities suggest a synthesis of these opposed traits. He was, for example, above all things courageous, and bound at all cost to be himself and speak his own mind. Having a profound detestation of hypocrisy and philistinism, he would rather give offense than be thought deliberately conciliatory. He would rather shock than soothe, because in this way he could at least be free from suspicion of buying favor by vulgar conformity." [15] Perhaps it is all best summed up by saying, as I already have said, that Barrett Wendell was Barrett Wendell.

But Wendell was a writer as well as a teacher. The two functions are in him closely inwrought, for the lectures he gave as a teacher he printed in books, and

[15] *Harvard Alumni Bulletin*—October 9, 1924.

at least one of his books became a text in college classes. Of course, too, his fame as a teacher will not directly outlast the life of those who sat in his classrooms. His books are pretty sure of being read for generations. In both of these relations, Wendell was an expositor and an interpreter. The qualities of his teaching inhere in his books. He deals with the greatest themes: *The Traditions of European Literature,* from the beginning to the year 1300; *The Literary History of America,* ever giving interpretations of education, democracy, and liberty. Both these books are marked more by scholarliness than by scholarship, and by scholarship than by scholasticism. They represent great trends, movements, tendencies, sympathies, syntheses. His *Traditions* have seemed to me to be the attar of rose of literary scholarship, fragrant, inspiring, impressive. To be able to read and appreciate such a work is evidence of literary responsiveness; to be able to write such a work is proof both of erudition and of sympathy. All his volumes are human documents. They do not smell of the lamp. Browning's Grammarian could never have written them. They have vision. They suggest the sky. In certain respects they can properly be called superficial. They do touch the surface. So also it may be said of the wheat crops. Profound, detailed, thoroughgoing scholarship, of course, has its abounding place. Wells of water and mines of coal, deep diggings into the depths, have their place and function. Let not the simple scholar quarrel with the positive scholar, neither let the positive scholar quarrel with the far-seeing, the deep-digging scholastic.

I have found myself in writing these paragraphs filled with the wish that Wendell might have been spared to complete a literary history of the whole Western world. His *Traditions of European Literature* covers a period down to 1300. His *Literary History of America* covers a period from the beginning of America to our own time. If only he could have lived, and been able to write the history of other parts of the Western world's literature from the year 1300 down to the present time, what a noble trilogy would have been the result. But in the vanity of regret, one cannot refrain from the wish for an interpretation more complete, for an achievement yet more lasting, for a comprehensive result yet more splendid.

My interpretation of my dear friend comes to its close. But as I conclude I find myself asking the question—what was the relation of his life to Life? What was his attitude toward the universe—if one may apply such a question to the individual? To this comprehensive asking I find myself answering in a threefold term: The first relation is one of curiosity: what is life? What is the totality of things anyway? Charles Kingsley once said that he looked forward to the day of his death with profound curiosity. Wendell looked forward to life universal, eternal, in the same mood, the mood of questioning, a mood, of course, characteristic of the great. The second relation is of submissiveness. To the omnipotence which invests us he bowed; to the omnipresence which surrounds he subjected his little limitations; to the omniscience which is about us as an atmosphere, he was reverently humble. His mood was the mood of Pascal. A third relation was the relation of faith—faith in the eternal goodness. Knowledge is limited. Faith was of the infinite, touching both time and space and all that in them moves.

XIII
EDWARD WILLIAMS MORLEY

BORN Newark, N. J., 1838; died February 24, 1923; A.B., Williams College, 1860, A.M., 1863. Professor of chemistry, Western Reserve College, Hudson, O. (afterward moved to Cleveland and named Adelbert College of Western Reserve University), 1869-1906; Emeritus 1906-1923; also professor of chemistry, Cleveland Medical College, 1873-88.

Author of many papers on chemical and physical subjects.

XIII

EDWARD WILLIAMS MORLEY

CHEMIST, INVESTIGATOR, TEACHER

Of the many scholars, scientific, classical, linguistic, historical, philosophic, sociological, who were my college associates for more than thirty years, none was more learned, more illustrious, more devoted, than Morley.

Edward Williams Morley was a child of the manse. He was also a graduate of Andover Theological Seminary. The principles underlying his religious parentage and training were the fundamental and permanent elements of his character. But early in his service as a minister (in Twinsburg, Ohio), he was offered a professorship in Western Reserve College in the neighboring town of Hudson, for in this service he had proved that his interest was rather scientific than theological or clerical. The college foundation bore the traditional title of ''Natural History and Chemistry.'' The professorship under this and other titles, as emeritus, he held until his death in the year 1923. His service covered fifty-four years.

Morley united, as not many college professors do

unite, great power as a teacher with equally great power as an investigator. His power as a teacher was primarily found in his knowledge, and quite as fundamentally in his devotion to the individual student. His power as an investigator is, of course, illustrated in his devotion to his many and diverse researches. His power as a teacher lives, and lives as long as do the lives of the hundreds of students whom he taught, and to whom he gave intellectual quickening. One of his students who became a professor of bio-chemistry says that "he received most of his education from Professor Morley, since he made so many stimulating suggestions in all fields of knowledge without at all interfering with his lectures in chemistry." His work as an investigator relates to at least two fields of nature. In one of these fields his work is completed and is done apparently unto conclusiveness. This work has given him place among the greatest of scientists. In the other field his work still progresses. The first field relates, as says his successor, Professor O. F. Tower, to "The densities of oxygen and hydrogen and the ratio in which they combine." [1] The field in which the work is still going on is the field associated with the name of Einstein. In the second field he collaborated with Professor A. A. Michelson "in developing the interferometer, an instrument for measuring lengths in terms of the wave-length of light. They used this instrument to determine the relative

[1] "Edward Williams Morley," by O. F. Tower, *Western Reserve University Bulletin*, August, 1923, p. 59.

motion of the earth and the luminiferous ether." [2]
With Professor W. A. Rogers he worked in measuring
the expansion of metallic bars; and also with Professor Dayton C. Miller, of the Case School of Applied
Science, he experimented upon the "velocity of light
in a magnetic field." He also assisted Michelson in
the first ether-drift experiment. In all these and other
experiments he became associated with his friend,
Charles F. Brush, and with Elias Loomis, of Yale,
who, long before Morley, was a professor in Western
Reserve College. The Michelson-Morley coöperation
and the earlier Loomis-Morley coöperation are among
the outstanding partnerships in scientific research.
Great in his discoveries and inventions, Morley was
also great in his associates, and they also were made
great through and in him.

These facts both prove and illustrate the breadth
of Morley's mind. His interests and devotions were
many, his chief interest however lay in the field of
the physical sciences. His intellect was at once comprehensive and concentrated. He recognized the differences between a vocation and an avocation. His
avocations, however, were several. He knew and loved
music. Playing the organ at the chapel service was
one of his minor services given to the college at Hudson. He learned Russian in order to read the Russian
chemical and other journals. But his vocation was
commanding, persistent, unrelenting.

The great and lasting results which Morley achieved
[2] *Ibid.,* p. 61.

arose from several causes and conditions. Among them
were his intellectual alertness, his comprehensiveness,
his patience, his laboriousness, and, be it added, his
skill in manipulation. His reasoning seemed to be a
series of intuitions. Conclusions followed swiftly on
insight. Yet, though being the master of immediate
intellectual processes, he was also patient. He revised
and re-revised his methods, measures and movements;
tested and retested his conclusions. Like Pasteur, he
examined all hypotheses contrary or similar. All possibilities of error, either personal or of conditions, he
sought to remove. More strongly than many scientists
he was able to say, ''This is the truth: I can no
other.'' It was also well that Morley's power was not
simply of intellect and of will: he had great skill with
his hands. In the poverty of the college he was largely
his own assistant, and the maker of his own apparatus.
He was, for instance, a skilled glass-blower, a skill of
the utmost value in his long experimenting process in
determining atomic weights. Gifted with all these
powers he used them to the utmost. He was among
the hardest of all workers ever known to me. He gave
full service as a teacher till the trustees of the college
offered him complete liberty respecting his interpretation of his duties, a liberty of which he did not fully
avail himself. Fourteen hours a day was a minimum
of the time spent at his tasks. He toiled to the limits
of strength. His wife has said to me that it was not
unusual for her at the close of the day to watch for
him coming home, questioning whether he might not

have fainted on the way. A speedometer which he sometimes used proved that in his walking to and fro, up and down, in the building wherein were his rooms, he frequently walked in a single day no less than twenty miles. Scientists are indeed hard workers, some would say the hardest; and no one of them was a harder worker than Morley.

As a scientist Morley's place is secure. It is by common consent among the highest. In the unique worth of this service I, of all men, should not pass over his worth as a teacher. For hundreds, if not thousands, of students rise up to bless him. Formally he taught chemistry, but he also taught every other subject. He especially taught English, and the oral use of our English speech. Precise himself in language, he demanded correctness and precision of all students. Oral slovenliness he abominated. Many a student have I heard say, ''Morley taught me English as no English teacher.'' Devoted to the students in ways both specific and general, he required of them an equal devotion to the subject of study. No tolerance had he for the shirker. Faithlessness easily stirred his indignation. He was profane without words. He could not suffer fools, either intellectual or moral. They quickened his abhorrence. But to the student highest, earnest, alert, laborious, he was devoted. His loyalty to truth, as I have intimated, was no less intense. From these two foci of devotion to truth and of laboriousness are swiftly and easily drawn the ellipse of his achieving life and rich character.

I cannot compare Morley to Pasteur in respect to the directness and beneficences of his service to humanity; but I can compare him to Pasteur in respect to the fundamental elements of scientific research. I cannot compare him to Darwin, for Darwin was not a teacher; but I can compare him to Darwin in respect to the intuitive vision, the comprehensiveness of understanding, the persistent patience, the humility of spirit, the prolonged and sober enthusiasm in which he pursued his researches.

XIV
HALDANE

Born July 30, 1856; died August 19, 1928. He was educated at Edinburgh Academy and the Universities of Edinburgh and Göttingen, where he studied philosophy under Lotze. Took first-class honors in philosophy at Edinburgh; called to the bar in 1879, and "took silk" in 1890. In 1885 he entered Parliament as liberal member for Haddingtonshire, for which he was reëlected continuously up to and including 1910; 1905, in Sir H. Campbell-Bannerman's cabinet as secretary for war, and carried out the reorganization of the British Army; 1910, appointed chairman of the Royal Commission on University Education in London; 1911, raised to the peerage; 1912, became lord chancellor. In 1924 he was lord high chancellor in the Labor Ministry of Ramsay MacDonald, and working chairman of the committee on imperial defence. On fall of Labor Ministry, Baldwin asked him to continue his long association with it; 1925, member of committee of Civil Research. He was elected first chancellor of Bristol University and was also lord rector of Edinburgh; received many honorary degrees.

Author: Life of Adam Smith; Education and Empire; Pathway to Reality; The Reign of Relativity; The Philosophy of Humanism; Before the War; Selected Addresses and Essays.

XIV

HALDANE

ADMINISTRATOR, PHILOSOPHER, FRIEND

THE mind of Haldane was weighty. It was one of the two weightiest minds I have known. The other belonged to Vinogradoff, professor of jurisprudence at Oxford. Vinogradoff's mind seemed to approach the ponderous. Such, however, was not Haldane's. It was neither ponderous nor heavy. It was alert though weighty, wise though knowing, broad though deep, altruistic though personal, it was analytical although not adverse to affirmation, it was logical although not free from emotions, it was independent yet coöperative.

The weight of Haldane's mind came from several sources. Early he became devoted to the search for the first principles of life and of all being. As a boy of seventeen he went from Scotland to Göttingen, and he went to Göttingen because Hermann Lotze was there. Of Lotze he says, "I had the privilege, boy as I was, of seeing him often in his study as well as of listening in his lecture-room, and to the end of my life I shall hold the deep impression he made on me—of a combination of intellectual power and the highest

237

moral stature. It seems to me but yesterday that he
used quietly to enter the lecture-room where we students sat expectant, and, taking his seat, fix his eyes
on space as though he were looking into another
world remote from this one. The face was worn with
thought, and the slight and fragile figure with the
great head looked as though the mind that tenanted
it had been dedicated to thought and to nothing else.
The brow and nose were wonderfully chiselled, the
expression was a combination of tolerance with power.
The delivery was slow and exact, but the command of
language was impressive. Our feeling towards him as
we sat and listened was one of reverence mingled with
affection.'' [1]

If Lotze gave to Haldane a new intellectual birth, it
was Kant and Hegel that brought to him subsequent
and consequent growth and development. They were
his ministers. For each was an apostle as well as a
disciple of first principles. The philosophers of the
Absolute, whether true or false in their metaphysics,
did breathe into their devotees a desire to understand,
and a will to be loyal to the results of understanding.
Science and metaphysics, mathematics and psychology, alike urge the student toward a knowledge of the
ultimate. The categories and derived inferences give
a sense of reality to the gropings of the individual
mind. The writings of Haldane, such as *The Philosophy of Humanism,* and *The Reign of Relativity,* offer
ample evidence of the eagerness of his search, the wis-

[1] *Universities and National Life,* by Viscount Haldane, p. 27.

dom of his methods, the sincerity of his devotion, and the solidity of his conclusions in the realm of the philosophy of the Absolute. Toward the close of his life he said, "It is enough to say that its essence (idealism) led me to the belief in the possibility of finding rational principles underlying all forms of experience, and to a strong sense of the endeavour to find such principles as a first duty in every department of public life. That is the faith that prevailed with me when at the Bar, when later on I undertook the reform of the Army, when I was Lord Chancellor, and when I sat on the Committee of Imperial Defence. It prevails with me today not less than in earlier days, and it helps in the endeavour to bring together the apparently diverging views of those with whom one has to deal." [2]

Haldane's was one of the great philosophic minds of the whole world in the concluding years of the nineteenth and the beginning years of the twentieth century. To change what is said in Antony and Cleopatra, in nature's infinite book of secrecy he had not only read a little, but of its secrets he had thought much.

In the interpretation of the philosophic mind of Haldane, religion fills a part both fundamental and constructive. For his religious principles and beliefs it is impossible to separate from the philosophic. If the religious beliefs sprang from the metaphysical prin-

[2] *Richard Burdon Haldane (Viscount Haldane)—An Autobiography*, p. 374.

ciples, it might also be said that the religious beliefs
were the flower and fruit of the metaphysical. Of the
religion of his youth he says, ''My religious outlook
was a genuine one. Its origin was a deep conviction
that the more experience is spiritual the more it is
real. My old master, Lotze, had influenced me towards
this conviction, and so had Hegel, whom I had been
studying as closely as the state of my then knowledge
permitted. With all this had come the further conviction that not only in philosophy but in science it was
true that no systematic knowledge is sufficient in itself
unless it leads up and points to first principles.'' [3]
In the little great book, *Education and Empire,* also
he defines and interprets. ''Religion may be defined
to be that aspect of the universe in which the relation
of man to God appears. . . . God must be conceived,
not as a force operating from outside in space; not
mechanically, as a substance or cause; not as a magni-
fied and non-natural human being, but as a spirit; as
mind; as the subject for which the world is object,
and in which the limited plane of human intelligence
appears only as a stage or phase.'' [4] ''It is an affair
of the *will* rather than of the *intellect,* of feeling
rather than of abstract knowledge. But just in so far
as it is so, it is the phase of comprehension in which
we realise for ourselves what philosophy points to,
but can do no more than point to. It gives us that

[3] *Ibid.,* p. 33.
[4] *Education and Empire,* by Richard Burdon Haldane, pp.
188-89.

direct and living contact which cannot be attained save in its practice.'' [5]

Perhaps the most informing and suggestive of all the interpretations of religion of Haldane is found in the fact that he once advised the members of the Workers Educational Association to read above all other books the Gospel of St. John and also Plato's *Interpretation of the Trial and Death of Socrates.* Plato's writing includes the Apology, the Crito, and the Phædo. Love, tolerance, forgiveness, understanding faith, are in both the Gospel and the essays. These fundamental elements are thus seen, heard, felt, in their highest, broadest, deepest meaning. Such was Haldane's religion.

This man of such philosophic absorptions, penetrations, relations, was also an outstanding administrator and statesman. He once said to me near the close of his long and diverse service, that he had held every office in the British government which he wished for, except that of prime minister, and for this office he had indeed no real desire. In the year 1923 he wrote to MacDonald, saying, ''To office I have no personal wish to return. I have spent ten years of my life in Cabinets, and pomps and ceremonies and stipends are nothing to me. But I do care for my ideals having a chance, and to secure that chance there are things that have to be seen to.'' [6] The record of such offices

[5] *Ibid.,* pp. 192-93.
[6] *Richard Burdon Haldane (Viscount Haldane)—An Autobiography,* p. 342.

is rather astounding.[7] He gives a picture of his typical day when he became Lord High Chancellor in MacDonald's government in 1923. "I used to go to the House of Lords just after ten each morning, and having seen that the judicial business of the day was in progress, spend an hour and a half in starting the day's work as Chancellor with my Secretaries. Sir Claud Schuster, the Permanent Head, was very quick and highly experienced. We got the work launched before twelve, and I then walked over to Whitehall Gardens, where the Staff of the Committee of Imperial Defence were at work. There, after settling the operations for the day with the Secretary, Sir Maurice Hankey, who was also Secretary to the Cabinet, I would often preside over a small meeting of the Chiefs of the Staffs of the three Services. We devoted much time to discussing possible emergencies which might have to be encountered. The Chiefs used to take away and to work out with their own Staffs the details of the counter-plans required. Later on they reported. The maxim I ventured to commend to them was based on old War Office experience, and I offered to have it put up in letters of gold. It was that 'Thinking Costs Nothing.' We accomplished a good deal of defence work of a permanent character in this period.

[7] Member of Judicial Committee of Privy Council; Rector of Edinburgh University; Chancellor University of Bristol; Gifford Lecturer St. Andrews University, 1902-04, House of Commons, Haddingtonshire, 1885-1911, Secretary of State for War 1905-12, Lord High Chancellor of Great Britain 1912-15 and 1924. Taken from British *Who's Who* for 1928.

"After a brief interval for luncheon I returned, either to Whitehall Gardens or, more often, to the House of Lords, to finish the business and correspondence of the day. I made a point of seeing each of my various Secretaries, and of consulting with them over the work with which they were entrusted, whether it concerned magistrates, or clergymen, or Home Office communications. At 4:15 I dressed and went fully robed into the House, and then took a good deal of part in the discussions. We introduced a considerable number of Bills, many of them of a not very controversial order. Questions about the policy of Government were constantly put to me as Leader of the House." [8]

The power for such work, so long continued, so complex, dealing with profoundest problems has been interpreted by one who knew him well. The minister of his ancestral church at Auchterarder, Dr. G. A. Frank Knight, writing soon after his death, said, "Legends floated through Auchterarder of his intellectual feats. It was currently reported and believed that he could dictate four letters on different subjects to four different secretaries at the same time and keep all the four hard at work! It was stated that when he became Minister of War he shut himself up one whole night in the War Office, and before the charwomen arrived in the morning he had read and digested forty volumes of Reports, which later formed the groundwork of his reforms in the Army." [9]

[8] *Richard Burdon Haldane (Viscount Haldane)—An Autobiography*, pp. 346-47.
[9] *The British Weekly*, August 30, 1928, p. 451, first column.

Undoubtedly the most constructive and perhaps the most enduring, at the present moment apparently the greatest of Haldane's work as an administrator, lies in his service as Secretary of State for War. For it was his early organization of the Expeditionary Force, and its prompt sending to France early in the summer of 1914 that may have saved the Channel ports from capture, and may have altered the ultimate decision of the Great War. In the first months of the war he was grossly assailed by his enemies in England. They did not know of his services as Secretary of War, and they did know of his German sympathies. He was accused of treason and treachery in direst forms. Such accusation he endured with philosophic calmness, and more than philosophic humor. He said to me once he received bushels of letters in fiercest condemnation. "What did you do with them?" I asked. "Gave them to a housemaid to burn." At the close of the war he received the following note from Field Marshall Haig: [10]

[10] Quoted in *Richard Burdon Haldane (Viscount Haldane) —An Autobiography,* p. 308 (footnote).

"MY DEAR LORD HALDANE,—There has been so much going on here that I have not been able to attend to my private correspondence. I therefore hope that you will forgive me for not writing to thank you sooner for your most kind letter.

"I appreciate very much indeed your kindly remembrance of my work with you at the War Office. For me that time will always stand out in my memory most prominently because the organization of our Army *for war* dates from then. Until you arrived at the War Office no one knew for what purpose our army existed! And I feel sure that all the soldiers who in those strenuous years were working at the War Office will bear witness to the all-important service which you then

Yet this philosopher who was also a great administrator and the greatest War Secretary, found his deepest public interest in the cause of education. As he wrote to MacDonald in 1923, "On this (education) I have been concentrated for years past, and there are definite reforms coming into sight without which my life-work would be thrown away. They do not require my presence at the Board of Education, but they do mean a definite Cabinet policy and some, though not a great deal of money." [11] In the literal sense of the word Haldane was a humanist. He was devoted to humanity, to humanity's enlargement, enrichment, development, happiness. He knew that education was the means, and that education was the method, for getting such enlargement and enrichment. Such devotion had an early origin. Entering the

rendered to the British Army in the Empire. You then sowed the seeds which have developed into the tremendous instrument which has vanquished the famous German Army and brought about a victorious peace. And where would we be to-day without the Imperial General Staff which was your creation and the Field Service Regulations (Part II Organization) which you forced through in spite of opposition from Army Council and Treasury?

"I and many soldiers with me, are greatly distressed at the ungenerous treatment which you have received during the critical phase in our country's history: and I hope the day is not far distant when the invaluable services which you have rendered to our Empire may be adequately recognized.

"With heartfelt admiration for the way in which you have done your duty and ignored all the spiteful criticisms of the Press which has attacked you, and again many thanks for your very welcome congratulations on what the British Army has done.—Believe me, Yours very truly,

'D. HAIG.' "

[11] *Ibid.*, p. 343.

University of Edinburgh at the age of sixteen, he was a student of the classics. His teachers were Seller, Blackie, and Masson. Among his fellow students were Andrew Seth, afterwards Professor Seth Pringle-Pattison, W. R. Sorley, and William A. Haswell, who became a biological professor in New South Wales.

Haldane's permanent interest in education had a twofold division. He recognized the right and the duty of giving the best education to the best minds. Such minds of his generation he knew intimately. He also knew the duty writ large of educating the democracy. The second duty became the more commanding as his life lengthened. He understood and felt the obligation of the traditional universities to give an education of the more democratic type and content. "Our common principle was one of faith in the effect of higher education on democracy. We did not indeed think that such education was everything. There were other phases of mental activity, such as religion and the love of the beautiful, which were not less important. But we thought that people whose minds were freed from the fetters of ignorance would develop these other phases more readily. We also thought that the student would feel that he had been assisted towards equality with his fellow-citizens, not absolute equality—for nature and circumstances would preclude that—but in the sense of having something more like even chances with his fellow-creatures. The Universities were under existing circumstances too frequently preserves for the sons and daughters of the rich. Our plans, if they could be carried into effect, would at least diminish for a large number the exclusion from the chance of self-development.'' [12] This movement for the education of the people took on special form in Adult Education. Of its Association he became honorary president. He said to his associates, ''Education and learning . . . were no mere means to an end. They were not there to create a class-consciousness, or even merely to get rid of class-consciousness. They were there to teach people that to all men and women the State should give the right to get such instruction as would free them from the depressing effect of circumstances for which they were not responsible, and which was preventing them from individually having a real chance in life.'' [13]

Haldane's interpretation of the function of the university I wish also to quote, and to contrast it with the memory of the reader of Newman's interpretation found in the seventh lecture of his *Idea of the University*. Haldane says, ''For the emancipated man has a high standard and his leisure is for him a precious thing. He knows how to use it and how to secure for himself intimate companionship and stimulation from the minds of the great ones who have revealed themselves without restraint in books. His is a different soul altogether from that of his narrow and ignorant neighbour. You will, by the way, find a good account of this in Plato. Him, moreover, the enlightened neighbour tends to stimulate by his example and thus

[12] *Ibid.*, p. 314.   [13] *Ibid.*, p. 321.

to raise the level of society. In his hours of labour the latter works hard and with concentrated purpose, because he recognises this to be his duty. He knows that he who will not work is not entitled to eat. In the quality of his daily effort and in its product he takes pleasure. He does not care if his station be a humble one socially, or if his reward be less than that of others to whom fortune has been more kind externally, for he realises that this sort of reward is neither the highest nor, by itself, satisfying. He feels that it is not in the form of such fleeting success that the highest justice makes its truest award. We are always more potentially than we take ourselves to be, and even to the best among us the very rough justice of the world does not always give the most. Real virtue finds its only satisfying reward in the satisfaction of doing the best without looking beyond the deed attempted."[14] Perhaps the chief difference between Haldane's interpretation of the function of the university and Newman's lies in this distinction:—Newman's interpretation relates to the making of the gentleman, Haldane's to the making of the man.

In a passage of more emotional eloquence than is usual with a Lord Chancellor, Haldane once reminded an audience that one hundred years before Germany lay shattered and crushed beneath the heel of Napoleon. What and who saved Germany, he asked. "It

---

[14] *Education and Democracy,* an address by Viscount Haldane delivered before the 52nd Annual Congress of the Co-operative Union, in Bristol, on May 25th, 1920, p. 6.

was the great men—men like Fichte and Von Humboldt, who called upon the German people to educate themselves. That has made Germany the great power which she is to-day. What we need is the recognition that in this problem of education lies our future; that on it depends our position as the leading commercial nation of the world, aye, and as the empire. The statesman who will realise that the problem exists, and who will set himself to it in the spirit in which Pitt set himself to the problem of a century ago, will have deserved well of posterity." [15] He tells the students of the University of Wales, "And it is in the Universities, with their power over the mind, greater in the end than the power of any government or of any church, that we see how the soul of a people at its highest mirrors itself. Your University life in this country of Wales is but young. We do not yet see how far it will develop. But what I know of the spirit of your people gives me the sense that the soil in which that young life has taken root is fertile in a high degree." [16]

From all that I have written regarding Haldane's philosophy, religion, and his manifold works, I hope that the personality of the man himself has emerged. For as Emerson says, though the man is greater than all his works, yet the greatness of the man does manifest itself in his methods and in his achievements. If

[15] *Education and Empire,* by Richard Burdon Haldane, pp. 86-7.
[16] *Universities and National Life,* by Viscount Haldane, p. 29.

a single word of interpretation were to be made for Lord Haldane, that word would be "comprehensiveness." For comprehensive was he in knowledge, in subjects of reflection, in writing, in reading, and in achievement. Comprehensive also was he in his moral and religious sympathies, as well as in the intellectual. In the breadth of his understanding he was quite akin to Archbishop Davidson. If one also cares to go back one hundred years, one finds a typical comparison in Faraday. He was blessed indeed with the virtue and the grace of tolerance, and his tolerance was not as the word at times seems to intimate, simply passivity. For his tolerance was strenuously active. In the great book *The Reign of Relativity* he says, "There may come to us, too, contentment of spirit, and a peace which passes our everyday understanding. We grow in tolerance, for we see that it is in expression rather than in intention that our fellow-men are narrow." [17]

In this breadth of understanding and of fellowship was ever manifest a deep sense of friendliness. Evidences of that friendliness are found in thousands of lives not only in England and Scotland, but also in Germany and the United States. Lord Morley once said that if he needed help he would first go to Haldane. At the risk of being altogether too personal, I venture to quote a letter which, near the time of his death, he wrote to me:—

"Some time ago you were so good as to send me

[17] *The Reign of Relativity,* by Viscount Haldane, p. 426.

your book on *The American and the German University*. I kept it by me until I should have time to read
it consecutively through. I have now done so, and
with great pleasure.

"Your impressions of the German Universities are
in full accord with my own. I was a student at Göttingen, with which I have kept up relations. I think
that you show very clearly what the influence
through the United States of the German Universities
has been, and also its real nature.

"Anyhow the study of your book has given me real
pleasure, for which I thank you."

This very personal study of one of the greatest of
all men whom it has been my humble happiness to
number among my friends, I cannot better close than
in words with which he closes his autobiography:—
"The best that ordinary mortals can hope for is the
result which will probably come from sustained work
directed by as full reflection as is possible. This result
may be affected adversely by circumstances, by illness,
by misfortune, or by death. But if we have striven
to think and to do work based on thought, then we
have at least the sense of having striven with such
faculties as we have possessed devoted to the striving.
And that is in itself a course of happiness, going beyond the possession of any definite gain." [18] "Our
duty is to work without turning our eyes to the right
or to the left from the ideals which alone can light up

[18] *Richard Burdon Haldane (Viscount Haldane)—An Autobiography*, pp. **376-77**.

our paths. It is not any finality attained that can ever be ours; what is ours can be no more than the best quality of which we are capable, put into the effort towards the attainment of what we have set before ourselves. The effort towards it is one which we daily find ourselves called upon to make anew. We have to think of how to live before we can learn how to die. God is not outside us, but is within our breasts, 'an almighty, ever-present Deity.' " [19]

[19] *Ibid.*, p. 366.

XV
HENRY JOHNSON

Born in Gardiner, Me., June 25, 1855; died Feb. 7, 1918. Received A.B., Bowdoin College, 1874; student at universities of Göttingen, Leipzig, and Berlin; Ph.D., Berlin, 1884; studied and traveled about five years from 1875; professor of modern languages, Bowdoin, 1877, librarian, 1880-83, and curator of Bowdoin Art Collection from 1894. Member Dante Society, etc.

Editor: Schiller's Ballads, 1888; Midsummer Night's Dream, 1888.

Author: Where Beauty Is, and Other Poems, 1898; The Seer, and Other Poems, 1910.

Translator: Les Trophées, José-Maria de Heredia, The Sonnets, 1910; La Commedia di Dante Alighieri, 1892-1911.

HENRY JOHNSON

SCHOLAR, TEACHER, POET, FRIEND

In a letter of the year 1915, sending to me a copy of his Dante, Harry Johnson (Henry is his formal name) said, "It is a great pleasure to write you these few words to ask your acceptance of a copy of my translation of the *Divine Comedy*, . . . Your personal belief that I have done what was possible to me and your acceptance of a friendly offering I know are to be counted on; the cold and critical estimate, who can tell what that will be? I am *primarily* indebted to Old Phillips for my first true acquaintance with scholarship. Do you think it strange that I fancy trying to do a long, hard piece of work is somehow a payment of an obligation?"

The allusion to Old Phillips has special meaning, for it was at Andover that we first met, and in the beginning of the fall term of 1869. Our fathers had been friends in their boyhood home in Industry, Maine. We were therefore prepared to like each other, and like each other we did from the early years of our teens. For Harry came to Andover at the age of fourteen. A bashful boy he was and silent, as became youth, and a certain diffidence or reserve seemed even in maturity to rest upon him as a beautiful robe.

After one year in the Academy he entered Bowdoin College. The terms of admission to the Maine college he was able to meet without the Senior preparatory year at a first-rate school like Andover. Following his graduation at Bowdoin, at the very proper age of nineteen, in 1874, he spent two years in travel and in study in Göttingen and Paris. His coming up, however, for his final degree was deferred. It was not until 1884 that Berlin, following his residence there and in Leipzig, gave him his Ph.D. In 1877 he was made professor of modern languages in Bowdoin. In 1880 he became librarian and later curator of the art collection of the college. In the librarianship he served three years, and in the curatorship for many. He also continued his teaching. From his election to the faculty in 1877 to his death in 1918, he remained a loyal and devoted son and servant of his Alma Mater. This length of service, of two score years, did not approach the almost unique length of term of a colleague, Packard, who served the college as teacher and librarian for sixty-five years, from 1819 to his death in 1884. It was of Professor Packard that Longfellow in his *Morituri Salutamus* sang, in his Bowdoin poem of 1875.

"Honor and reverence, and the good repute
　That follows faithful service as its fruit,
　Be unto him, whom living we salute."

The richness of Harry's life lived with his associates, and for and with the undergraduates, was as beautiful and holy as was the number of the years of their common service.

Bowdoin was and is and ought to be a small college. It is small in the number of its teachers. It is small also in the number of its undergraduates. In Johnson's early time the number of the teachers was no larger than fifteen. " . . . the fifteen men of the faculty could not sit together for long without becoming pretty well acquainted, for better or worse, with each other's salient traits. The internal administration of Bowdoin was the composite result of the individual psychologies of these close-gathered men, their mutual checks and reinforcements." Professor Burnett in his biography of Hyde interprets several of the number. Among them are Chapman, " . . . in English, vigorous conservator of custom, a gentleman throughout, with a sly humor devoid of malice in the corners of eye and mouth." There was Houghton, " . . . in Latin, urbane and travelled, conservative, compact in wit." "There was Little, the Librarian, idealistic, aspiring, self-sacrificing, withal emotional, hesitant, a little anxious, yet devoted to climbing in the high mountains." Of Johnson, Burnett says, " . . . epigrammatic, scholarly, gentle, whose strongly felt emotions forced the counter-check of an almost fierce devotion to facts." [1] With men of the type of Chapman, of Houghton, and of Little, and of the beloved Packard, an elder statesman, Harry lived his life, did his work, and fulfilled his destiny.

Harry's life and character were a union of the

[1] *Hyde of Bowdoin,* by Charles T. Burnett, pp. 142-143.

scholarly, the æsthetic, and the religious. He was a scholar in Italian, French, and German literatures. In modern, as in most, languages, the scholar may take on one or several elements or relations. The chief characteristic may be either philological, historical, grammatical, comparative, or æsthetic. With Harry the relation was æsthetic. He taught Bowdoin boys both the elementary and the advanced courses, and in his teaching he was a faithful master. Sitting in his classroom, I have seen, heard, and felt his faithfulness. His students loved him, and these students, long become graduates, add to their lasting love admiration and beautiful appreciation. Coming back to Bowdoin it is not unusual for them to say, "I learned most from Professor Johnson, not perhaps irregular verbs, but the big things of life. He influenced me most of all my teachers, though he may have let me through too easily."

In his teaching the student ever felt the forcefulness of the emphasis on the element of truthfulness, truthfulness both ethical and intellectual. "Yes, but is that exactly what the French says?" is a comment which President Sills says Johnson frequently made on a translation offered by a student in his classroom. In this emphasis the breadth of his learning was also manifested. In his knowledge of Shakespeare he held a place with the scholars. In his knowledge of Latin he was a translator, for instance, of Lucretius, whose versions were commended by the wise; and in his knowledge of European history he seemed almost like a specialist. In his teaching, moreover, one felt the soul of the devotee who appreciates literary beauty. His was the artistic soul. For Henry Johnson was a poet and a translator of poetry. In all his verses the artist was heard singing. As the head, too, of the art department of the college, a department among the richest of all college collections of pictures, one recognized in him a wise judge and enriching interpreter.

I am constrained to believe that Harry's verses are, and will remain, the most commanding evidence both of his æsthetic soul and of his religious faith. Of all these forms of his creation, the translation of Dante is noblest, and may prove to be the most enduring. Ignorant as I sadly am, I cannot write worthily of the translation, but this work of Harry's, begun in 1892 and lasting until 1915, does move me as does no other translation. Has not Dante himself said that no poetry can be translated? Yet having in mind the translations of the Cambridge interpreters, both in poetry and prose, Charles Eliot Norton and Longfellow, one is constrained to believe that Harry's attains a high place.[2]

[2] The following letter was received by Johnson from one who has been called the foremost scholar in Romance philology. It is taken from the *Bowdoin College Bulletin* of June, 1918, a bulletin having President Sills's noble interpretation of Johnson:

(Translation)

Florence, May 27, 1915.

ESTEEMED COLLEAGUE,

America may truly be proud of its Dante studies. The invaluable Concordances, the singularly sound and well balanced edition of the divine poem that Grandgent has produced, the

Some cantos in the *Divine Comedy* lead one into the holiest shrines. In the Inferno, in the first canto, are the verses which interpret the familiar passage of the meeting of Virgil and of Dante.

" 'A poet was I, and I sang that just
　　Son of Anchises, who came forth from Troy
　　After the burning of proud Ilium.

translations, constitute a triad that has not its equal elsewhere. Nor elsewhere is there anything that compares with the Dante Collection of Cornell University with its precious catalogue.

I have not here at hand the versions that have preceded yours; fruit of so long and persistent labors. But this version seems to me truly excellent; and it has never happened to me in reading the Commedia translated into any language whatsoever that the original echoed constantly in my ear in the way that it does here. A most excellent decision, the preservation of the strophe, giving up entirely the rhyme. The rhythm is essential, because from it is determined the whole movement that the thought takes in the expression. The rhyme on the other hand, is a secondary matter, so much so that, treating of the *canzone*, Dante could say in the De vulg. Eloq. II, IX 4 (Oxford ed. II, IX, 28) that "it is not of the essential art of the *canzone*." To preserve it meant to force one's self to contortions of every kind and to subject the thought to the word.

To Dante as to a sublime guide are turned the eyes of the Italians in this anxious moment of their history. The boundaries indicated by him in the direction of the east, the noble monument, far superior to all the others, which was erected to him at Trent, speak to us a language that could not be more potent. But how, too, beside this, and in a way far more important, does he appear maker and welder of our unification! The problems that now torture us, solved—if we shall so far succeed—we must strive that he become for us ever more teacher of moral loftiness.

With feelings of gratitude and of profound regard, I esteem it an honor to profess myself

Your devoted servant,

Pio Rajna.

But thou, why turn'st thou back to such distress?
   Why not ascend this mountain of delight,
   Which is the source and cause of every joy?'
'Art thou then, pray, that Virgil, and that fount
   Which pours abroad so wide a stream of speech?'
   Began I, answering him with bashful brow;
'Honor and light of other poets, now
   May the long study and great love avail me,
   Which made me search thy volume; for thou art
My Master and my Author; thou alone
   Art he from whom that fair style has been taken,
   Which has done honor to my name.' "

In the last canto of the Paradiso are these sacred
verses:

"Not that more than one single semblance was
   Within the Living Light on which I gazed,
   Which is forever such as it has been,
But through my sight which took on strength in me
   Looking thereon, one sole appearance seemed
   Transformed to me, as I myself was changed.

      *   *   *   *   *

Oh, how far short is speech, and oh, how weak
   For my conception, which, to what I saw,
   Is such, to call it little is not meet.
O Light Eternal, that alone abidest
   Within Thyself, knowing alone Thyself,
   Self-known and knowing, lovest and dost smile!"

Are not these verses indeed as moving to the heart
as are the emotions which any scripture can offer in
thought, feeling, imagination, faith?

For Johnson's religious faith was quite as fundamental and constructive as were his æsthetic belief and imagination. By nurture, as well as by natural feeling, his faith was elemental. It was a quiet reserved faith as became his character. It voiced itself rather in terms of the imagination than in the testimony of the prayer-meeting, though he was a regular attendant at the Wednesday evening service of prayer. The booklet *On Sacred Themes,* a tract of only fourteen pages, sings his creed. The very titles of its poems are significant—"Love's Stewardship," "Glory," "Light of Light," "The Coming," "Immanuel," "Heavenward," "Prayer," "Thanksgiving," "Consecration," "Faith." The first of these, "Love's Stewardship," is characteristic of the man:

"Thy love it was that gave me birth
And made me share this goodly earth;
My home, my friends, my all, are thine,
The use of all alone is mine.

Forgive me that I sought to live
As though I took and would not give;
I promise Thee that I will share
What Thou hast given in my care.

The gift of cheer if I withhold
And leave Thy love to me untold,
Give me no courage when I cry,
And when I need Thee, be not nigh.

What though my talent be but one,
My single task shall yet be done;
I will be true, and give each day
The best of my own self away."

Another hymn of the collection, "Consecration," was sung at his bier.

These hymns seem, indeed, to be a simple rendering of the simple trust, belief and consecration of Longfellow—Longfellow, an early predecessor of Harry in the historic chair at Bowdoin.

With Harry's æsthetic appreciation and with his religious spirit, there went along a certain emptying of his heart into the heart of his friends. It was a beautiful altruism, a substitution, a certain wistfulness of feeling, a oneness of interpretation and of emotion, which stood for the fullness and nobility of his character. His face possessed a certain yearning, a yearning for the acceptance of himself by yourself, and also an equal yearning for himself to accept you. His manner was sympathetic, without a breath of softness. I do not think of his weeping in sympathetic love, but I do think of his having a feeling for a distressed friend which was too deep for tears. His speech was an interpretation of the best,—often perhaps an interrogation of the best in himself,—in you, in books, in nature, in men, in God. His mood was the mood of worship. He was a priest at the altar. In every place of beauty he built a shrine. His constant prayer and aspiration ever seemed to be toward the eternal. He lifted the earth unto heaven; and he gave heaven unto the earth. In the two sonnets, "When He Shall Come" and "The Rain," we feel his religion both as faith and as beauty.

When He Shall Come

I have already come. I begged the bread
Which you refused Me at your door,
Me, asking what I needed, nothing more,
From you who from My bounty had been fed.
I have already come. In vain I plead,
Not on some far, forgotten day of yore,
Not in a speech unknown, unheard before,
This morning, here, it was My voice which said:
  "Have you some work to do? I cannot find
  A man that wants a laborer, although
  I have tried hard; and I have come to you."
It still goes echoing, echoing in my mind,
  A voice forever calling, clear and low:
  "Have you some work, have you some work to do?"

The Rain

The clouds that all the morning frowned in vain
Were sailing lower, sweeping now the tops
Of the high hills, till oftener threatening drops
On face and hand told of the coming rain.
The sky became of one soft hue again,
One interfusing gray, which scarcely stops
Its work till the old cliff-face, that outcrops
Defiant, seems to wear a softened strain.
  O spirits of the never-resting wind,
  Stay your swift course till ye shall take my prayer
  To Him who sent you with the rain today:
Thou who dost live in all, in world and mind,
  Let me too in this double being share,
  Let me be and build after Thee alway.

Bowdoin College has had rather a deep than a broad
influence in American and world life. Yet its breadth
is not to fail of appreciation. For it gave an educa-

tion to Longfellow, to Hawthorne and to others not
unworthy of such leadership. Like Bowdoin College
is Johnson's life: it touched the deepest elements of
the personal character of his students, influencing
profoundly their emotions and broadening their intellectual culture and character. His translations, moreover, unite him with one of the greatest of the lasting masters. His own poems sing the deathless songs
of the human heart. Like Bowdoin, too, and like the
whole State of Maine he was the soul of friendliness.
Like the two rivers on whose banks he lived and died,
he moved toward limitless horizons, ever reflecting the
images of Heaven.

XVI
CHARLES ALBERT DICKINSON

BORN Westminster, Vermont, July 4, 1849; died at
Corona, Calif., Jan. 9, 1907; graduate of Phillips
Academy, Andover, 1872; Harvard University,
1876; Andover Theological Seminary, 1879. Pastor
of Payson Memorial Church, Portland, Maine,
1879; Kirk St. Church, Lowell, Mass., 1882; Berkeley Temple, Boston, Mass., 1887-1900; Pastor
Emeritus, Berkeley Temple, 1901-07.

XVI

CHARLES ALBERT DICKINSON

A FOUNDER OF THE INSTITUTIONAL CHURCH, FRIEND

A FRIENDSHIP which began in my teens, which grew in the years of formal education, and which is now held in loving and lasting memory, bears the name of "Dick." "Dick" was Charles Albert Dickinson. Dickinson became "Dick" to me as a schoolmate in Phillips Academy at Andover, and "Dick" he remained as a classmate and a roommate at Harvard and Andover Theological Seminary. *Our* "institutional" relations cover no less than eight years, a rather unique record. Our rooming together at Harvard was for the Freshman year only. A death in the family brought his mother to Cambridge, and for three years his mother's home was his.

On graduation at Andover Seminary, Dickinson entered upon his life's work as a minister. Churches in Portland, Lowell, and Boston he served in succession. To Congregational churches in Portland and in Lowell he brought first-rate preaching, and wise, loving pastoral care. To the Boston church he gave not only these qualities, but also peculiarly able elements of administration. For he became its minister for the

269

purpose of transmuting an old and somewhat decaying church into what was then called an Institutional Church. The epithet "Institutional" was first used, so far as I know, in this sense by President Tucker of Dartmouth. In this service, beginning in 1887, Dickinson continued thirteen years. An institutional church is perhaps the most commanding in its call for a large budget. For its works are manifold and far-flung. What in earlier decades of the last century Maurice had tried to do in London, and what in the later decades Hugh Price Hughes had tried to do, Dickinson sought to do in Boston. His work and works embodied the distinct social conception of Christianity, and of the church. Societies, institutes, brotherhoods abounded. Classes in all sorts of practical endeavors were as many as are the societies and fraternities of the typical college. The works went out, too, beyond the church walls. Rescue missions were founded; and homes for young women and for young men begun. A floating hospital for sick babies was launched, which lasted for some thirty years. A home for friendless children in his own home town of Westminster, Vermont, was established, and is continuing under changed conditions. The mottoes were "All things to all men to save somebody;" "all things to help everybody and anybody who needs help." But in the midst of such manifold services preaching was not neglected; for Dickinson was among the most efficient of all preachers of his time.

Among the members of the new church in Boston

was one who bore the name of Frank G. Pratt. Pratt and Dickinson were fellow students at Andover. Ill health obliged Pratt to give up his studies. Coming to Boston he presently became an associate of Daniel S. Ford, the owner of a great paper—*The Youth's Companion*. Pratt earned and received rapid promotion. He became Dick's chief financial support in the church. The promise seemed assured of a long and useful coöperation of Pratt and Dick. The assurance was that this church would become the lengthened shadow of two lives. Pratt's wisdom was no less great than his generosity. Upon Pratt Dick leaned, and Pratt always supported. After slight warning Pratt died. The corner stone on which both were building was taken away. Pratt's passing marks the beginning of anxiety, financial, executive, ecclesiastical. Dick's great soul in its idealism struggled with the problem of the support of Berkeley Temple. In this struggle he was aided and blessed by a devoted wife, whose worth in consecrated helpfulness and efficiency no words can intimate. But the load was too heavy. The result was that Dick's health broke, and broke not to be mended.

While devoted to his churches, Dick was also one, and perhaps the chief one, in coöperation with its founder, in carrying on one of the great church works of the nineteenth century, the Christian Endeavor Society. Francis E. Clark had become the pastor of the Williston Church two years before Dickinson began his work at the other end of what Longfellow calls the "City Beautiful." With this movement from its beginning, and for many years, he was in close knowledge, sympathy, coöperation. On no one more fully, in the early years of the great undertaking, did the founder depend. Dickinson was counselor, guide, an acting president at the great meetings of the organization, a co-editor and co-owner of its newspaper. If Clark was the John Wesley of the movement, Dickinson was its Charles Wesley.

Broken in health, broken in purse, but not broken in spirit or in courage, Dick went to California in the year 1900. In California his partially restored health allowed him to preach in leading churches, and to take up other work. But the struggle, valiant and pre-determined in its result, was not for long. He died in the year 1907, at the age of fifty-eight.

Nature did much for Dick. Its chief intellectual gift to him was imagination. He thought in pictures. Truth made its appeal to him in individual images rather than through general, comprehensive terms. Of the two types of mind, the philosophic and poetic, his was the poetic. He belonged moreover to the order of the seers. He was an apostle, a prophet. What ought to be was to him quite as significant as what was. He saw visions, he dreamed dreams. Idealism was one with the poetic impulse. Early was this poetic impulse felt, and to the last it continued. His college classmates recognized its worth, and made him their class poet. His associates in one of the most remarkable movements of the church of the century appreciated it, and summoned him as their singer.

Its results live in hymns which have found a place in the hearts of men and in the history of the church. The last lines of his class day poem at Harvard prove his poetic power, and illustrate also other great qualities of his character:

> A youth pursues a rainbow bright
> Far up the rugged mountain's side,
> But when he gains the crowning height,
> The radiant bow, thrice glorified
> Above the far horizon lies;—
> "Oh, give me wings," the urchin cries:
> So we pursue the future's bow,
> The distance widening as we go.
> The mountain-top we've gained to-day,
> But, lo! our rainbow, far away,
> With tenfold brilliance spans the sky.
> On eagle's wings we now must fly
> Far o'er the passion plains of life,—
> Above all selfish, earth-born strife.
> What though our beacon bow shall fade
> And turn to mist?—be not dismayed.
> Heaven's fadeless beacon flames beyond:
> On, brothers, on, none dare despond;
> Be ours a purpose firm and sure;
> Be ours a manhood staunch and pure.

Dick also wrote verses which have become hymns. The most popular of them probably is that entitled "O Golden Day."

> O golden day so long desired,
>   Born of a darksome night,
> The swinging globe at last is fired
>   By thy resplendent light.

And hark! like Memnon's morning chord,
  Is heard from sea to sea
This song: One Master, Christ, the Lord;
  And brethren all are we.

The noises of the night shall cease,
  The storms no longer roar;
The factious foes of God's own peace
  Shall vex His church no more.
A thousand, thousand voices sing
  In surging harmony
This song: One Master, Saviour, King;
  And brethren all are we.

Sing on, ye chorus of the morn,
  Your grand Endeavor strain,
Till Christian hearts, estranged and torn,
  Blend in the glad refrain;
And all the church, with all its pow'rs,
  In loving loyalty
Shall sing: One Master, Christ is ours;
  And brethren all are we.

In Dick were also two great qualities which are closely associated. In him was a genius for friendship and also a charm of personality. He cared for folks and folks cared for him. Entering college at an age when most boys are graduating, he yet was free from any air of superiority, or of patronizingness. In him was found no assumption. He took his place as a freshman with the freshmen. He fought our class battles with the humblest of us, and he sang the songs which we adopted, songs which he wrote, with the best and with the worst singers of us all. He was jolly with the jolliest, happy with the happiest, sympathetic with the sorrowing. There was in him what George Eliot calls "a laughter of the intellect." Sympathy clothed him, and went out from him as an atmosphere.

In this common and hearty air of friendliness, there was also found an element of personal charm. His face was a face of sunshine and of cheer. His smile was beautiful. His form was tall and willowy, his shoulders sloping as if he wished to come close to you. His voice was full and sweet, at times tremulous, indicating a tender heart, and a manner sympathetic, responsive, gracious. His speech was flavored with wit, his walk and conversation breathed sympathy with each of men's moods. Yet in his friendships he was discriminating without being finical; refined without a touch of fastidiousness; pure without an intimation of coldness; and cultured for a college boy without remoteness or indifference.

Like Stevenson, Dick early retired from the marching ranks. He watched his companions going forward to their victories. Regret was in his soul, but no complaint trembled on his lips. His death reminds one of Keat's "Valedictory," which he spoke to Severn. The name of neither is writ in water. One may apply to him certain adjectives which he used in his class poem. He kept his purpose "firm and sure," his manhood "staunch and pure." One can believe that "heaven's fadeless beacon" still guides.

XVII
THEODORE CHICKERING WILLIAMS

Born in Brookline, Mass., July 2, 1855; died May 6, 1915. A.B., Harvard University, 1876; Litt.D., Western Reserve University, 1911. Minister of Unitarian Church, Winchester, Mass., 1882, All Souls Church (Unitarian), New York, 1883-96; in Europe, 1897-99; headmaster Hackley School, Tarrytown, N. Y., 1899-1905; in Europe, 1905-07; headmaster Roxbury Latin School, 1907-09 (resigned).

Author: Character Building, 1894; The Making of Man (Phi Beta Kappa Poem), 1894; translation, Elegies of Tibullus, 1905; Virgil's Æneid, 1907; Poems of Belief, 1910; Georgics and Eclogues, 1915.

XVII

THEODORE CHICKERING WILLIAMS

MINISTER OF THE CHURCH UNIVERSAL, FRIEND OF VIRGIL,
SYMPATHETIC SOUL

As the river of life lengthens, its channel narrows. If the channel deepens as well as narrows, one may indeed be thoroughly content. This remark applies to Theodore Chickering Williams, or Teddy, as I called him.

For Teddy made three rich contributions to life: the earliest as a preacher; for he followed a great preacher in an age of great preachers, Henry W. Bellows, as minister of All Souls (Unitarian) Church in New York. For no less a period than thirteen years he upheld the dignity and power of this pulpit at once personal and historic. This service he began at the age of twenty-eight. His second contribution was as a school-teacher. He was the first principal and in many respects the founder of the Hackley School on the Hudson, a school becoming historic. Later he came into a noble succession of principals of the already historic Roxbury Latin School. The third contribution lay in his poetry: poetry of his own verses and hymns, of his translations from the Latin, and in

279

particular of his translation of the Æneid. His river of life deepened as it narrowed.

As a preacher Williams represented and continued the Boston tradition. He followed by a long interval Channing, and by a less long one Gannett, James Freeman Clarke, and the Peabodys. Rather akin to them was he than to Theodore Parker or to Edward Everett Hale. His sermons were of the classical type. The message he spoke was simple in style, deep in, and creative of, thought, as deep as the audience would accept, teeming in both inspiration and aspiration, but rather the more in aspiration. I once asked a distinguished minister about the preaching of Williams. His answer was the remark made concerning Christ, "And he took a child, and set him by him." Each sermon was a worthy union of the divine and of the human.

Of his school teaching Williams finally became very weary. He wrote me near the close, saying: "I don't enjoy my job. It does not bring me in contact with interesting people, or call out my best powers, but just *tires* me. I am blue, deeply, darkly blue. I am not *good* enough to teach school, but I *am* too intellectual. It *bores* me." But to his teaching he clung as a duty till the task was done. Then he found freedom, the freedom of the upper air of thought and imagination. At last he won his wings.

In this threefold offering as preacher, as teacher, and finally and comprehensively as poet, are seen and felt one controlling and constructive method and motive. And that is the spirit of the artist. Teddy possessed the gift of imagination and of taste. In the beautiful he exulted; it clothed him as a garment; it inspired him as a prophet; it ruled him as a king. His special use of this gift lay in the power of words, words voicing sentiment, vision, creative imagination.

Even Teddy's prose, spoken or written, and early prose, too, proved his artistic sense in the use of words. For he was the class orator of his class of '76 at Harvard. Election to this office was and is the highest honor which the class can bestow upon one of its own members. A re-reading of his oration, after an interval from first hearing it of more than fifty years proves how worthily given was this under-graduate and graduating distinction. I now quote from it in order to show the consummate worth and controlling force of his early artistic impulse and in-terest. The extracts also prove the intellectual matu-rity of his youth. In answer to the question, ''What are our best equipments for the duties of life?'' he says: ''Not the Greek moods or the chemical analyses, but sound judgment, the power of choosing well, of resolutely following up the choice, and that unhesi-tating trust in the veracity of your own convictions by which the courage of self-reliance is distinguished from the perversity of self-will. It is these moral qualities that seem to me of more value than any intellectual acquisitions.'' [1]

[1] *Baccalaureate Sermon and Oration and Poem,* class of 1876, p. 22.

That Harvard gave, as it still gives, such equipment is proved by what he further says: "In the best sense, Harvard is Puritan still—in the moral dignity of her aims; in the high spiritual significance of her mission in American society; in the position which she holds there in the vanguard of intellectual inquiry, —Puritan in her reverence of truth. Just as in the old days it was ever her purpose to make the intellect the servant of the character, and to send forth her sons, not merely as scholars, but as upright and godly men, able and willing to cope with the spiritual and worldly perplexities of the community in which they lived; so she sends us forth *now,* to meet, as best we may, the many-sided and far-reaching problems of the intellectual world of to-day, and to confront the complex conditions, the new and formidable obstacles that are presenting themselves in American society." [2]

But the artistry of Teddy's mind through the pen in the use of words is yet more impressively illustrated in his poems. These poems take on several forms. Perhaps the most widely known of them are found in his hymns, hymns which are sung in many churches in England as well as in America. He takes his place with Oliver Wendell Holmes, with Samuel Longfellow, with Gannett, and with Hosmer as one of the great singers of the Unitarian Church, a church conspicuous in the recent decades for its writers of hymns.

The hymn which has become a song of the Church

[2] *Ibid.*, p. 26.

Universal is perhaps the following for it voices a lasting need and a filling of the need of the human heart:

> When thy heart, with joy o'er flowing,
>   Sings a thankful prayer,
> In thy joy, O let thy brother
>   With thee share.
>
> When the harvest sheaves ingathered,
>   Fill thy barns with store,
> To thy God and to thy brother
>   Give the more.
>
> If thy soul, with power uplifted,
>   Yearn for glorious deed,
> Give thy strength to serve thy brother
>   In his need.
>
> Hast thou borne a secret sorrow
>   In thy lonely breast?
> Take to thee thy sorrowing brother
>   For a guest.
>
> Share with him thy bread of blessing,
>   Sorrow's burden share:
> When thy heart enfolds a brother
>   God is there.

Williams' patriotic songs, too, have fire, force, fervor. His songs of belief, moreover, are genuine, noble out-pourings of the aspiring winged spirit. His sonnets, likewise, and other poems that are in many respects sonnets, serve to illustrate his skill. I must be content with a quotation of only one of his verses, and this merely an extract from what he writes under the

painting by Sodoma of the "Thorn Crowned Christ."
The picture itself belonged to him; beneath a copy of
it, which he gave to me, he wrote these lines:

"Thou in thy morn of youth joy-flushed and proud
   Didst picture forth thy scourged and bleeding Lord,
   His thorns a crown, his blood the sign sublime
Of life self-offered. He heeds not the loud
Taunt of the world, but meets its whole vile horde
Alone with God's love, overcoming time."

But to Teddy, as to most of us, the river of life
narrowed as it lengthened. It came to leave its
preaching and its teaching relations, and to confine
itself more and more to poetry. And in the poetry,
narrowing, it confined itself still further to his friendliness for Virgil. His translation of the Æneid has
been called by a most competent scholar, Samuel Ball
Platner, the best rendering, English or other, ever
made. And one does not forget Dryden, or Conington,
or William Morris. Of his own methods and purpose
Williams himself has said, "My first aim has been lucidity. I have tried to make the narrative move swiftly
and clearly; and to minimize (without loss of accuracy) the frequent artificiality and entanglement of
the original phrase. Though seeking a poetic diction,
bold and vivid phrases, a vocabulary rich in emotional
association and words of appealing sound, I have
sacrificed much to the avoidance of foreign idiom,
and have not attempted the impossible task of bringing over the full magic and suggestion of every Virgilian phrase. Yet having made movement and lucid-

ity the prime requisites (after accuracy), I have lingered long to avoid the commonplace. Only genius can attain the grand style. The translator of it must often be in the plight of the ass who tried to wear the dreadful semblance of the lion. Yet the attempt is obligatory. There must be stateliness and force. The middle way must be found between artificiality and commonness.'' [3]

In this period of the two thousandth anniversary of the birth of Virgil such a word interpreting such a work makes a peculiar appeal to the thoughtful imagination.

Teddy was, as he describes Virgil, a dreamer. He was indeed, also like Virgil, the idealist, the detached, the contemplative mind. In his dreams and in his contemplations he heard the inner voice, and the outer as well, for in him opposites seemed to unite as in other valiant souls. He was devout, yet playful; self-centered, yet companionable; devoted to the immediate task, yet having vision; master of prose, he was even more master of verse; mature with the mature, he was a youth with the youth. Of many foreign experiences, he was yet born and he died within sight of the State House dome. Possessing richest friendships, he was generous in his own giving of affections. A gentleman he was, at home in any society. On a tablet placed on the wall of his church, King's Chapel in Boston, are inscribed these lines of his own writing

---

[3] *The Æneid of Virgil,* by Theodore C. Williams. Introduction, p. xxvii.

(not of course for this purpose) : he "could share the whole world's tears, and still be glad." The vision of God is promised to the pure in heart. His vision of the divine and of the eternal was clearer than is given to most.

His face came to take on a look which Newman's, seen in his portraits, had in his early years. The face, too, like his whole movement, had a certain detachment which Emerson's wore. This detachment from this world, his waiting for the inspired and inspiring voice, are caught and set forth by a noble sculptor, Mrs. Nathaniel Horton Batchelder, in a marble once placed on the walls of the church where he preached for the early middle period of his beautiful life.

XVIII
PEABODY AND BOWEN

ANDREW PRESTON PEABODY, born in Beverly, Mass., March 19, 1811; died March 10, 1893. At the age of twelve admitted to Harvard College; with two exceptions youngest graduate. Taught Middleton, Mass., Meadville, Penn., Portsmouth, N. H.; graduated, Harvard Divinity School, 1832. While a Divinity student served as proctor, and instructor in Hebrew. After graduation was tutor in mathematics; became minister in Portsmouth, N. H., 1833, serving twenty-seven years; 1860, appointed preacher to the University, and Plummer Professor of Christian Morals, an office which he filled, both active and emeritus, till his death; acting President of Harvard, 1862, and 1868-69; overseer, 1883-93. Editor of North American Review, 1854-63. Published many volumes and more than 100 sermons and reviews.

FRANCIS BOWEN, born in Charlestown, Mass., September 8, 1811; died January 2, 1890. Graduated from Harvard with first honors in 1833. Taught mathematics, Phillips Exeter Academy, 1833-35. 1835-39 Harvard, tutor in Greek, instructor in Mental Philosophy and Political Economy; 1839-40, in Europe; literary studies, Cambridge, 1840-52. 1842, published edition of Virgil and also Critical Essays on Speculative Philosophy; owned and edited North American Review, 1843-54; for six years edited and published the American Almanac and Repository of Useful Knowledge. In 1849, published Lowell lectures, two courses on the Application of Metaphysical and Ethical Science to the Evidences of Religion; 1850, appointed McLean Professor of History, holding the office six months; 1853-89, Alford Professor of Natural Religion, Moral Philosophy, Civil Polity; professor emeritus, 1889-90.

XVIII

PEABODY AND BOWEN

PHILOSOPHERS, INTERPRETERS

It was a great assemblage of great men who were enrolled in the Harvard University faculty in the first years of the eighth decade of the last century. The simple calling of the academic roll is moving. Benjamin Peirce, Agassiz, Oliver Wendell Holmes, Asa Gray, Sophocles, James Russell Lowell, Ezra Abbot, Wolcott Gibbs, Child, Lane, Winlock, Cooke, Charles Carroll Everett, Dunbar, Goodwin, Langdell, Bôcher, Gurney, J. B. Thayer, Adams Hill, Henry Adams, William Everett, Goodale, Shaler, Palmer, William James, J. B. Ames, Charles Eliot Norton—such men with their associates formed the Harvard University faculty, undergraduate and professional.

Yet from the list I have purposely omitted two names, Andrew Preston Peabody and Francis Bowen. For these two names had a meaning more intimate, more personal, representing an influence more formative and constructive than most others. Each embodied the Harvard heritage. Each was a graduate, and each the first scholar in his class. They were, be it at once said, of opposite relations and types. Peabody's place was as "Preacher to the University, and Plummer Professor of Christian Morals." Bowen's designation was "Alford Professor of Natural Religion, Moral Philosophy, and Civil Polity." Their personalities were quite as unlike as were the two broad fields covered by their professorial connotations. Their personalities, too, exceeded by much the value and significance of their professorships, important as the Alford Professorship was and is. Peabody might be called professor of the heart, as indeed he has been called, and Bowen professor of the intellect. In his service Peabody continued for thirty-three years (1860-93), Bowen for thirty-six years (1853-89), with another year as emeritus.

Even in their bodies they seemed to be quite as unlike as in their field of learning and in the constitution of their minds. For Peabody was tall, strong, laborious, inclined to stoop, enduring, slow-moving, yet vigorous, walking from Cambridge to Salem, twenty miles, of a Sunday morning to preach at the end of his Sabbatical stroll. Bowen was slight, cadaverous, afflicted at times in the classroom with a wracking cough, a man of the Kantian type. He says of his master, Kant, that at the end of his life he "dried up rather than died." Some way Bowen was so frail and fragile that it seemed to us hot-blooded Juniors a wind might have lifted him and borne him to the skies. Peabody carried in his face a solar radiance, which seemed to shed forth a general benevolence. "And he wist not that his face shone." Bowen bore an expression which apparently intimated the marks and lines which he ascribes to Kant's countenance. Peabody came to his chair from the ministry, and had no other training for his teaching than that which the scholarly pastorate of wide reading and broad interests allows. Bowen read philosophy and worked in the severer cognate subjects from his graduation in 1833 to his election to the Alford Chair twenty years later. Each edited the *North American Review* at two different periods, Bowen from 1843 to 1854, when he owned the quarterly, and Peabody from 1854 to 1863.

Peabody was ever the incarnation of simplicity and of kindness, of generosity and of love. He embodied the charity of the 13th chapter of 1st Corinthians. Once, asking him what my mark was in a course of ethics, he replied, "I have given you what I seldom give any man—a perfect mark." So benignant his look and so tender was his trembling voice as he said "A perfect mark," I tried to look grateful and happy, too, but in my look of gratitude I am sure there was a bit of amusement, for I knew it was hard to get a mark lower than 97. Francis G. Peabody says, "Among the myths which gathered about his name was that of a student who inquired what mark he had received in examination, to which the kindly doctor is said to have replied, 'A very good mark indeed. By the way, what is your name?' "[1]

Bowen, on the contrary, was critical, careful, con-

[1] *Reminiscences of Present-Day Saints,* by Francis G. Peabody, p. 30.

servative. I received marks in his courses in philosophy almost as much lower than I thought they ought to be as those given by Peabody were higher than they should have been.

Peabody was the traditional absent-minded professor, walking on the street with one foot on the curb and one foot in the gutter. Bowen was always *present-minded,* self-conscious, keen, alert. Bowen was conservative enough; Peabody was yet more conservative. President Eliot once wrote me about Peabody, saying, "I was never much interested in Dr. Peabody. He was too conservative and absent-minded for me." Peabody was serene; Bowen gave the impression of being easily irritated, probably a false impression. Peabody seemed to dwell constantly in the upper intellectual and emotional regions. Among his favorite studies was mathematics; and apparently he could have become a professor of the subject; but he was otherwise ordained from his birth. Bowen also at times seemed to be remote, but usually his task was immediate and direct. To Peabody the epithet tranquil could be applied, but who would think of applying it to Bowen? Peabody had a most benevolent, even benignant, influence over the Freshmen required to take his course in elementary ethics, an influence continued in his elective courses. His general power was felt in his two acting presidencies, following the terms of Felton and of Hill. Bowen brought his mind and the minds of his students into close grips with such philosophers as Descartes, Spinoza, Malebranche, Pascal, Leibnitz,

Kant, Schopenhauer, Fichte, Schelling, Hegel, and
von Hartmann. His courses in philosophy were really
noble and formative experiences. One of the best of
expositors, he helped to make his students feel at home
in the whole realm of modern philosophy. He trained
his students to think on all subjects by training them
to think on the deepest themes. Peabody ever seemed
to find the soul of goodness in things morally neutral
or even evil. Bowen had his detestations. They were
embodied largely in the ''dirt philosophy.'' He was
convinced that this ''crass'' philosophy was intellectually unsound and ethically pestiferous. He also was
equally convinced that the traditional interpretations
were sound. He says, ''I accept with unhesitating
conviction and belief the doctrine of the being of one
Personal God, the Creator and Governor of the world,
and of one Lord Jesus Christ, in whom 'dwelleth all
the fulness of the Godhead bodily;' and I have found
nothing whatever in the literature of modern infi-
delity which, to my mind, casts even the slightest
doubt upon that belief.'' [2]

Peabody's preaching was, like Thomas Arnold's,
marked by simplicity and earnestness. Bowen's teaching was direct, personal, progressive, insistent,
formative.

Both Peabody and Bowen began to write early and
they wrote much. With Peabody it was *multa*, with
Bowen *multum*. Yet the variety, as well as the
amount, of writing of each was marvelous. Peabody
published a dozen or more volumes, but the sermons,

[2] *Modern Philosophy*, by Francis Bowen. Preface, p. vii.

reviews, and articles were numberless. About one
hundred and ninety titles of his writings are included
in the Harvard Library catalogue. Bowen early published an edition of Virgil. The years previous to the
beginning of his professorship, as well as the thirty-
six years of its active continuance, were fruitful.
There lie before me as I write his volume on *Logic,*
his *American Political Economy,* his *Hamilton's Metaphysics,* and his edition of De Tocqueville's *Democracy in America.* And these are only the companions
of a dozen other volumes.

A student once said of Peabody the Saint, as reported by Francis Peabody, ''I like to see his light
burning as I pass his house . . . and know that the
old man is there.'' [3] His love for all and the love of
all for him endured through the college generations.
For Bowen there was unbounded respect and a keen
sense of noble and lasting intellectual indebtedness.
Each lived the elevated life, immortal even while walking with us mortals, the one of deep and high feeling,
the other of a thinking equally deep and high. Bowen
helps to disprove Burke's remark that, ''nothing can
be conceived more hard than the heart of a thorough-
bred metaphysician.'' [4] Peabody refutes the current
belief that the man of a great big heart cannot be
shrewd, wise, thoughtful, intellectually influential and
even constructive.

[3] *Reminiscences of Present-Day Saints,* by Francis G. Peabody, pp. 38-39.
[4] *Writings and Speeches of Edmund Burke,* Vol. V, p. 216.

XIX
CHARLES FRANKLIN HOOVER

BORN Miamisburg, Ohio, August 2, 1865; died June 15, 1927. Ohio Wesleyan University, 1882-85; A.B., Harvard, 1887, M.D., 1892; universities of Vienna and Strassburg, 1890-94. Practiced in Cleveland, Ohio, 1894-1927; visiting physician, at Cleveland City Hospital, 1894-1907, and at Lakeside Hospital, 1907-1927; teacher of physical diagnosis, 1894-1907, and professor of medicine, Medical College of Western Reserve University, 1907-27. Commd. maj., Med. R. C., April 15, 1917; served with Base Hospital, Unit No. 4, in France, May-September, 1917; President, Association of American Physicians, 1926-1927.

CHARLES FRANKLIN HOOVER

THE UNDERSTANDING PHYSICIAN

OF all professional men, doctors are the most personal; lawyers the most public-minded; ministers a fitting union of both the personal and the public-minded. Doctors talk the least, lawyers talk much, ministers talk more. Lawyers write much, ministers write yet more, doctors write least. But what doctors do write is of the best. In evidence of the worth of the writing of doctors let me name Oliver Wendell Holmes, Weir Mitchell, Harvey Cushing, and Dr. John Brown of Edinburgh, the author of *Rab and His Friends*.

Of course the members of these three historic professions write technical papers and volumes, and in a profusion about equal, although both lawyers and ministers excel doctors in their literary creativeness. The doctors are still the more and the most silent. Like the priest at the confessional, they deal with the individual. Their consulting room is a personal sanctuary, their diagnosis an individual interpretation, their prescription an intimation of forgiveness and

297

an assurance, it is to be hoped, of salvation. Do not *salvus* and its derivatives stand for health? These paragraphs and others to follow are illustrated or have illustration in four doctors about whom I wish to write. They were indeed guides, philosophers, and friends.

Charles Franklin Hoover had been called by a competent judge the best physical diagnostician in the world. Dr. Walter Wesselhoeft of Cambridge once said to me, speaking of Dr. Weir Mitchell, "Mitchell could see right through you." What is perhaps more important, Hoover could feel right through you. His touch on you was revealing, revealing above the touch of any other physician known to me and to many. He wrote on the increasing value of the laboratory with its new and significant instruments of precision. To all these tools he would give full credit. But he also felt and wrote that the present tendency is to overvalue these tools and assets and perhaps to underrate the coördinating clinical methods of personal history and of bedside examination. For he himself says, "The exercise of intelligent clinical observation should be to a physician the most fruitful source of intellectual satisfaction. In this kind of work he can always gather new knowledge by employing originality, and he must be original to do it. Such work is more satisfying than to repeat tests which have been devised by the originality of others. A photographer derives some pleasure in a photographic reproduction of a painted picture, but how inferior is such pleasure compared to that of the original painter. When a complaining doctor leans too heavily on laboratory support for comfort in his practice, it probably means that he has failed to strengthen the powers that lie within his grasp. When by his perspicacity, a doctor makes a diagnosis of an obscure case he has a glint of the same Divine fire that lit the mind of Democritus when he said:

'Rather would I explain the cause of a single fact than become king of the Persians.' '' [1]

Often, therefore, do I think that Hoover was quite as much a philosopher as a physician, as much a psychologist as a diagnostician, as much a humanist as a scientist. Once he said to me he felt that the medical graduates are liable to be like the squirrel ''that collected hard nuts in the autumn and lost its teeth in the effort. In other words, when the winter of life comes to a man who has spent his life in collecting facts and has lost his philosophical teeth, he will have an old age of spiritual starvation.'' [2] He also said, ''The conquests of science have freed us from many superstitions but it has not silenced the great trumpet calls of God, immortality and duty.'' [3] Hoover believed that ''education must inseparably hold science, philosophy and the humanities.'' [4] He reasoned that it is of the ''greatest importance for one in his early

[1] Manuscript, paper on *The Reputed Conflict between the Laboratories and Clinical Medicine*, pp. 15-16.
[2] Manuscript, address to students, p. 2.
[3] *Ibid.*, p. 3. [4] *Ibid.*, p. 4.

years to acquire some conception of the history of human thought so that he can in later life shape his reading toward an enlargement of his knowledge of a subject that must have a great interest for an educated man.

"The memory of my own undergraduate years is inseparably and gratefully associated with two teachers: one a professor of Greek who sought to impress his students with the beauty of the philosophy of the structure of language and the other who expounded Greek philosophy and the English writers on Ethics. The memory of these two teachers recurs with increasing frequency and gratitude because under their guidance some acquaintance with subjects was acquired that have in my later professional years been an unfailing and deepening solace of my life when the technics that have furnished the business of the past forty years have ceased to monopolize my interests." [5]

What I have written gives proof of a personality high, broad, deep. Its formation began, as with most, at a time long before he was born, and in a land far-off from the place of his birth. Hoover was of Holland ancestry. His reverence for his forefathers possessed him to the end. In one of his last visits to Holland he sought out the tomb of William of Orange, and gratefully laid flowers on the grave of the great Stadtholder. The sense of reverence and the piety of the Holland people emerged early in his youth. His

[5] *Ibid.*, pp. 4-5.

wife tells me that at the age of thirteen he asked his father to establish family prayers. While still in his teens he thought much of becoming a minister. His father, however, without opposing his wish, decided that so fundamental a choice of life's long results should not be made so early, a wise conclusion based on general grounds as well as special, as is proved by the ultimate career.

At this time of youth he tried especially hard to experience what is known in religious terms as conversion. In subsequent life he not seldom told of his endeavor to be converted. But he declared he did not succeed. He could not create the symptoms! He was unable to feel, to do, to experience as the converted feel, do and experience. That the feeling was genuine and the desire sincere, there can be no doubt. But his was not the typical regeneration. Possibly one might say that his new birth began in his age of unconsciousness.

While Hoover was in the midst of his medical career there was perhaps an intimation of the return of the early religious feeling. For he considered seriously giving up his career in America and going to Hankow as a missionary-physician, or teacher.

The soberness of that early life did not, however, stop fondness for fun and for sport. While a student at Ohio Wesleyan he was guilty of going to a theater to see a play of Shakespeare. This guilt especially was incurred while the class was studying the very play which was presented on the stage. For such offend-

ing he was asked to apologize. He refused. Other
offenders also refused. He was, therefore, with them
expelled. Twenty-five years later he was offered his
degree but refused it. A spirit of independence, as
well as of love for happy adventure, possessed him
in youth as well as in age.

Hoover's general education was completed at Harvard. At Harvard, as he said, it was George H.
Palmer who had a mighty influence over him as over
thousands of other men.

Such reverence, and piety, such breadth of education, and of training, were fostered and intensified in
all the years of his studentship in the Harvard Medical School, in Vienna, and in Strassburg. The richest
achievements were won in all the lengthened service
of the most relentless of professions, and in the doing
of the duties of a great chair of medicine and of research. But the foundations were laid broad and
deep, and they were able to bear, as they did bear, the
weight of wisdom pure and applied. For his mind was
both analytical and synthetical. He saw things immediately, individually, independently. He also saw
things as a whole. The last time I met him while he
was still in health he told me he was reading Har-
nach's *History of Christian Doctrine*. The last
time I met him as he lay in bed we discussed
Dickens. Among the constant companions of his
travels were Gibbon's *Roman Empire*, and Lecky's
History of Civilization. He saw phenomena in
the light of a very uncommon common sense. The

value of common sense is a platitude. The value
of uncommon common sense is a principle. Individual facts he saw, heard, felt, clearly, accurately.
The meaning of these facts he interpreted soundly.
Application of the interpretations he made logically.
His appreciations were both of the individual and of
the race.

There was also in Hoover a certain force of intellect,
of heart, of conscience, and of will, qualities and elements which may comprehensively be called masterfulness. One was enlightened and moved by his understanding. One felt his emotions, for he—this
philosophical diagnostician—had them. One was
quickened by his conscience, for he obeyed the imperative of Kant, "I ought," and Luther's self-under-
standing, "I can no other." He had a will which
expressed itself fully and freely and yet in restraint,
sometimes in gentle scorn and more often in fitting
appreciation of antagonistic interpretations and conclusions. But under all conditions one recognized
and felt a certain masterfulness of his whole character.

In method and point of view Hoover represented
the union of the conservative and of the progressive.
Normally a conservative, he was also determined, as
his secretary, Achsa Parker, has reported to me, that
"no new remedy that had merit or the promise of merit
went untried at Lakeside." She adds, "I was particularly interested in his account of the first use in
Cleveland of thyroid extract for cretins or morons.
One time at City Hospital a small boy, a very stupid

boy, was 'tolled in' (his expression) by his sister. They decided to try thyroid extract on him, and requested him to return. Within the appointed time the boy returned with his sister, but this time the boy came in first and confidently announced, 'Do you know, I am a good deal better.' The news spread through the hospital, and in no time the boy was surrounded with eager internes and staff physicians. Considerably daunted, the boy made his escape as soon as possible and never came back!''

Dr. Hoover's methods with his classes were rather personal than formal. His lectures were delivered so swiftly that no stenographer could keep up with his pace. In fact he seemed to think that the technical details of his interpretation were of less importance for the records than the general impression which he left upon his students. Valuable as definite suggestions were and are, the point of view of the practitioner was quite as important as specific directions. These students were moved by him as he was moved by Osler and by other great teachers.

In Hoover's applications of truth and in his appreciations one sees and feels a peculiar sense of piety toward the heroes of humanity. He lamented the ease and swiftness with which the successive generations forget their predecessors. He, a philosopher, had a poet's feeling of regret in the failure to remember the great ones of the past. His feeling was permanent. He was unlike the French people, who, in a fit of enthusiasm, may change the name of an avenue in Paris to commemorate a man or an achievement, and again change this name after a generation, having forgotten its special significance. He felt that the race is human and deserves respect. He also felt that the heroes are humanistic and deserve worship. His placing flowers on the tomb of the great Stadtholder illustrates his feeling. This respect for humanity and his care for individuals were most manifest in his devotion to those who are sick, and especially to the sick who are poor. His heart went out toward them in great tenderness, and they in turn loved him. The hospital wards were sanctuaries for his blessed ministries. He was worshiped as a priest.

In his loyalty to sound principles and to wise methods, he yet felt little rancor for some practitioners who followed a practice which seemed to be based on quackery. Of course at times he was stirred, as he ought to have been stirred, by indignation. But in this keen sense was mingled also a sense of pity for the misguided. Indignation draws away strengths from a practitioner of medicine, as well as of law, and most practitioners have no strength to spend in ways so vain. They need all their force for the honest practice of a necessary and honest profession.

It is one of the most pathetic of all ironies that this man, best of diagnosticians, lay for months in his last illness doubtful of the cause of his illness. The doubt also belonged to other great diagnosticians. No examination, no test, no experimentation revealed the cause. It was not till the end had come and examinations were made which only death allows that the cause came to be known. It was apparently proved that growths due to moulds of the lung were the primary cause. Apparently, too, the infection was received from a machine which he made in research for the true nature and cause of breath sounds. Of this machine a colleague, Dr. Blankenhorn, has given me this description and interpretation.[6]

[6] "In the course of editing a proposed book on Physical Diagnosis, the doctor became dissatisfied with the accepted teaching on the nature of the breath sounds heard about the chest. In elaborating his own theories as to the cause of breath sounds, he resorted to a device designed by himself and largely built with his own hands, which would imitate noises produced in the respiring lung. In assembling the material to make this device, a large rubber bag was used which, unfortunately, had been a long time in the laboratory and used in previous experiments in a way to fill it with moisture and dirt capable of generating moulds. In using this appliance, the doctor blew his own breath into the apparatus and inhaled from it in a way to expose himself to moulds and dust which might be within the rubber bag. The peculiar way in which he did this breathing removed the natural guard which ordinarily defends the lungs and air passages against the germs of disease. It came about then by accidental means that he was, in enthusiasm of his experiment, utterly unconscious of the fact that he might be inhaling deep into his lungs the spores of a deadly infection. After a short period of these experiments, the doctor was taken ill with a very mysterious fever. This fever was due to an infectious granuloma of the lung as was shown by autopsy.

The course of the illness was most distressing to his many associates and pupils, because his own science and art apparently could not be brought to his aid. During the long weeks of his illness, and after numerous tedious examinations and consultations, no satisfactory diagnosis of his disease was proposed until his lung was extensively involved and treatment failed. During this period of uncertainty the doctor showed

Hoover died a martyr to science, as have scores of others, like Walter Reed and Gorgas.

a fortitude most unusual and an abiding faith in the adequacy of the medical attention which he received from his own pupils who managed the case. He resented all suggestions that council be brought from afar and from other schools, insisting that if his own men could not cure him no one could. His problem, however, was thoroughly studied by all available council, and men from Baltimore, Philadelphia, and Boston were consulted in the various aspects of his disease. He was treated aggressively for mould infection of his lung when that was finally agreed upon as diagnosis, but all known methods of treatment availed nothing and he died rather abruptly from gangrene of the lung.

It is a tragic fact that medical science has made little advance in the study of these moulds. In this instance it seems doubly tragic in that his active pursuit of medical knowledge should thus be stopped by so mysterious a disease."—Personal letter of Dr. M. A. Blankenhorn, 18 April, 1930.

XX

FRANK EMORY BUNTS

BORN Youngstown, Ohio, June 3, 1861; died Nov. 28,
1928; graduated U. S. Naval Academy, 1881;
served in U. S. N., 1881-83; M.D., Western Reserve
Medical College, 1886. Professor of surgery, Western Reserve Medical College, 1893-1928; Director
of Cleveland Clinic Foundation, Director Cleveland
Trust Co. Major and surgeon 1st O. Vol. Cav.,
Spanish-American War; Lieutenant Colonel, Medical Corps of U. S. A., commanding General Hospital No. 9, B. E. F., World War.

XX

FRANK EMORY BUNTS

THE BELOVED PHYSICIAN

''There are men and classes of men that stand above the common herd: the soldier, the sailor and the shepherd not infrequently; the artist rarely; rarelier still, the clergyman; the physician almost as a rule. He is the flower (such as it is) of our civilization; and when that stage of man is done with, and only remembered to be marvelled at in history, he will be thought to have shared as little as any in the defects of the period, and most notably exhibited the virtues of the race. Generosity he has, such as is possible to those who practise an art, never to those who drive a trade; discretion, tested by a hundred secrets; tact, tried in a thousand embarrassments; and what are more important, Heraclean cheerfulness and courage. So it is that he brings air and cheer into the sickroom, and often enough, though not so often as he wishes, brings healing.

Dedication to 'Underwoods.'

R. L. S.'' [1]

I MAKE this long extract, for Bunts was a sailor, a soldier and a physician. Seldom occurs such

[1] *The Life of Sir William Osler,* by Harvey Cushing. Vol. I, p. 232.

a union, either in the prose of writing or in the prose of living. Such a triple union may be said to constitute poetry.

It is sometimes asked what are the exterior marks of a Yale or of a Harvard graduate. It is also constantly declared that it is easy to detect an Oxford or a Cambridge graduate. Often have I thought that the beholder could easily infer that Bunts was a graduate of Annapolis and not of West Point. Of course he had not the gait of the sailor, but he had both the gait and the set of shoulders of the midshipman. Two years of service, however, in foreign seas following his graduation at the Naval Academy, in 1881, proved that the admiral's stars were not to be his guiding stars. He was by nature and grace destined to be a physician.

But from his years of naval education and of service he carried forth, above all else, the bearing of a gentleman who well embodied Newman's historic definition. Born in the great steel-making town of the Mahoning valley, his hand ever seemed to be firm, vigorous to grasp and to hold, but also it was not without the velvet glove. Altruism was his mood, intellectual and moral. He knew and felt the best of the world. His appreciation of that best was deep, broad, constant. I have seen and heard his appreciation as he mingled with medical groups in Rio de Janeiro and Buenos Aires. That appreciation I have ever seen and heard and felt as he mingled with bankers and with directors of great trust companies. He was at home in any society composed of those who embody the cardinal virtues and the graces which are also cardinal. In this personality were found humor, wit, and tactfulness. The apt story sprang to his lip. Responsiveness clothed him as a garment. Cheerfulness looked from his eyes, smiled in his face, spoke by his tongue. The gospel of optimism was declared by his vigorous walk as well as by his happy talk. The best was his. Of the best he made a yet better.

The life and career of Bunts were marked by successive enlargements and by a constant spirit of progressiveness. Beginning his great service under limitations of the lack of means, he yet began it with high hopes. Doing each duty nobly, and entering into every opportunity with wisdom and zeal, he moved forward unto largeness and greatness. The progress was slow but it was real, and it suffered no regress. From general practice he entered into emergency surgery, largely railroad, and from emergency surgery he passed on into the general surgical practice. While still a surgeon, he founded, with other surgeons, Crile and Lower, and with John Phillips as the head of the medical service, the Cleveland Clinic. It remains and shall remain as a monument to his professional wisdom, courage, coöperativeness, and achievement. He was indeed a man of and for and by Cleveland.

Among his makers, who was also a maker of Crile, was Dr. Frank J. Weed. Of Weed, Bunts has written in an autobiographical sketch, called *A Triple Alliance,* "It is not easy to analyze one whom we admired and loved so much as we did Dr. Weed. He was not a product of higher education. He was a graduate of the Wooster Medical School and a student and later assistant of Dr. G. C. E. Weber of Cleveland, who was at that time, perhaps, the most outstanding surgeon in Ohio. Certainly his association with this great surgeon must have been of the greatest value to him, but there was an innate ability which distinguished him throughout his only too brief career. His ability to 'size up' a patient's troubles and to base a prognosis upon them without the intricate and scientific aids of today was unequaled by any one whom I have ever met. He was big of body and equally big of heart. His was the cheerfulness of manner and deep interest in his patient that made his entrance into the sick room a longed-for event. They trusted him and loved him, so that I have heard them say, 'Why! Dr. Weed, I'd rather die under your care than live under that of another physician.' Dr. Weed was a great friend of the younger generation of physicians and probably started more of them on their way to success and usefulness than any other surgeon in Cleveland." [2]

With such experiences and upbringing it was natural that the life and career of Bunts should be of valiant service and of sympathy—not of sympathy with happiness only, but also and yet more needed, of sympathy with those whose lives are clothed with drab-

[2] *A Triple Alliance*, Manuscript, written by Dr. Bunts in November, 1928, p. 1.

ness and sackcloth, and with those whose souls are
filled with a spirit of heaviness. His gentleness made
him great. His feeling for his fellows was not forced
on one as an opiate or laid on one as a prescribed
anodyne. But he moved about the sufferer as a quiet
atmosphere, that gave soothing till the edge of pain
was dulled and the heart's ache quieted.

Bunts was thus a noble coöperator and comrade
in life's experiences. Such co-working and co-living
were felt in the hospitals' daily round and in the professor's lecture. It was also felt in the field of the
soldier, for, as I have said, Bunts was not a sailor.
He was indeed a soldier-sailor or a surgeon-soldier.
In the two great wars fought in his life time he
served. Major, lieutenant, colonel, commanding general in the medical corps, represent the great offices
he filled. For this mannerly gentleman, this skilled
surgeon, this humanness of large, rich, and happy
relations, this citizen of America, was above all else
a patriot, brave without sternness, loyal without bigotry or narrowness, serving his God and his country,
a man without fear and without reproach,—the happy
warrior.

XXI
JOHN PHILLIPS

BORN Welland, Ont., February 19, 1879; died May 15, 1929. M.B., University of Toronto, 1903; honor graduate, silver medalist. Came to United States in 1903, naturalized citizen, 1918. Instructor in medicine, Western Reserve University, 1906-10; demonstrator of anatomy, 1906-07; assistant professor of medicine, 1910-19; assistant professor of therapeutics from 1919; assistant visiting physician, Lakeside Hospital, 1910-19; cons. physician at St. Johns Hospital from 1919. Captain Medical Corps, U.S.A., 1918. A founder and trustee of Cleveland Clinic Foundation, dir. of medicine since 1921.

Contributed about sixty articles to various medical magazines; wrote section on Diseases of Pleura, Mediastinum and Diaphragm, in Cecil's Textbook on Internal Medicine, 1927.

XXI

JOHN PHILLIPS

THE FAITHFUL PHYSICIAN

THE mediæval medical writings, I am told, are distinguished by at least two characteristics: first, by proof that the older doctors had a knowledge and a skill which were prophetic of the knowledge and skill of the younger brothers of the present generation; and, secondly, by proof that these elder practitioners used instruments which we are inclined to believe are modern. These writings, moreover, prove that the mediæval doctors were philosophers; they were fond of speaking, of thinking, of writing about the problems which belong to the science and the art of medicine of every generation. If they knew less, they reasoned more. If they dreamed more, they also questioned more, and most.

As I write of these two qualities of skill and of instrumentation of the early period, I call to mind the name of John Phillips. For Phillips had taken the mediæval bath. Each case as it was presented to him, apparently new in itself, was not to him new: it was the successor of scores or hundreds of other cases in both diagnosis and therapeutics which the books had made known to him. The new cases continued the teachings and the interpretations of the former generations.

For Phillips was a follower and disciple of Aristotle, as well as of the school-men, and also—to take a long leap—of John Stuart Mill. He was given to the tracing of causes and results. His belief in the law of causality was constant and deep. He was, as Dante says of Aristotle, the master of those who know. One may add, moreover, that he was the master of those who relate knowledge to knowledge. Each sickness represented the law of causality. The cause might lie down deep and be obscure. The cause might take on genealogical relations of the family as well as biographical of the individual. The apparent cause might be found in the exterior environment, being, however, really only an occasion. The cause, especially in cases of hypochondria and neurasthenia, might seem to have small relation to the effect. It was for him to follow every clue, to trace the slightest evidence, to analyze and to synthesize all phenomena. He sought to reach the *ding-an-sich* whence emerged the phenomenon. To such searching and researching he gave himself with fullness of devotion. He gave, too, of his time—his time was eternity, like that of Browning's Grammarian.

Such permanent inquisitiveness represented unique solidity of intellectual power and equally unique force of will. His mind was not facile, its operations

were not swift. His literary style, as seen and felt
in his papers, was characterized by lucidity, directness, and weight. These papers were rather Aris-
totelian than Platonic. They lacked literary charm.
His style was devoid of picturesqueness. In reading
his papers his speech was monotonous, as his paragraphs were without beauty. But the matter was
compact, the suggestions germane, the inductions
inevitable, the lessons apt, timely, pregnant with great
meanings.

Vitally associated with such a constitution of intellect and of forceful will was another element equally
constructive. It was the element of loyalty to the
truth. For truth he sought, and when found he bore
to it unswerving allegiance. Every patient he felt
had a right to the truth. No evasion was to be suffered, no concealment to be attempted. Of course
proper place and time were to be commanded, and
fitting opportunity to be made available, for inevitable
revelations. "Should a doctor tell a patient that death
is certain?" is a form of a most frequent question.
This writing is not the place to argue the answer,
but it is safe and true to say that Phillips could tell
a patient that death was certain in such a way as
to inspire him to make a more vigorous attempt to
live. The mind of Phillips was brought into vital
touch with the mind of the patient; the will of Phillips was brought into vital touch with the will of the
patient; the heart of Phillips was brought into vital
touch with the heart of the patient. One may change

Christ's remark and say, "Ye shall know the truth, and the truth shall make you well."

Physicians as I know them seldom speak scornfully of their patients, though they know their weaknesses, their inconsistencies, their sinfulnesses. Yet for them they seldom have a mood of scornfulness. Of all men, Phillips yielded the least to any such temptation. Rather his sympathy was deep, broad, and full of understanding. Subject himself to depressions at times, these depressions were often caused by the absorption of himself in the aches and anxieties of the sick. No one was a "case"; each was a friend. Coming home of a night tired, "gone," he was asked the reason of his suffering. His answer was: "I have had to tell three mothers this afternoon that their little children can never be normal. Their minds will never be more than half a mind." The piercing agonies of the mothers had gone as a knife into his own heart also.

This sympathy was not confined to the sick only. For Phillips was a teacher and a professor of medicine. To his students he gave of his knowledge; to his students he gave of his inspiration unto wisdom; to his students he gave of the quickening power of his life. His students came to him to talk about their problems—and medical students have problems more numerous and deeper than most. He loved them, and therefore they loved him. This love was both of the heart and of the will.

The ending of this life at the age of fifty was the

result of what is known as the Clinic disaster of the 15th of May, 1929. One of the four doctors who controlled this house of health, it yet killed him. The inevitable ignorance of preserving films cost him and all of us his life. But his death and the death of many others have resulted in discoveries which it is believed will avoid like catastrophes. In his death, as in his life, Phillips was a savior of men.

XXII
CARL AUGUST HAMANN

BORN Davenport, Iowa, January 26, 1868; died Jan. 12, 1930. M.D., University of Pennsylvania, 1890. Practiced in Cleveland from 1893; professor of anatomy, 1893-1912, professor of applied anatomy and clinical surgery from 1912, Western Reserve University School of Medicine, also dean; visiting surgeon of St. Vincent's Charity and Cleveland City hospitals.

CARL AUGUST HAMANN

THE TRUSTED PHYSICIAN

I HAVE just come from a Memorial Service the like of which I have never known. It was a service of silence. Besides the reading of the Bible and a few selected passages of Milton, besides the dirges of organ, of orchestra, of voices, besides the repetition of the Hippocratic and other oaths, no words were spoken. No laudation was attempted; no interpretation ventured; no edification risked. I saw no tear; I heard no sob.

"Nothing is here for tears, nothing to wail
    Or knock the breast, no weakness, no contempt,
    Dispraise, or blame,—nothing but well and fair."

It was an academic service, memorial of a beloved teacher and scholar. It was a professional service, memorial of a skilled, self-sacrificing surgeon. It was a human service, memorial of a man divine in his manfulness. Silence.

The silence was sign and symbol: for Carl August Hamann was a silent man. The silence of his speech and life were fittingly typed by the silence of all in his death. Yet in both death and life the silence was vocal. Each mind spoke its own eulogy. Each heart told its own sorrow, each conscience felt the sense of duty which guided and inspired Hamann's life. Each voice sang its own memorial eulogy and elegy. Written tributes of the associations of which he was a member were presented with only a formal word of their origin spoken. More silent and more vocal than all else was the white robe of the surgeon and the black robe of the teacher which lay on the altar as if waiting for him to put them on again.

There were two elements in Hamann which seem to me to be of peculiar and almost unique worth. The first is the confidence which he quickened. The silence of the service was emblematic, the silence of the hour spoke for the silence of his life. Silence quickens faith. We distrust eloquence. Boastfulness we abhor. The boastful man is first cousin of the quack, a half-brother of the scoundrel. Silence quickens imagination, and imagination bears its own proofs and convictions. Confidence in Hamann was based on both knowledge and feeling. One knew that this surgeon was skilled. The skill was based on both experience and knowledge. Hamann came to his professorship through the chair of anatomy. This confidence was also formed on the assurance of absolute integrity. The unconscious patient in his helplessness knew he would be dealt with fairly, honestly, truthfully, in benevolence, and in beneficence. The sick man lay down to sleep with the feeling which the mystic has as he rests back in the infinite love of his God, knowing that the "eternal God is thy refuge, and underneath are the everlasting arms."

There was also in Hamann the deepest sense of obligation. In his last days he said not infrequently, "I do not want to die. I have not yet met my obligations to humanity." Like Paul he felt himself to be a debtor. He realized the obligation of giving happiness, of restoring health for sickness, of inspiring strength for weakness, of creating working power for uselessness, of giving guidance to the lost, hopefulness to the despairing, light for darkness, comradeship for loneliness, contentment for misery, of quickening a grip on the infinities in the very finiteness of time and space, and of inspiring loyalty to the spiritual in place of absorption in things. He felt the one comprehensive obligation of meeting obligations.

Such a character may well "quiet us in a death so noble."

XXIII
RAYMOND AND SEELYE

JOHN HOWARD RAYMOND was born New York City, March 7, 1814; died at Poughkeepsie, August 14, 1878. Student at Columbia College; graduate of Union College, 1832; law student New Haven. Entered Baptist Theological Seminary, Hamilton, N. Y., 1834; student, tutor, professor in Theological Seminary and allied Madison University, 1834-50; professor of English, Rochester University, 1850-55; president Brooklyn Polytechnic, 1856-64; president Vassar College, 1865-78.

LAURENUS CLARK SEELYE was born Bethel, Conn., Sept. 20, 1837; died October 12, 1924; A.B., Union College, 1857; Andover Theological Seminary, 1858-59; universities of Berlin and Heidelberg, 1860-62. Ordained Congregational ministry, 1863; pastor North Church, Springfield, Mass., 1863-65, prof. rhetoric and English literature, Amherst, 1865-73; first president Smith College, 1873-1910, president emeritus, 1910-24.

XXIII

RAYMOND AND SEELYE

FOUNDERS

UNIQUE similarities, and diversities equally unique, prevail in the foundation of colleges. The motives moving Johns Hopkins were unlike the motives influencing Senator and Mrs. Stanford in establishing the University bearing their name. The purposes, too, which inspired the Duke family in transforming Trinity College, North Carolina, into Duke University, and with the change of name vastly to enlarge its functions and to increase its endowment, were unlike the purposes which ruled the Maryland and the California founders.

But the ideals and visions which controlled the two first presidents of two outstanding colleges for women are quite as similar and significant as are the unlikenesses prevailing in the conditions and aims of the founders of the great universities in Baltimore, Palo Alto, and Durham.

The similarities forming the characters and prevailing in the careers of Raymond of Vassar and of Seelye of Smith begin with the beginning of these foundations and continue to the end of their lives. In a narrow sense, Raymond and Seelye were contemporaries. Their official careers formed a continuity, Seelye taking up his work in 1873, some ten years after the foundation of Vassar and five years before the lamented death of Raymond, and carrying it forward unto a consummate triumph in 1910. The middle year of the later decades of the last century is indeed significant. Vassar was actually opened to students in 1865, Smith and Wellesley in 1875, and Bryn Mawr in 1885.

A principal remark to be made regarding the likenesses of these two first presidents is that each interpreted women as just as capable of the higher education as are men. That humanity is divided into male and female was, of course, in general, of primary importance, but that primary importance was in a sense secondary as regards education. That woman was to be educated as a human being, and not as either a drudge or a doll—her historic functions— and not in turn fundamentally as a wife or a mother, was a conception foremost, a condition formative, and constantly prevailing. In the early publications of Vassar it is said that the purpose of the college is "to found and perpetuate an institution which should accomplish for young women what our colleges are accomplishing for young men." [1] The purpose is also interpreted as "to devise a system of intellectual

[1] *Life and Letters of John Howard Raymond*, edited by his eldest daughter, p. 561.

training which, while adapted to the special wants of
the sex, should be of as high a grade relatively, and
should accomplish essentially the same ends, as the
American college for young men, in other words, to
devise a system of *liberal education for women*." [2]
The trustees of Vassar affirmed "that the larger the
stock of knowledge and the more thorough the mental
discipline a woman actually attains, other things being equal, the better she is fitted to fill every womanly
position, and to perform every womanly duty, at home
and in society. At the same time, they could not but
see that there are specialties in the feminine constitution, and in the functions allotted to woman in life;
and they believed that these should not be lost sight
of in arranging the details of her education." [3]

Ten years later we find the essence of this doctrine
perpetuated in the formal statements made at the
foundation of Smith College. It is said that the trustees "would secure to young women a culture fully
equivalent to that afforded to young men by our best
New England colleges, and yet differing from that as
woman differs from man in her physical and mental
constitution, and in the sphere of her active life." [4]
It is further interpreted that "It is the wish of the
Trustees to realize as far as possible the idea of a literary family, in which young women may not only
enjoy the best facilities for intellectual discipline, but

[2] *Ibid.*, p. 562.   [3] *Ibid.*, p. 563.
[4] *The Early History of Smith College, 1871-1910*, by L.
Clark Seelye, p. 12.

may also receive a social refinement and culture, which will enable them to feel at home in the best society, and to conduct themselves with grace and propriety in any sphere of life.'' [5] In the president's report for 1904-5 as a summation of what Smith had already begun to accomplish it is said, ''The general culture which produces sound judgment is a good preparation for any vocation to which a woman may be called.'' [6]

A similar likeness prevailed in respect to the conception of the character of teaching and of the worth of the teacher. Of Vassar it is said at the close of Raymond's first decade, ''The aim of our training is, not to inculcate a particular creed or system of belief, but to furnish the youthful mind with the well-established and undisputed results of past inquiry, to inform it clearly in respect to the great questions in philosophy and science which now divide the thinking world, and so to develop and discipline its faculties that it shall be able in due time to form its own opinions, and to understand and explain the grounds on which those opinions rest.'' [7] To Seelye, in turn, the actual work of teaching and the worth of the teacher himself were of primary significance. The personality of the teacher was absolutely primary. In his inaugural address, Seelye said, ''Teachers are not mere literary or scientific treatises—at least ought not to be. Their personal character must impress

---

[5] *Ibid.,* p. 22. [6] *Ibid.,* p. 127.
[7] *Life and Letters of John Howard Raymond,* edited by his eldest daughter, p. 598.

itself with greater or less force upon all who come under their instructions.'' [8] His daughter, who is also his biographer, says, ''The ability to teach was far more important than the development of a department. A teacher must be able to get the point of view of his pupils; he must be able to draw knowledge out of them as well as to put knowledge into them.'' [9]

To these two presidents the element of religion in the life and work of the college was fundamental. Both Raymond and Seelye were of a religious origin, inherited religious traditions, and were surrounded with religious atmospheres and conditions. They were preachers of the Calvinistic faith. Bred in a Christian home, serving as officers in a Christian college previous to their great presidencies, each held the same conception of the worth of the Christian faith in the liberal education of women. In Raymond the emotional side of this faith was the more dominant, in Seelye the intellectual.

Each, too, had been a student of theology, and had been recognized as a minister before becoming a teacher or a president. Of Raymond it has been said that his earnest wish and endeavor was that Vassar, ''while in no sense sectarian, should yet be interpenetrated with the principles of a pure and ennobling Christianity. It was education, in its complete and highest sense—education crowned with practical godliness—that he aimed to give to those committed to

[8] *Laurenus Clark Seelye,* by Harriet Seelye Rhees, p. 192.
[9] *Ibid.,* p. 193.

his care." [10]   In the year 1868 he wrote to Miss
Lyman, "the lady principal," absent on account
of ill health, on the occasion of special religious
services in the college, saying, "Pray for us, and
especially for me, that wisdom may be given to direct
and moderate without checking or chilling this spirit
of benevolence, and to secure for permanent use, in
the future the momentum of this wonderful impulse in
the right direction." Many graduates of Smith declare, "that the most valuable things about their college course was the effect upon them of President
Seelye's deep spirituality, his convincing faith, the
saneness and sincerity of his religion which was a
pervasive force in the college life." [11]

The change which has come over the colleges in
respect to the place and function of religion, since
Raymond died in 1878 and since Seelye retired in
1910, is nothing less than revolutionary. The change
has at least three elements: first, religion as a force
in the development of character of the undergraduate
has become less constructive. Its atmosphere is less
constant, less pervasive, less vital, less vitalizing. The
second element is the fact that religion is made less
personal in all the diverse relations of the college.
It may hold its place, as it probably does, in the heart
and will of the individual; it has certainly lost its
place as an integral part of the communal life. It has

[10] *Life and Letters of John Howard Raymond*, edited by
his eldest daughter, p. 711.
[11] *Laurenus Clark Seelye*, by Harriet Seelye Rhees, p. 300.

fallen from a major interest to a very minor one. Third, religion has abdicated its emotional power and function without gaining a corresponding intellectual force. In the former time, perhaps its power as an emotion was too forceful. Certain interpretations, indeed, which Raymond made bore intimations rather of the revivalist than of the philosopher. Yet, nevertheless, this interpretation was sincere even if ill proportioned. In the present time religion in the college is in peril of lacking a sense of feeling sufficient to influence the will. The ill proportion continues, however, in different relations from decade to decade.

The revolution shows itself in colleges for men as well as in colleges for women in at least two immediate forms of administration. One form lies in the lack of attention to the distinctly Christian character of candidates for professorships. The emphasis is placed, as indeed it ought to be placed, on the intellectual worth and power of candidates. But it should not be placed there to the exclusion of other evidences of academic value and efficiency. A second form of the declining influence of religion is manifest in the narrowing function of the chapel service. At the present moment I am not writing of the substitution of voluntary for required attendance, but I am writing of the whole abolition of the service. I am also writing of the fact that, if the service is still held, its religious content is in many colleges largely eliminated.

To Raymond and to Seelye the daily chapel service was of primary worth. Raymond used the service as a special means for inspiring students unto right choices. One of the students says, "The appeal was always first to the understanding of the students, then to their moral dignity." [12] The early graduates of Smith remember in particular the prayers of their president. "Prayer was for him no narrow individualistic petition, it was a supplication for strength, wisdom and grace, a thanksgiving for mercies received, a true communion with God." [13] Another graduate says, "We had the prophet who wrestled with God at morning prayers and revealed to us as from some peak the scope of the task before him and us. I was one of the first to go forth from morning prayers in a state of exaltation, but it has since been the unforgettable experience of a multitude of young women." [14]

In causing or suffering this revolution or fundamental change in the emphasis laid on religion, the American college is losing one of its most formative forces in the culture of manhood and womanhood. The fact that these academic changes are essentially identical with similar changes in the whole community may serve to give a reason for the changes; but the reason does not serve as an apology. Of course such a declension does not intimate that there

[12] *Life and Letters of John Howard Raymond,* edited by his eldest daughter, p. 685.
[13] *Laurenus Clark Seelye,* by Harriet Seelye Rhees, p. 301.
[14] *Ibid.,* p. 303.

should be a return to the evangelistic atmospheres
and pietistic methods which Mr. Durant introduced
and used at the college of his foundation. Excess
is quite as pestiferous as abstinence.

The influence of the Christian faith over students
gets its worth far more from the character of the
officers of the college who embody this faith than
from the formal exercises of religion, even if these
exercises be apt, sincere, and wise. The influence,
of course largely unconscious, which Raymond and
Seelye gave forth, was constant and pervasive. These
men represented the older type of college president.
Their dignities rested on them normally and naturally.
Their very presence commanded respect. Their attitude of intellectual understanding was characteristic.
But also it was said that no one knew Raymond who
had not heard him thundering and seen him lightning. Reverence for their presidents was among all
students a normal mood. Testimony of such a feeling among Vassar students abounds. I knew Seelye
for many years, and my own feeling was one of most
respectful regard. A sense of personal and reverent
affection belonged alike to students and teachers.
Writing of a chance talk which a Smith student had
with her president, she says, "It has been part of
the warp and woof of my life ever since." [15] Each
president united an understanding and appreciation
of the daily undergraduate life of the student with a
vision of her future years.

[15] *Ibid.,* p. 150.

This feeling of reverence was perfectly consistent with a certain mood and method of administrative autocracy. The autocratic method and mood are perhaps most unfitting in the new president of a new college. In the beginnings both Raymond and Seelye had to make laws, to establish regulations, to form rules, to intimate prescriptions, and possibly to determine proscriptions. The contrast between the wisdom and caution in administration of the first two presidents in Vassar and Smith and the evangelistic enthusiasm of one who was virtually the first president of Wellesley is deep and wide. In Mr. Durant's religious emotionalism is, of course, found the reason. But such zeal is hardly an excuse for a willingness to break up the academic routine to hold revival meetings. Of course a wise president, be he ever so new, will create the atmospheres out of which proper decisions will emerge through general discussion. Of Raymond it is said in the formative years, "The deliberations of the Faculty have been conducted with unprecedented harmony and vigor, and with satisfactory results. It is cheering to the President, and full of happy augury to the institution, to see this body becoming more and more a unit and a power in the College, through an increasing spirit of mutual respect and a practical coincidence of views among the Professors, *which is all the more intelligent and the more likely to be permanent because it is reached through the freest and most earnest discussion."* [16] Profes-

---

[16] *Life and Letters of John Howard Raymond*, edited by his eldest daughter, p. 583.

sor Backus, greatly beloved by students, in the first
years wrote of Raymond soon after his death, "He
brought to his task an unwearying patience, well developed power of observation, a cautiousness that
seemed at times to border on cowardice, but it was
the cautiousness which attends the heroic man. His
ear has been attentive to the voice of duty, and when
she has bid him act, he has been the man of courage.
This quality of caution in President Raymond has
been of incalculable value, not only to Vassar College, but also to the great educational interests which
it represents." [17] In the president of Smith, the
element of autocracy was more present and more constructive than in Raymond. His daughter writes of
his "benevolent despotism." [18] Mrs. Jennette Lee
also says, "I think I have never heard him 'lay down
the law,' yet he remains to me almost the finest example of an autocrat I have ever known." [19] With trustees, too, as well as with faculty, the same personal
and official mood was manifest. Even if he declared
that the trustees were alone responsible for decisions,
it was recognized what was the origin of the ultimate
decision and also what they would be. "On one
occasion the head of a department went to him to
ask if the trustees were going to grant his request
for an extra teacher. The president replied soberly,
'I cannot forecast the action of the trustees.' 'Oh,
well,' said Professor Stoddard, 'you tell me what you

[17] *Ibid.*, p. 714.
[18] *Laurenus Clark Seelye*, by Harriet Seelye Rhees, p.
189.
[19] *Ibid.*, pp. 188-89.

are going to recommend and I will do the forecasting!' '' [20]

But in his autocracy Seelye possessed the priceless virtue of patience. He was also serene, and at times humorous, even when his policies were overruled, as they were, and as they are indeed and perhaps occasionally ought to be of every progressive college president. But when a decision was reached, even if contrary to his own judgment, that decision was to be enforced. President Wilson once said of a member of his cabinet that he had a unique way of continuing a debate after a decision had been reached. In Seelye there was no such sense of unfitting prolongation. A decision was decisive and definitive.

But, as I have already intimated, the form of the government of a college, whether democratic or autocratic, was of no importance to either Raymond or Seelye in comparison with the worth of the teaching. Government was only a scaffolding for the instruction. The emphasis on teaching, laid by both Raymond and Seelye, has been continued by their successors. The student was after all the final cause, the ultimate goal. However full the course of study, however wise the method of administration, however rich the endowment, however influential the teaching, the student represented the comprehensive, consummate and controlling end.

The worthiness, however, of the end and the adequacy of the education which each college offered,

[20] *Ibid.*, p. 197.

did not prevent criticisms and antagonisms. Antagonisms and criticisms would inevitably arise in the early periods of the first colleges. But they continued beyond the foundation of both Vassar and Smith. These oppositions were based in both instances, first, upon the assumption that women are intellectually inferior to men, and therefore are incapable of the typical liberal education; secondly, that the health of women is not so robust as to bear the rigors of the higher education; thirdly, that the primary function of woman is wifehood and motherhood; and, fourthly, that the higher education may have a baneful effect on the moral nature of women. This last criticism took on the form of an interrogation asked by a so-called religious paper, in which it is anxiously questioned whether the culture of the intellect as pursued at Smith does not "deaden the susceptibilities and substitute for the quick moral and spiritual intuitions of women the slower and less trustworthy processes of the reason?" [21]

Of course the history of the last half century proves the incredible foolishness and silliness of such criticisms. But they were made no less at the founding of Smith College in the eighth decade of the last century than at the founding of Vassar in the preceding seventh. This criticism had to be met and was met by the two great presidents.

The interpretation and the meeting of these criticisms had at least one fundamental value: a definite

[21] *Ibid.,* p. 164.

organic unity in each college was thus established and promoted. Such an integration of the indefinite and manifold forces was of peculiar worth. For a certain amount of emotionalism seems to be needed at the beginning of great institutions or of great human movements. Presently, however, intellectual, administrative, and executive forces need to be created, the purposes to be made definite, the methods orderly, and the whole procedure wise, in order that adequate results may emerge. In 1867, two years after its opening, the president of Vassar wrote, ''The conviction strengthens within me that I must see this College business through—through at least this first period of uncertainty and doubt and embryonic confusion, until it has won a determinate and recognized place among the institutions of Christian culture, and commenced the career which wise and firmer hands shall guide to blessed results.''[22] A Smith student who became a professor in the college, writes that in her judgment Seelye's most distinctive service ''besides his strong influence for good taste and good sense, was his giving it the life and spirit of an organism.''[23]

In the very beginning of each college, as well as throughout the administration, each president, like most presidents, was called upon to raise money for endowment and for meeting annual expenses.

[22] *Life and Letters of John Howard Raymond,* edited by his eldest daughter, pp. 646-647.
[23] *Laurenus Clark Seelye,* by Harriet Seelye Rhees, p. 187.

Indeed, the endowment for the whole first decade of Vassar College was only $306,000 and the endowment secured in the second decade was only $168,000. It may be added that in the third decade 1885-94 the gifts for endowment were $331,437.33. In the fourth decade they were $545,944.49. In the fifth decade they fell to $276,980.24. But in the following decade the whole endowment rose to more than four millions, and at the present writing it amounts to more than seven millions.

The history of the endowment of Smith College is equally significant. In 1875, the value of the buildings and grounds was only $125,000, and the endowment was only $328,000. The increase of these two values is significant although not quite so significant as the values of the year of the foundation. In the year 1910 the buildings and grounds represented a value of $1,535,124. (A Letter from Smith College, dated Nov. 16, 1929.) The investments show a corresponding increase. In 1910, thirty-five years after the college was opened, the endowment was only $1,285,-031. In 1917 it had increased to $2,242,591. Three years afterward it became $3,157,155. In five years after it had increased to $4,277,062. In 1929 it amounted to $5,292,865.

But, be it said, that despite financial hardships and stringencies, each college was able in those early years to keep out of debt, a result which is as desirable as it is uncommon. It may also be added that Seelye had the reputation of being one of the most, if not the

most, skilled of all college financiers. He seemed to
be able to invest funds safely and remuneratively.
He was also able to install economies. He had a
way of making dimes count as if they were dollars.

In the struggle for money and in the promoting
of the great purposes for which money was so dire-
fully needed, a specially precious element characterized these two great presidents. Both Raymond and
Seelye kept the college free from what may be called
"fads" and "isms." They were able to prevent their
colleges falling into the perils of educational idiosyn-
crasies. The peril of such academic tangents is constant. The peril was and is threatening in a cause at
once so conservative and so progressive as the higher
education, as it is indeed present in education of every
type. Of course in all such tangential movements
were found both superficialities artificial and elements
fundamental. "Short cuts" is the shortest phrase for
describing these fads. "Special courses," too, is a
term used for interpreting the method of getting a
presumed education without willingness to pay the
cost. Against such methods and atmospheres and
movements each of these presidents was a constant
and ardent foe. A student who ultimately became a
teacher in Vassar writes of Raymond's exposition
"of the purposes of the College curriculum, the necessity of its symmetry, the close inter-dependence of its
parts, the fallacy of that policy which would work it

out in a slovenly or hasty or one-sided fashion." [24]
The present president of Radcliffe College, who was a
student and became dean of Smith, Miss Ada L. Com-
stock, writes that "President Seelye's undistorted
vision seems to me to account for the directness, the
simplicity, the sanity of the Smith organization." [25]
The sanity of Raymond and of Seelye was of untold
value in the formative years of each college.

Yet the emphasis on the severer studies did not prevent a proper emphasis on what are usually called
the "lighter decorative studies" of the curriculum.
Music and painting are the chief subjects included
in such a classification. The present department of
fine arts at Vassar represents the essential understanding and appreciation of its first president. In
the early consideration and foundation of Smith College, the determination of Seelye was fundamental
and constant that the fine arts should have a high
place in the curriculum. As at Harvard, under
Charles Eliot Norton and John Knowles Paine, the
fine arts came to occupy a high place, so likewise did
they in the first years of Vassar and of Smith.

The two presidents were also alike privileged to live
to see the fruitage of their plantings. The harvest
was more complete for Seelye, but even after the brief
period of thirteen years Raymond was not without his

[24] *Life and Letters of John Howard Raymond*, edited by
his eldest daughter, p. 664.
[25] *Laurenus Clark Seelye*, by Harriet Seelye Rhees, p. 186.

glorious and satisfying reward. In the very midst of his career a trustee wrote to Raymond saying, "having achieved a triumph not less honorable to you than fruitful of beneficent results to women." [26] In 1878 Vassar had become a leader in the higher education of women, a leadership which the newer institutions which had just begun at Wellesley and at Northampton were glad to follow, and also in certain respects to divert from. To Seelye a yet more abundant harvest in immediate results was given. With an active service almost three times the length of Raymond's, which was continued by an additional fourteen years, Seelye through the great qualities of inspiration, understanding, judgment, caution, progressiveness, and through the coöperation of trustees, students, and graduates made Smith College the largest in the number of its students of the independent colleges for women. He was, in his united humility and pride, content.

Soon after his death, a Vassar student wrote a poem concerning her president. It is also an interpretation of Seelye quite as truly as of Raymond.

> "O strong soul, by what shore
> Tarriest thou now? For that force
> Surely has not been left vain!
> Somewhere, surely, afar,
> In the sounding labor-house vast
> Of being, is practiced that strength,

[26] *Life and Letters of John Howard Raymond,* edited by his eldest daughter, p. 621.

Zealous, beneficent, firm!
Yes; in some far-shining sphere
Conscious or not of the past,
Still thou performest the word
Of the Spirit in whom thou dost live.
Prompt, unwearied as here!
Still thou upraisest with zeal
The humble good from the ground,
Sternly repressest the bad!
Still like a trumpet dost rouse
Those who, with half-open eyes,
Tread the borderland dim
'Twixt vice and virtue; reviv'st,
Succorest!—this was thy work,
This was thy life upon earth.'' [27]

[27] *Ibid.,* p. 691.

XXIV
FRANCIS AMASA WALKER

Born in Boston, Mass., July 2, 1840; died in Boston, January 5, 1897; graduated Amherst, 1860; studied law; fought in the Northern army during the whole of the Civil War. After the war, became editorial writer on the Springfield, Mass., Republican. In 1869, was made chief of the government bureau of statistics; superintendent of the ninth and tenth censuses; commissioner of Indian affairs. From 1873 to his death his work was educational, first as professor (1873-81) of political economy and history at Yale, and then as president of the Massachusetts Institute of Technology.

Author: The Wages Question; Money; Land and Its Rent; General Political Economy; and other works.

XXIV

FRANCIS AMASA WALKER

LABORER IN GREAT CAUSES, LOYALIST,
FRIEND OF STUDENTS

In the year 1883 John Hay wrote from Sienna to
Francis A. Walker in a line of characteristic verse:
"Walker renowned in war, in peace and the hearts
of reformers." [1] These phrases happily intimate that
Walker would have won high place in any vocation
to which he might have applied his first-rate powers.
In fact these powers he did use as a soldier, as a sta-
tistician, as an economist, as a writer, as a teacher,
and as a college president. His many-sidedness was
characteristic. President Hadley is reported as saying that, "Walker knew more things worth knowing
than any other man of his acquaintance." [2] And
John H. Gray, economist and professor in several colleges, said, "I know of no other American who
reached so high a rank in so many different fields of
activity. He gave shape and value to American statistical work through his influence on the United States

[1] *A Life of Francis Amasa Walker,* by James Phinney Mun-
roe, p. 209.
[2] *Ibid.,* p. 152.

census and the American Statistical Society. He took an admirable and influential part in American military history. He was a distinguished author in the field of Economics and one of the founders of the American Economic Association. He gave shape and significance for a time far beyond his own day to technical education through his relation to the Massachusetts Institute of Technology. He was a good citizen and a great scholar and distinguished organizer and administrator and a loyal and beloved friend.'' [a]

But the diversity of Walker's abilities and the richness of his services as now seen in review are summed up in economics and in college administration. His place in economic research and exposition are evidenced in the seven years between 1876 and 1883. In this short period he wrote several books which fifty years ago were called great: *The Wages Question, Money, Money in Its Relations to Trade and Industry, Land and Its Rent,* and *Political Economy.* As texts their present use has become small. But they remain as influences in economic thought and theory. Since the time of their writing, however, the prevailing interpretation has passed over from the mechanical type to the biological; the theory and the trend of theories in economics have come to take on the intellectual and scientific atmosphere of the present age. The Wage Fund theory has given way to the theory of compensation as depending less on

[a] *Ibid.,* pp. 337-338.

the element of machinery and more on the productivity of the workman. Walker's books, therefore, help to put an end to the old half-truths and to bring in a broader interpretation of economic fact and a wiser creation of economic theory.

But the greater and the greatest contribution which Walker made, and perhaps the most enduring, was made through his presidency of the Massachusetts Institute of Technology. This presidency resulted in Walker's surrender of leadership in American economic thought. This surrender was undoubtedly both voluntary and involuntary. An executive college office and reflection on theories of economics were and are inconsistent. Philosophy and administration are traditional enemies. They were such in the career of Patton of Princeton and also of Hadley at Yale. Some would say that the price which Patton and Hadley paid was too high, but this opinion would not be universal. Some also would affirm that, despite his great work as president, Walker also paid a too high price. But anyway, he did pay the price, and apparently without regret.

Walker's presidency, beginning in 1881, covered essentially the last two decades of the last century, ending only with his death in 1897. Fortunate in the presidency of its virtual founder, Rogers, it was certainly no less fortunate in Walker himself. For Walker had a conception of scientific education as both technical and general.

Every type of professional education moves between

the Scylla of specialization and the Charybdis of generalization. If it move too far to the side of specialization, it suffers the peril of the ill adjustment of the subject or of the victim to a world in which training may fail to find its proper application. If it move too far toward the side of generalization, it in turn incurs the risk of the lack of a power to deal properly with insistent specific problems. In the first instance one cannot see the forest because of the trees. In the second case one cannot see the trees because of the forest. Necessity is laid upon us to see both the trees and the forest. The specialist succeeds, if he succeed, in finding the proper niche in which to use his trained power. He fails, if that proper condition be not available. The humanist succeeds, if he succeed, if he have a wide and broad opportunity for the application of his talents native and acquired. He fails, if he fail, through vagueness.

In his theory and in his practice Walker avoided both perils. He recognized that the Institute was to be true to its name, Technology. He also recognized that the worth of the offering which the graduates might make to life was to be determined in large part by their personal character, by the richness of their intellectual endowment, by understanding, by poise, by moral thoughtfulness, by patience, and by idealism. He also had a generous appreciation of the value of language and literature, of history, and, of course, of political science and economics, as values enriching to the general intellectual endowment. He furthermore did not fail to believe in these general subjects as adding to the worth and efficiency of the engineer himself.

Walker's idea of the nature of education is well interpreted in a paragraph in his report for the year 1886. In his account of the work of the class then graduating, he said, speaking of the four years of the course: "Those years had been spent in the work, not of decoration, but of construction; not in polishing the surface, but in building up the substance of mind and character. Little time or thought had been expended in memorizing facts previously ascertained, or in rehearsing the opinions of others; but from the first day's exercise in the laboratory of general chemistry, through all their course, these young men had been taught to see with their own eyes and think with their own minds, weighing, probing, analyzing, testing for themselves, the substances and appearances which formed the subjects of their study, until, through the development of their perceptive powers, through the formation of a habit of careful, discriminating, and minute observation, and through the exercise of the faculty of judgment, the least gifted of them had become capable, as evidenced by the severe test of our thesis requirement, of selecting a field of investigation, isolating the subject matter, eliminating for the time everything alien or adventitious, providing all the conditions of a true experiment, and, through the application of approved tests, making an actual contribution to human knowledge. This is what we deem education in the best and fullest sense of that term.'' [4]

This judgment, expressed with characteristic succinctness and weight, is reinforced by his opinion of the worth of the so-called small college. A graduate of Amherst when Amherst had less than two hundred and fifty students and a faculty of seventeen members, he ever held that the value of education gained by close relationships of teacher and classes was greater in institutions of a few students. He also held that the worths of friendships were better fostered in the smaller than in the larger institution. In this opinion, however, many graduates of the large college would not agree. In the small college, however, as his career at Amherst illustrates, the opportunity is broader for getting a discipline for leadership. This discipline is based at least in part upon the holding of the many and diverse undergraduate offices. To some men, however, this presumed advantage is gained at a too high intellectual price. College politics, class politics, easily pass from being avocations to the order of vocations.

To the interpretation and application of his conception of education, the Institute gave a fairer and fuller opportunity of usefulness than many colleges offer to the president. Without being an autocrat, Walker was master in his own domain. He was a leader. Free from the absoluteness of the commanding general in the field, he yet was distinguished by

[4] *Ibid.*, pp. 248-49.

the directness and forcefulness of the military régime. He was, however, rather a governor than a ruler; the president of a democratic republic than a monarch. He yet was and is known as "General Walker," and "President." He was indeed a loyalist: a loyalist to his friends and co-workers, a loyalist to his country, a loyalist to his native commonwealth, a loyalist to his cities, New Haven and Boston, and, above all, a loyalist to the Massachusetts Institute of Technology.

In his loyalties, however, his emotions were not suffered to blot out the sense of intellectual proportion and distinction. He saw clearly what relation a school of technology should bear to the community, he understood equally well the demands which the community may make on the agencies of the higher education. He also saw and appreciated the contributions which the community should make to the higher education. The communal and the institutional relations are mutual. Above many presidents he also recognized the importance of the proper adjustment of each department of education in college and in school to every other department and to the whole life of the institution. He understood that in academic affairs there obtains the essence of the doctrine of state rights and of federalism. He also appreciated the distinct, the coördinate, and the coöperative relation of trustees and of the teaching staff. He realized that these relations require constant watchfulness in the avoidance of collisions and conflicts. Such crises are always disturbing and sometimes disastrous. His experience taught him, as every college president is taught, that personality in the administration of a college is of a worth far greater than regulations or laws. The president, too, like every teacher, is to be an ideal for students' inspiration and following. To his students Walker was indeed an embodiment of the human best. A welcome to his office was constantly in waiting for each and for all. His interest in his students was deep and unfailing, for he was a gentleman loving and loved, both chivalric and sympathetic: as his successor President Compton, in a personal letter to me, says, "he created an esprit de corps among students and alumni."

The influence of Walker as a personality cannot be too strongly emphasized. Its value among the students was of the highest type. Professor Davis R. Dewey of the Institute writes me saying, "Until General Walker came, I doubt if very much attention had been given to questions of the physical or social welfare of students. The Institute was regarded as an institution for the advancement of knowledge, pure and simple. With the growth of the student body, however, under General Walker's administration new problems of student welfare of course arose, and General Walker was responsive to these needs." The Secretary of the Trustees, too, of the Institute says, "The popularity of the president among students bore fruit for years after his death. In their love for General Walker an unusual alumni loyalty to the Institute developed. This was felt far more than ten years after the Walker presidency. . . . General Walker's appreciation of better living conditions for students is realized by reviewing his annual reports to the Corporation. A student house—under direction of the Y. M. C. A.— was first established while he was president. . . . The sympathetic treatment of student and faculty began with him.'' Professor Dewey also says, ''Although giving no instruction and never meeting the students in a class, save possibly some two or three times a year when called upon for a special lecture, yet he knew, I think, every man of the graduating class each year, and could also address by name scores, if not hundreds, of other students of the school. He had their complete confidence and admiration. He never addressed the students on questions of discipline, for such questions did not arise under his administration, but every student with whom he came in contact,— and scores saw him at one time and another in his office—felt an inspiration in personal contact and by the unconscious influence of the manliness of their president.''

Walker's influence as a president among other colleges was felt in and through the Phi Beta Kappa more fully than perhaps through any other academic agency. For his associations with the Society began as an undergraduate at Amherst in 1860. In 1883 he was made a senator, being a member of the first group of officers. He served for no less than five triennia, to his death, in 1897. In 1889 he gave the commencement address to the Brown chapter on *The Growth of the Nation,* a theme peculiarly fitted to him as su-

364 Friends of Men

perintendent of the census. In this address he pointed out the peril of "admitting to a nation, so fortunately built up, great hordes of peasants from the most down-trodden European regions." [5] Four years later, in 1893, he gave the address before the Harvard chapter, in which his subject was *College Athletics*. In this address he distinguished between the evils and the worth of college sports. Like the address of Charles Francis Adams, given on the same platform of Sanders Theater, *A College Fetish*, it was both commended and condemned, but it was sane, and it was influential.

Walker, therefore, goes into the structural history of the United States as a wise interpreter, as a leader and supporter of great causes, federal and educational, as a friend of students and all men. He was called "General"; he was called "President"; he was called "Frank." Each name is fitting: for it is descriptive and interpretative.

[5] *Ibid.,* p. 334.

XXV
WILLIAM PEPPER

Born in Philadelphia, August 21, 1843; died July 28, 1898, at Pleasanton, California. He was educated at the University of Pennsylvania, graduating from the academic department in 1862, from the medical department in 1864; 1868, he became lecturer on morbid anatomy; in 1870, lecturer on clinical medicine; from 1876 to 1887 professor of clinical medicine; in 1887 succeeded Dr. Alfred Stillé as professor of theory and practice of medicine; elected provost in 1881, resigning in 1894.

Author: A Text-book on the Theory and Practice of Medicine; edited the System of Medicine by American Authors; and other books and papers.

XXV

WILLIAM PEPPER

DIAGNOSTICIAN, PROVOST, CITIZEN

THERE are no less than a score of colleges and universities which are the outward sign and symbol of great personalities. These personalities may have been founders or re-founders. Their powers may have coöperated actively in the primary and favoring conditions of each institution. Their powers may also have vanquished antagonisms of environment and atmosphere in the laying of foundations. But at all events their character has become the characteristics of their institutions. The life of their institutions has been born and nourished of their life. Their personal life still flows and will flow in the institution.

Among such created institutions, and among such creating personalities are: Leland Stanford University, bearing the marks of the co-founder, David Starr Jordan; the University of California, in which the service of Wheeler stands forth as preëminent for length and constructiveness; the University of Minnesota, through which the personality of Northrop was impressed on the whole Northwest; the University of Michigan, representing the enriching charac-

367

ter of Angell; the University of Chicago, possessing
the vigor, vision, and "coruscating abundance" of
Harper; Oberlin, standing for the equanimity, fairness and patience of Fairchild; Cornell, bearing the
name of one of its founders, still in purpose and
environment the University of Andrew D. White;
Johns Hopkins, the creation of the enthusiastic and
devoted Gilman; Princeton, refounded by McCosh,
uniting a revolutionary atmosphere with Scotch philosophy; the University of Virginia, still rejoicing in
the architecture and schools of its founder, Thomas
Jefferson; Yale, still vital after one hundred years
with the forces which the elder Dwight and his co-
operative followers gave to it; Vassar, shaped and
molded by Raymond and by Taylor; Smith, bearing
the name of a woman whose bequest gave it being,
yet the child of the love and patience of Clark
Seelye; Brown, through the vision and wisdom of
Wayland, helping to establish the elective system in
all colleges; Williams, still perpetuating the name
and personality of a great teacher and friend, Mark
Hopkins; Dartmouth, standing as the foundation of
Eleazer Wheelock, yet pervaded by the universal
good will of Tucker; Harvard, the mother of us all,
coming to a new youth in the service of Eliot.

Yet among these and all other colleges stands the
University of Pennsylvania which, in its later decades, accepts the name of Pepper as a re-founder, as
in its first and following years it rejoiced in Franklin
as its founder and supporter.

Pepper once said to me that, "after the days of

Benjamin Franklin the University went to sleep. It slept in peace till I came one hundred years after. When I came it woke up, and there was trouble, and there has been trouble ever since.'' Pepper was indeed a trouble-maker for the Philadelphia Friends.[1] But of course he was much besides a trouble-maker. For in his troublesomeness there were other elements.

The troublesomeness characteristic of the boy and of the man were needed. For the University of Pennsylvania had for its whole history been ''sedate, conservative, respectable; quiescent in the belief that the methods of education which were wholesome for the fathers must be wholesome and all-sufficient for the sons and grandsons.''[2] The troublesomeness of Pepper sprang out essentially of an energy which came nearer to a fullness than has belonged to any college president. It was also an energy complete and overflowing which belonged to Pepper not only as provost of the University of Pennsylvania, but also at the same time as a professor of medicine, as a practitioner of medicine, and also as an author of great

[1] "The story is told that long ago a company of Philadelphians were staying once at a summer hotel, and had retired for an afternoon nap. This was suddenly cut short by a tremendous noise in the hall. One exasperated guest opened her door to expostulate, when she caught sight of a four-year-old boy in pink kilts marching down the hall, armed with two sticks, and alternately beating on the doors and shouting at the top of his lungs: 'No one shall sleep in this house this afternoon, I say, if I can help it!' It was William Pepper. Fifty years later the story was told to some friends, one of whom added: 'And no one has slept in Philadelphia for years because of that same William Pepper.' " *William Pepper* (1843-1898), by Francis Newton Thorpe, p. 459.

[2] *Ibid.*, p. 334.

medical works. Pepper was indeed three men, or
perhaps rather more than three men, wrapped up in
one personality. The chief executive of a university
normally fills at least four positions, or holds four
relations: the first relation is to the students, to whom
he is a friend; the second relation is to his associates
of the teaching staff, to whom he is an inspiring counselor; his third relation is to the members of the
Board of Trustees, to whom he is a guide, a philosopher, a watchman on the walls of an academic Zion;
the fourth relation is to the public, to whom he is to
be an interpreter and an inspirer. The office of the
president of a great university lies like the kingdom
of heaven, four square. Not a few of the presidents
represent this quadruple of diversities of service, and
also an amount of labor which is sufficient to command the powers of at least a quartette of executives.
Leaving out his relations to students, Pepper embodied the other relations with fullness, efficiency, and
glorious achieving. "His love of work and ceaseless
activity were a disease, incurable, but encouraged by
more activity. He fed upon work, and yearned for
it even when supposed to be resting. The centre of
greatest activity was the centre of his affections, and
the truest picture of the man is of one consumed by
work. He was given to putting himself into perspective, subjecting himself, as it were, into viewing and
noting his own activity. With him the greatest day,
the happiest day, was the busiest day. Eating seemed
like a waste of time; sleeping was a necessary evil.
Action, action was life. Thus at intervals of years

he made records of a typical day, which began soon
after midnight of one day and closed late after midnight the next.''[3] His laboriousness deserves all the
alarming and mouthfilling epithets prodigious, colossal, killing.[4]

In his manifold services Pepper maintained a

[3] *Ibid.*, p. 523.

[4] "His habit of working all day and every day as hard as
was in him may be illustrated by outlining an average day
of his life. He arose at a quarter of seven, took a cold sponge
bath, and was in his office at 7.15, from which time he dictated letters and opinions for an hour, breakfasting while seeing patients, which together with all sorts of business occupied
him till 11.30. His medical lectures, twice a week, occurred
at twelve or one, as the roster committee might arrange. Till
half-past two he was in consultation, and usually in his office
from half-past two until four. His luncheon, always a light
one, was taken in his office. He was in consultation till 7.15,
excepting the time—usually 5.30 to 6.30, four times a week—
given to lectures. He dined often with company at home or
elsewhere. He was again in consultation from 8.30 until ten,
from which later hour he dictated to one of his stenographers
until past midnight, frequently till 2.30. This division of
time, with minor variations, was maintained habitually. He
insisted that such labor was only possible by moderate, slow
eating, thorough chewing, and short naps of five minutes at
any time or place. . . .

"On one occasion, at a theatre-party which he was giving,
after some fifteen minutes, he excused himself, and was gone
three-quarters of an hour. Remaining a short time, he excused himself again, and was gone nearly as long. He then
returned for a moment, and excused himself a third time. He
had appeared at three functions, at two of which he had made
formal addresses; the third disappearance was for a consultation. While under great pressure of work he occasionally
worked thirty-six or even forty-eight hours without interruption except for a bite of food. This was in the last five years
of his life, while he was devoting all his energies to civil
affairs."

William Pepper (1843-1898), by Francis Newton Thorpe,
pp. 457-58.

sound interpretation of the idea and of the worth of a university. In an address given in the year 1890, on the close relationship between Columbia of New York and the Philadelphia University, he said, "The essence of a University is a breadth of view embodied in its organization which makes it keep in touch with all the intellectual needs of the people; an atmosphere of freedom which encourages individuality and original thought; and a richness of equipment in library and museum and laboratory which stimulates research and investigation. The tendency to conservatism in such an institution is inevitable; the danger is of too tenacious adherence to tradition and of blind disregard of the tendencies and needs of each new generation. The more closely in touch it is with a great community—the current of whose life-blood is thick with seething thoughts and plans—the less likely is conservatism to harden into apathy." [5]

In his constant interpretation of the idea of the university, he also quite as constantly referred to the forces necessary for its support. "It is difficult to compute the resources needed for the work of a great University. It is to draw to it the great scholars of the world, to accumulate the treasures of the past and the present, and to illustrate knowledge in all its branches; to provide ample endowment for research and for scientific publications, and to enable worthy students to do advanced work freely or at nominal cost. The annual cost of maintenance must be large,

[5] *Ibid.*, pp. 286-87.

many times larger than the total income of any American University to-day. But if it is seated where it may do not only this, but may also make itself the true centre of a vast community, influencing profoundly its social life, and elevating and quickening its intellectual life, there are needed not only vast material resources, but the widest and most generous co-operation."[6] "The wise use of wealth, the gifts of genius and the acquirements of learning, the fine qualities of personal character and of public-spirited citizenship, these challenge our highest admiration, as they have that of all vigorous and progressive nations. And it is precisely these excellences that the influence of a University fosters and develops."[7]

The seriousness of the conditions to which the higher learning should minister were ever present to him as an unrelieving anxiety. "We are trying in this country an experiment in civilization of grand proportions and commensurate risk. Even if the tide of immigration has begun to ebb, there are elements in the problem before us well calculated to arouse anxiety. We are trying the incomparable experiment of trusting to the power of education, religious and secular, to enable sixty millions of people to govern themselves."[8] The university, receptive, responsive, coöperative with the community, obedient to every worthy command, becomes a beneficent power of the community at large. It at once leads and follows the intellectual intimations of the community.

[6] *Ibid.*, p. 287.   [7] *Ibid.*, p. 288.   [8] *Ibid.*, p. 289.

In this leadership of the community, and to Pepper the leadership was far more constant and far more commanding than the following, he founded in the University of Pennsylvania schools such as the Wharton of Finance and Economy, added Institute after Institute to the number of well-nigh a score.[9] In fact under Pepper's constructiveness the University of Pennsylvania became an outstanding university of the world.

To the achieving of these great results in creating or re-creating a historic university in a historic city, he brought not only tremendous working power, as I have intimated, compelling energy, but also many other qualities which were constructive. For a university is a coöperative agency and institution. In this coöperativeness Pepper was eager to bear his share of responsibility. Of course this share was

[9] The Wharton School of Finance and Economy,
    The Biological Department,
    The Department of Philosophy,
    The Department of Physical Education,
    The Veterinary Department,
    The Auxiliary Department in Medicine,
    The Training School for Nurses,
    The Post-Graduate Course in Law,
    The University Library,
    The Graduate Department for Women,
    The Biddle Law Library,
    The Department of Archæology and Paleontology,
    The Department of Hygiene,
    The Semitic Department and of Assyriology,
    The Department of American History,
    The Department of Architecture,
    The Wistar Institute of Anatomy and Biology.
    William Pepper (1843-1898), by Francis Newton Thorpe, p. 339.

chief. In fact this responsibility was so great and was so fully carried by him that he made himself a necessary, an essential, factor.

For Pepper possessed the quality of inspiring others in his great educational evangelism. Yet at times his colleagues faltered in the unflagging quest in which Pepper led them. "The financial burden upon him was heavy to bear. Some of his associates in the Board of Trustees, upon whom he depended for assistance, were wearying in well doing, and the labor of supporting and administering the University fell wholly upon him." [10] Yet usually his associates yielded to his commanding enthusiasm. "He was naturally a leader of men, and his unselfishness secured their fidelity. The result was inevitable; committees, Councils, Legislatures yielded before him in recognition of his superior insight as to the best method of promoting the general welfare." [11] With women in particular he had much influence in securing both loyalty and gifts. In fact his coöperation with women had upon him an influence quite as great as that which resulted for them in their co-working with him. He was thus transformed from a somewhat conservative supporter of the higher education of women to a devoted, enthusiastic believer and a progressive leader.

Yet in all of Pepper's coöperativeness there was a certain masterfulness, a masterfulness which belongs to great spirits. He had a habit of overlooking the

[10] *Ibid.*, p. 282.　　　　[11] *Ibid.*, p. 471.

small and the petty, and of giving himself to the
great, the primary, the fundamental, the constitutive.
His general method and special methods were direct.
A desire to be useful possessed or obsessed him. The
desire was so evident that it helped to disarm criticism and to cast out antagonism. His very presence
was stimulating. There was a certain splendor in his
manner, manners, personality.

This masterfulness was a cause and also a result in
part of his skill as a medical diagnostician. This
skill was, of course, in its beginning a foundation
professional, but it became also of a general type. He
sought for facts diligently, he put facts together ra-
tionally, he compared facts and weighed evidence
carefully, he inferred new truths logically, he did the
duty of new truths skillfully, faithfully, triumphantly.

Pepper also had, as is necessary for every president, a keen sense of proportions. He recognized the
diversity of values. Dr. Horace Howard Furness said
of him, after his death, "His perspective was always
true. At a glance he distinguished the permanent
and the transitory. Therefore it is that the institutions with which he was connected or which he
guided will for many a year to come follow out
the lines which he in his clear-sighted wisdom laid
down." [12]

There is, furthermore, another element to which I
must refer which is also constructive. It is an element at once primary and secondary. It is primary
for it is necessary, it is secondary for it is derived.

[12] *Ibid.*, p. 535.

That element is courage. Does not Aristotle say that courage stands midway between timidity and rashness? Pepper's courage was a union of caution—in every undertaking he provided against the possibility of defeat—and also of audacity, for he took up work and works which were not supported with full reasonableness. He was in a sense hot-headed and warm-hearted. He was never, however, harebrained. His courage was the courage of the great adventurer.

There was one advantage, however, which Pepper did not possess. This is the advantage of being loved by his students. His own nature was to love deeply, and he was loved deeply by those who knew him. But his students did not know him. His students admired their provost, they were acquainted in general with his great qualities. His works met their eyes wherever their eyes turned. His medical students heard his lectures and read his great textbook. But they did not and could not love him as students of Brown University loved Faunce, or of Dartmouth, Tucker. For they did not know him. In college, as in other concerns, love is the result, or should be the result, of acquaintance and knowledge. The Pennsylvania students had little or no opportunity of knowing Pepper, and his opportunity of knowing them was equally meager. Therefore a most coöperative, happy, and useful part of academic life was lacking. But this lack had at least one compensation. This was found in the acquaintanceship which sprang up between the graduates and Pepper. For to the graduates, and in particular to those of the medical department, he felt himself specially related. His recognition of their work was constant and deep. "They have carried with them to all parts of the world the lessons there learned, not only in medical science, but in medical ethics and in medical enthusiasm; and they have returned dutifully the benefits they received by an unswerving support of all her measures for the advancement of medical education and of all the highest professional interests." [13]

There is one virtue belonging to intellect, to heart, and to will which Pepper did not possess, the virtue of patience. He was not willing to wait for conclusions. Indeed, he was inclined to hurry the process which leads to conclusions. He hardly realized that a university is a growth (not a manufacture) and that growth takes time. It was hard for him to appreciate the Scriptural truth that their strength was in their sitting still, and that in quietness one is to possess his soul. His constant wish and will were to be up and doing. Yet, despite the lack of this elemental virtue and beautiful grace, he did his great work, lived his long and short life, and died at the age of fifty-four. Had he possessed the patience of Eliot he might also have lived and worked to Eliot's fourscore and ten. Perhaps, however, he would have said, "It is better as it is." He preferred fifty years in America to a cycle in Cathay; but if he could have had his cycle in America!

[13] *Ibid.*, pp. 256-57.

XXVI
EDGAR FAHS SMITH

BORN York, Pa., May 23, 1856; died May 3, 1928. B.S., Pennsylvania College, 1874; A.M., Ph.D., Göttingen, 1876. Instructor in chemistry, University of Pennsylvania, 1876-81; professor of chemistry, Muhlenberg College, 1881-83, Wittenberg College, 1883-88; professor of chemistry, 1888-1911; vice-provost, 1899-1911, provost, 1911-20, University of Pennsylvania. Member Jury of Awards, Chicago Exposition, 1893; member U. S. Assay Commission, 1895, 1901-05; adviser in chemistry, Carnegie Institute, 1902; trustee Carnegie Foundation, 1914-20; president Wistar Institute, Philadelphia, 1911-22. Member of Electoral College, Pennsylvania, 1915; Commission of Public Safety; Commission for Revision of Constitution of Pennsylvania, 1919; College and University Council, 1911-20; State Council of Education, 1920-22; research asso. Carnegie Institute, 1915, 1918; appointed by Pres. Harding to board of technical advisers, Disarmament Conference, 1921.

Author: Classen's Quantitative Analysis; Richter's Inorganic Chemistry; Smith & Keller's Chemical Experimentation; Richter's Organic Chemistry; Smith's Electro-Chemical Analysis; Theories of Chemistry; Chemistry in America; Atomic Weights; Robert Hare; James Woodhouse; Chemistry in Old Philadelphia; Atomic Weight of Boron and Fluorene; James Cutbush; Priestley in America; and many others (see footnote of a following page).

XXVI

EDGAR FAHS SMITH

PROVOST, TEACHER, INVENTOR, FRIEND

OFTEN have I wished I might make a book seeking to interpret the most loved teachers of our colleges. What a rich treasury it would indeed be of dear souls loving and loved. In it I would tell of "Old Peabo" of Harvard, who embodied the great phrases of Paul's eulogy on charity. Included, too, would be Shaler, also of Harvard, of whom it was said, "Late in life he was fond of telling the story of his once having overheard two students talking together. 'Where's the old man?' asked one. 'Hush!' said the other, 'if he hears you call him old man, he'll walk your d—d legs off.' " [1] Chief among the worthies would be North of Hamilton, whose other and more affectionate name was "Old Greek." Of him a graduate wrote, "Professor North, I love you because you inspired in me a desire to do my best and to realize in my life what God has made possible." [2] Of course,

[1] *The Autobiography of Nathaniel Southgate Shaler,* p. 369.
[2] *Old Greek. A Memoir of Edward North with Selections from his Lectures,* S. N. D. North, p. 138.

too, a place would be had for Garman of Amherst.
Of Garman, Principal Stearns of Andover has written:

"To him hundreds of Amherst men owe the best inspiration of their lives. Those who have enjoyed the
privilege of sitting as disciples at his feet realize as
none others can what a rare privilege has been theirs.
He taught us the beauty of truth. Through him the
spiritual world was brought near and its glory revealed. He made us feel the presence of the Divine
within us, and he stirred as few men have been able to
do within the hearts of his pupils the desire to serve.
The wonderful influence he exerted over the minds
and lives of his students was unique in the educational
world. Sluggish minds were stimulated to activity;
careless minds were taught the value of accuracy;
indifference was changed to eager desire. To many an
Amherst man the most sacred and cherished memory
of college days will always be that morning hour in
Walker Hall where intellect was quickened and ambition aroused." [3]

The interpreter also would not leave out Wright of
Middlebury, who held higher hopes for his students
than they had for themselves. One of these students
wrote to him saying, "I am trying to catch up with
your ideals for me." In the list I should want to
include from wholly different zones Osler, the teacher
of medical students in three universities, Jowett of
Baliol, and Tholuck of Halle, a theologian gifted with
wit and humor, and with paternal love for his students.

[3] *Letters, Lectures and Addresses of Charles Edward Garman*, by Eliza Miner Garman, p. 581.

Yet as noble, as inspiring, as formative, as loved, and as loving as any other of the noble group is Edgar Fahs Smith. Of the fourteen provosts of the University of Pennsylvania I have known four: Pepper, the re-founder, the inspiring teacher; Harrison, the watchful and insistent financier; Penniman, the present head, the faithful conservator and the broad-minded administrator; and Smith, whom Penniman succeeded, and of whom I now write in a way most personal.

On the campus of the University of Pennsylvania, within sight of a laboratory which he planned and in which he worked, stands a statue bearing this inscription:

EDGAR FAHS SMITH
Provost 1911-1920
Teacher   Inventor   Friend

The four words represent the four-square relation of his life. Each word, illuminating, represents either the service he gave, or the contribution he made, or the relations he held. I cannot but believe, however, that the last word, Friend, is the more and most revealing.

The nine years of his provostship were perhaps the most trying of all the decades of his life. He accepted the great office and undertook its duties under the earnest persuasiveness of the board of trustees. He was reluctant to give up his daily and double work of teaching and of research. Technically, during his administrative period, he continued his professorship. The opportunities of the professorship were his life. He, however, accepted the provostship under the promise, as he understood, that he should have no responsibility for the financial relationships of the university. Especially did he insist that he should be free from any specific or implied duty of raising funds either for endowment or for meeting current expenses. For such undertakings his immediate predecessor, Harrison, had peculiar power. Hardly, however, had he been placed in the provostship when it became plain that the trustees were relying on him for important financial duties. He once said to me, with tears in his voice, "It almost killed me." Possibly one might soberly say that the financial condition became a cause which ultimately contributed to his death.

Of course one might add that Smith should have known! For he is not the first of college presidents who have learned that honest and high-purposing boards of college trustees sometimes allow themselves to give happy promises of immunity from specific labors in financial administration to a newly elected president, promises which it seems later so easy to forget or to neglect.

Yet it is as teacher, as inventor, and as friend that, as declares the monument, the personality is most beautiful and preëminent. This trinity of great forces and qualities are wonderfully joined together in a noble unity of personality. Edgar Smith's service as teacher opened the door to friendships, and the friendships ministered unto his work as a teacher. His teaching, too, was constantly reinforced by his researches, and his teaching contributed certain human impulses unto his investigations. His work was indeed a unity, as his personality was a unit. Too many teachers make their teaching and their personality independent parts of their one character. Such divisions or subdivisions are, or at least should be, impossible.

But to these three constructive elements are to be added—and the addition could have fittingly been written on his monument—his service as a writer. For his books, biographical and theoretical, were the normal expression of the studies of the laboratory and of the library. Their number is indeed colossal, and their variety nothing less than immense.

This is not the place to give in detail the contributions which he made, through writing and research, to chemistry organic, inorganic, analytical, electro and historical. To name even the investigations, the experiments, the discoveries, would bear both the writer and the reader too far afield. Perhaps the most important contributions were those devoted to electro-chemistry,—

". . . a domain in which he was a pioneer and soon became a recognized leader of international reputation. In the hands of this master craftsman, the electric current became a tool of undreamed usefulness and possibilities, opening up wholly new methods of ana-

lysis, separation and determination. About half of all
the research papers he published were based upon new
applications of the electric current. His introduction
of the rotating anode together with the employment
of currents of high amperage and high voltage
marked a new epoch in the development of electro-
analysis. His books on electro-chemistry quickly became and have since remained the standard texts in
this country, while the Harrison Laboratory was soon
known throughout the world for its leadership in this
branch of chemistry.'' [4]

His biographies of chemists, too, numbered more
than a score, and his interpretations of chemistry
historical and theoretical almost an equal number.[5]

[4] *Science,* May 31, 1929, p. 560.

[5] Separate books, brochures or articles have been published
by him concerning the following chemists: Theodore G.
Wormley, Jr. (1897), Robert Empie Rogers (1905), George
F. Barker (1907), Fairman Rogers (1909), Robert Hare, an
American chemist (1917), James Woodhouse (1918), James
Cutbush (1919), Franklin Bache (1922), James Curtis Booth
(1922), Samuel Latham Mitchill (1922), Charles Baskerville
(1923), Jacob Green (1923), Matthew Carey Lee (1923), Mar-
tin Hans Boye (1924), John Griscom (1925), James Blythe
Rogers (1927), Priestley in America (1920), Priestleyana
(1922) and the Priestley Medal Lecture (1926). More general
treatises, written wholly or largely from the historical point
of view, were: "Chemistry in America" (1914), "Men of
Science from the Keystone State" (1914), "Chemistry in
Old Philadelphia" (1918), "The American Spirit in Chemistry" (1919), "Progress of Chemistry" (1921), "Our Science"
(1922), "A Half Century of Mineral Chemistry in America,
1876-1926" (1926), "Observations on Teaching the History of
Chemistry" (1926), "Bromine and Its Discoverers, 1826-1926"
(1926), "Early Science in Philadelphia" (1926), "Fragments
Relating to the History of Chemistry in America" (1926), "A
Look Backward" (1927), "A Glance at the Early Organic
Chemistry of America" (1927) and "Old Chemistries" (1927).
Science, May 31, 1929, p. 564.

To the scholar even, and to one who is not a scholar, it is inevitable that the thought and heart turn to Smith as a friend. For as a friend I knew and loved him. As an adopted son of the University of Pennsylvania I join with tens of thousands of the real sons of Alma Mater in declaring that he was chief among our dearest. Toward him one has the feeling which an American soldier declared in saying that he went to France for flag and for country, but that he went over the top for mother. For Smith helped his students to carry chemistry into life. Its methods were life's methods, its principles life's principles, its prophecies, its rewards constructive of life's happiness. To his students he was at once a father and an elder brother. Their sorrows were his sorrows, their triumphs his triumphs, their achievements gave to him a sense of glory. With their slowness of advance or with their rapid progress he sympathized, and in the rapidity and height of their advancements he rejoiced. His simplicity, his altruism, his sense of reality, his sturdy honesty, the depth of his thoughtfulness, the breadth of his tolerance, his vision of ideals, inspired, quickened, moved his students. His devotion to them was structural and formative in manhood. He was their friend. He wrote, as a last sentence to his interpretation of Wetherill, "He was one of those Golden Natures who help us form Ideals of Life." The sentence itself we have a right to think of as autobiographic.

XXVII
BENJAMIN IDE WHEELER

Born Randolph, Mass., July 15, 1854; died May 3, 1927; A.B., Brown University, 1875, A.M., 1878; Ph.D., University of Heidelberg, 1885. Instructor in Latin and Greek, Brown University, 1879-81; instructor in German, Harvard, 1885-86; acting professor of classical philology, 1886-87, professor comparative philology, 1887-88, Greek and comparative philology, 1888-99, Cornell University; president of University of California, 1899-1919; president emeritus, from 1919; Professor of Greek literature, American School of Classical Studies, Athens, 1895-96; lecturer, Harvard University, 1898; Roosevelt professor at University of Berlin, 1909-10.

Author: The Greek Noun-Accent, 1885; Analogy in Language, 1887; Introduction to the History of Language, 1890; Dionysos and Immortality, 1899; Organization of Higher Education in United States, 1896; Life of Alexander the Great, 1900 (translated into Russian); Unterricht und Demokratie in Amerika, 1910. Editor department of philology in Johnson's Cyclopædia and in Macmillan's Dictionary of Philosophy and Psychology.

XXVII

BENJAMIN IDE WHEELER

PRESIDENT, SCHOLAR, TEACHER

Royce, Schurman, Wheeler: three great names in American scholarship and academic administration; three great names, too, representing unities made, and names also standing for inevitable separations. Wheeler and Schurman were colleagues at Cornell in the last decades of the last century. Royce and Schurman were once considered together by President Eliot for appointment to the philosophic faculty of Harvard. Royce was selected, thus beginning a career of unique distinction and worth. If Schurman had been selected, he would not have gone to Cornell as Sage Professor of Philosophy in 1886, neither would he have been elected president of Cornell six years later. In case Schurman had been appointed by Eliot to a Harvard chair, Wheeler would have been made president of Cornell in 1892. For there was a large body at Ithaca who were shouting "We want Benny Wheeler." In this realm of prophetic imagination or of imaginative prophecy I may add a remark which Moses Coit

Tyler once made to me, that he had often thought
Schurman, who was born on British soil, "ought to
have gone to England and entered the House of
Commons. For Schurman's speaking was just the
kind of speaking that the House of Commons liked."
But Schurman did enter diplomacy, a calling in
which silence has peculiar rights and duties, coming
finally with happy distinction to an ambassadorship
which his Cornell predecessor, Andrew D. White,
had filled. From the new university on the Pacific,
Royce came to the ancient college on the Charles;
and from the shore of Cayuga's waters went Wheeler
to the Pacific coast. Such transformations, such
successions, such likenesses, such unlikenesses,
such surprises, for three American scholars and
teachers!

Yet with all their dissimilarities of origin, of conditions of intellectual service, it would be hard to
find three American scholars who more fully embodied
the one essential element of scholarship and of human service: abundance of life. Each of them incarnated the divine intimation of the value of the
fullest life. The evidence of Wheeler's incarnation
of the intimation, in the judgment of his colleagues,
is found in the title of the book containing his papers
and addresses, *The Abundant Life.*

The most evident, and indeed apparently superficial, element of Wheeler's character and achievement is seen and felt in the style of his writing. What
are the forces and factors which create and constitute

one's English style? It is a simple question, but the
answer is complex. Yet the truth is that the style is
the man. But, leaving out this fundamental element
of character, one may ask what are the creative causes
of Gibbon's noble, majestic, ever-flowing paragraphs?
What are the influences that formed Macaulay's
stately and regimental periods? What are the intellectual forces that sharpened Hawthorne's chisel for
carving out Hilda, Hester and other immortal characters? What give to Matthew Arnold's pen hesitan-
cies, repetitions, critical moods, which yet move forward toward weighty conclusions? The questions
have relations to Wheeler's style. For Wheeler had
a power as a writer which belongs to few college
presidents. It was a style unique in its affluence. Its
richness belonged to both content, phrase, sentence
and paragraph. Its words wove a fitting garment for
the idea. The idea spread out like a broad and flowing robe into well-knit paragraphs. It was a style
formed on the classical model. It had a philological
basis, but it does not smell of the lamp. As one reads
its pages one feels the influence of the Greek mood
and tense. Vistas of thought open, words are used
which belong only to the scholar in Plato and in
Sophocles. But it is a style vital with the quickening
spirit of modernity. Many years ago I heard the
beloved Andrew Preston Peabody say that when he
was editor of the *North American Review* he could
easily detect whether an article submitted for publication was written by one who was classically

trained. Each page of Wheeler's writings bear evidences that he had taken the Greek bath.

As I have intimated, style is apparently superficial. But style is really characteristic and significant. It bears evidence of the essential manhood of the man who writes. The wealth of Wheeler's English is an intimation of the richness which he bore to the universities which he served: Brown, Harvard, Cornell, California, and of the richness which he received from them. That wealth had many parts fundamental, constructive, complex.

The relation which unites (and sometimes separates) a college faculty and its president is, on the whole, one of the most important relations of the academic life and procedure. Herein lie wisdom, inspiration, good will, confidences, coöperation, progress, tolerance, achievement. Herein also are found the opposite elements and qualities, alas! The history of the University of California is a history distinguished by brief terms of its presidents. The record is most significant:

Henry C. Durant	1870-1872
Daniel C. Gilman	1872-1875
John LeConte	1876-1881
W. T. Reid	1881-1885
Edward S. Holden	1885-1888
Horace Davis	1888-1890
Martin Kellogg	1893-1899
Benjamin Ide Wheeler	1899-1919
David P. Barrows	1919-1924
William Wallace Campbell	1924-1930

In fact the list of the occupants of the office is a union of wisdom and of unwisdom, of happiness and of unhappiness. In the year 1869 the office was offered to General George B. McClellan and it was declined. Wheeler became president in 1899 and continued for twenty years. His administration covers one-third of the entire academic history. At the present writing, in the first days of 1931, the third president since his retirement in 1919 is in office. Wheeler's long term was most effective in winning results academic and communal. The longer the length of the term of a college presidency, the greater is its efficiency; and the shorter the less. The length of service and efficiency are at once both cause and effect. Wheeler's term was, therefore, remunerative in richest values.

Of the relation of faculty and president in university administration Wheeler spoke in his inaugural address words of wisdom:

In the real university life, the president must be a teacher among teachers, a colleague among colleagues, and the spirit of coöperation, not the spirit of authority, must determine their work together. The educational policy of the university must arise from within, from the body of teacher-colleagues, and not be imposed from without by either president or governing board. Leaving aside the conception of the university as a business organization, the real university must be a family life in which loyalty of each member to the whole shall be the divine inspiring breath.[1]

[1] *The Abundant Life,* by Benjamin Ide Wheeler. Edited by Monroe E. Deutsch, pp. 38-39.

After seven years of service the seriousness and complexities of the office had apparently begun to weigh on Wheeler, for in the year 1906 at the inauguration of Houston as president of the University of Texas, he said:

There is no more difficult and complicated task to which an American citizen can address himself. Let him combine all the energetic skill of a business man, all the intellectual subtlety of a scholar, all the commanding grace of a diplomat, all the persuasiveness of an orator, and all the magnetic force of a leader; he will yet find the demands of the position greater than he can meet.[2]

But after nine further years of service a still further seriousness and solemnity had come to rest upon his interpretation of the office. For with both wit and solemnity he said to his colleagues of the state university:

The relations of corporation and faculty became in the state universities the prototype of the relations of regents and faculty, between which two resides the president as automatic coupler, alternately squeezed and stretched, or in more violent collisions, alternately forced up into dangerous eminence and dragged beneath the wreck. Fortunate operation of the university machinery consists in a proper distribution of powers and tasks between the three elements: regents, faculty, president.[3]

But even if the president is "alternately squeezed and stretched" and sometimes "dragged beneath

[2] *Ibid.*, p. 134.   [3] *Ibid.*, pp. 126-127.

the wreck" he is still the permanent uniting force
and personality.

The office of the American college president has
rewards many, diverse, lasting, richest. The office is
also subjected to not a few pains and even penalties.
The hardest of all these pains to bear is the duty of
the exclusion of unworthy colleagues. Such a duty
weighed on Wheeler as it weighs upon every worthy
president. The proper method, however, of perform-
ing this duty is the one which Wheeler proposed. It
was the method of action by one's colleagues. He
says,

In proceeding against a professor for incompetency
no step should be taken without full and careful conference with his nearest colleagues in the faculty, pref-
erably in a body as well as individually. The professors themselves above all others should be vitally interested in helping establish the standards of their
profession by aiding in the excision from the teaching
staff of dry rot, incompetence, indifference, and mis-
fits . . . the president, whose path is sad enough at the
best, will be relieved of a lonesome duty which brings
him today the chief misunderstanding and odium
attaching to the administration of his office.[4]

More fundamental in constructiveness, more comprehensive in administration, far more imperative in
authority than either faculty or president, stands the
university itself. The whole university, the single
institution, is the mother of all. Wheeler's understanding of the university is among the ablest of all

[4] *Ibid.,* pp. 129-130.

interpretations which he gave to the forces and conditions of the higher education.

Among the choicest treasures of the American university, among the most fundamental of all its elements, lies the element of freedom. Freedom from political partisanship, freedom from religious bigotry, freedom from a sociological bias, are essential and constructive. The fact of freedom applies equally to the state and to the privately endowed university. The emphasis on this principle both in the pursuit of truth and in administration Wheeler constantly lays down and with force and discrimination:—

If the university is to hold the confidence of the public its pursuit of the truth must be absolutely free. Not that it should speak with any official authority or set any seal or stamp upon its products, or strive to standardize the truth, but that it should be known to seek and see with eye single to the facts. It cannot utter finalities or provide the ultimate recipes for life and conduct, for its freemen will differ and clash in the future as they have in the past; the sanctions of its authority with human kind will rest solely on the disinterestedness, the sincerity, and the integrity of its attitude and its labors.[5]

The purpose or the method of securing endowment for the college is a motive or condition often referred to as impairing academic liberty. The frequency of its sinister application, however, is far less constant than is the public belief regarding it. Upon the possibility of its evil influence, Wheeler says,

[5] *Ibid.*, p. 156.

The things at stake in the freedom of the American universities are too high and precious, that the pursuit of endowments should be suffered to affect the attitude or judgment of the man at the head, or his public expressions or acts suffered to count as repayment of benefits received. To appoint your college presidents solicitors of bounty is to make them jesters at the tables of the rich.[6]

Also, in general, he says,

A state university should certainly lend no aid to partisanship of any kind, but on the other hand I have no hesitation in expressing my conviction that if the conditions of public control require that any field of human interest and social need which demands investigation for the social good must be excluded from the purview of the state university because of such control, then the basis of organization is false, and public control is a mistake. A university with blinders on is no university at all. But in actual experience I am persuaded this difficulty does not in any real form exist.[7]

One of the most serious of the evil effects of the lack of freedom in the university is the limitation which it lays upon the search for truth. Such an effect is an unspeakable evil. Its pestiferous character is well expressed in a Founders' Day address in the year 1916, at the neighboring university at Palo Alto:

If our walls are to bear but one inscription, let these five words standing at the entering in of its

[6] *Ibid.*, p. 157.   [7] *Ibid.*, pp. 139-140.

gates tell what the university is for: *To Help Find the Way.*

"Help," because we are a social body and share our tasks; "The way," because our goal is the truth; "Find," because our mode is that of search.

Our path shall be the plain straight ahead. We will abjure the maze and drive for the open. We will annul the mysteries and shake off the barren formulas of authority. We will set the man above the schedule, and the truth above the form.[8]

In this voyage of discovery there is found one element which has peculiar value. It is the virtue of the steady mind, the willing hand. With aptness and wit he says:

Desirable as it is that a state university should be ever keenly sensitive to the conditions and needs of its community, it cannot be a university if it is swept about by every wind of doctrine, if it is overset by every wave of change. The university is the compass-needle, not the weathercock.[9]

But before every other element of the university, however, constitutive and constructive, that element which we call personal character is most fundamental, and is to be made dominant. On the very day in which he assumed office, speaking to the students, he said:

It is what goes over into spinal marrow, what goes over into real life that makes us; and what we are likely to gain from our university life is not bits of knowledge, is not maxims and rules for getting this

[8] *Ibid.,* p. 174.　　　　[9] *Ibid.,* p. 143.

or that; but after all it is this one thing that we talk so much about and understand so imperfectly—it is character. The men you tie to are men of character. As I grow older I come less and less to respect men of brilliancy and to tie to men for their characters. And what men are going to get out of their university life is not what is pumped into the pail, but what goes over into life. And it comes not only from the lecture room, but from association with the best minds they find in the faculty, alumni, and student body—association with the whole life and character of the University. This University is a living thing. The real University is alive. Blood pulses through its veins. The spiritual life of the men who have gone before is in it. It is not a thing of buildings, of statutes, of courses—it is a thing of life. What you will get out of this University that is worth your while, that will stand by you, is what you will get out of association with it as a living thing.[10]

The university belongs to the individual, it also belongs, and more, to the whole community. It belongs to the individual in a sense active, laborious, coöperative.

It must be admitted that nowhere in all the wide world is there a keener sense of, nowhere a stronger demand for, the qualities of personal force and character which inhere in the totality of personality and are entirely independent of tinseled acquirement—than just here in America. Nowhere is there so pronounced a need for the plain article, men. The mere specialist, sharp as a needle and equally broad, will find poor acceptance. I doubt indeed if anywhere in

[10] *Ibid.,* pp. 25-26.

the world, present or past, was ever found so large an opportunity and so natural a place for the liberal education in its fundamental sense as here in the land of freemen who are free after a larger plan than the world has ever yet known.[11]

As an element in the university's constitution and administration, Wheeler gives peculiar heed to the individual student. The search for truth is, of course, central, both progressive and continuous, but with it is to be united the human process and product—the student himself. If the student become the scholar, it is well. If the student, not becoming the scholar, yet becomes the man complete, it is better and best. In his first address at the university, delivered primarily to the students, he said:

Almost the only consolation I have this morning in entering upon my work is the belief that I am going to know you and to have to do with you intimately; for all this work of the presidential office is burden and care. It is only done in order that the real thing may be reached, the real object, the bringing forward of a university made of students. I want you to find in me—to believe from the beginning and throughout, that you have in me a personal friend. I shall regard my mission here a failure if that is not the case. I want you to come to see me, and come to me as persons. . . . Please do not be afraid to come about petty matters, little matters. What interests you will interest me. And I hope I am going to have time enough to know about your petty affairs.[12]

[11] *Ibid.*, p. 182.   [12] *Ibid.*, pp. 24-25.

His remark reminds me of another college president, now serving, of whom one of his colleagues said the boys come to talk over with him their love affairs.

In the score of years of his administration, Wheeler refers constantly in his many addresses to his relation to students and their relation to him. He also emphasizes specific elements which constitute their own individual character. He frequently points out the forces which make for their welfare in the present and for the long future. The worths which the great subjects of study give to the whole character of the student he touches upon with noble truthfulness and wisdom. Mathematics teaches one "to think consecutively, hold the mind with a firm grip to the problem in hand, and force it to step surely from premise to conclusion." [13] The sciences fit one "to see facts, brush aside the cobweb illusions of fancy, hope, and prejudice, and boldly, serenely, and heroically face the facts." [14] The humanities, too, give the priceless blessings of ability to reason in the terms which life offers:

. . . in incomplete syllogisms and not be tied to the syllogism of the logician and mathematician. Contingent reasoning is the form of reasons we all apply in dealing with the common emergencies of human experience. That inestimable gift we call good judgment, a thing inhering in a larger whole we term good sense, deals with this type of reasoning and employs, to gather its premises, those insights or intuitions

[13] *Ibid.*, p. 184.   [14] *Ibid.*, p. 184.

which in their chastened form yield the superb indefinable touch of taste.[15]

In general, the most precious teaching for the student is the teaching of life itself:

Life is begotten of life, and it will remain in the future as it has been in the past, that the health of the spiritual life passes neither from book or subject but from the life of the master to the life of the pupil. The greatest education is the giving of life, and the greatest teacher was one who came that ye might have life—and have it more abundantly.[16]

Yet in the whole educational process it is the grace of sympathy, the gift of altruism, which adds worth to the study of the individual themes. As he tells the graduates of the class of 1907:

. . . you have missed the largest value of your training if through it you have not acquired some added suppleness of mind and heart to see the world from others' eyes, to think their thoughts with them, to measure the weight and meaning of their motives and desires. At least half the total effort of education is expended toward this end. Reading, literature, history, social and political science, and philosophy make this their direct goal. The true interpretation of literature or the appreciation of any other form of human art, sculpture, painting, or music, is a process of entering into spiritual accord by the solvent of human sympathy.[17]

Yet the sense of altruism, the graces and graciousness of deep human sympathy are to be made

[15] *Ibid.,* pp. 184-185.   [16] *Ibid.,* p. 101.   [17] *Ibid.,* pp. 56-57.

consistent with personal independence. As he declares to the class of 1905, on its graduation:

The sooner a man learns that only what one gets for himself is really one's own, the better. This consciousness of absolute self-responsibility, this sure knowledge that one's fate is at the certain mercy of one's own acts and choices brings with its first unfolding the appalling lonesomeness of the mighty deep— alone with one's fate and one's power to control it; but until one has thus been once alone, he has never yet been once a man. You have heard good advice already to the full; you have had your minds made up for you already too long. You have now got to decide for yourselves, and having decided take for yourselves the consequences.[18]

As the means and method for nourishing this sense of independence, the power of will has supreme worth:

It is power of will more than power of mind that differentiates them. Must and ought have fifty times more stuff in them than might and could. . . . Having lost faith in their own wills they had ceased to plan their own work and went drifting on through life swept with every current and chance breeze and never reached a wharf or delivered a cargo.[19]

To the class, also, of 1904 he says with forceful directness:

What each one of you is to be in life will depend chiefly on what you *will to be*. It has been found in the history of every college class that a certain num-

[18] *Ibid.*, p. 52.　　　　[19] *Ibid.*, p. 103.

ber of those whose scholarship has been poor turn out
to be successful men—and a certain number of high
students prove failures. So far as my experience goes,
it is on both sides the will that is in play. The fact is
that good scholarship in college is more a testimony of
self-control and the power to force one's self to do
duty than it is to brains; and this is really the reason
why the great proportion of the successful men come
from the upper half of the college classes. The thing
above all others that gives a man success is his grip on
himself. It is his self-steering power. Will is keel and
rudder—whereby the craft can cross currents and
eye the wind—whereby it can go where it *planned* to
go, and not merely drift on the currents of the *Zeit-
geist* and be driven about by the fickle winds of opinion or the gusts of impulse and wrath. But on the
other hand it must be remembered that stubbornness
is no evidence of the real strength of the will. Stubbornness is merely a stranded log painted to resemble
a steam yacht.[20]

In the exercise of such independence the intellectual
and the ethical virtue of distinguishing between the
more and the most important, and the less and the
least, is of consummate worth. He says, speaking to
the class of 1914:

Some people seem never to know any difference between the footnotes and the headlines. What is true
about knowledge is true about the general business of
living; sooner or later, if you are going to live the
life of wisdom, you will have to make up your minds
what things are for you worth while—what things are
worth while *for you*, you and your goal being what

[20] *Ibid.,* pp. 46-47.

they are, and you will have to gather together the will to do those things which are worth while, and leave out those things which are meaningless.[21]

This sense of independence is to prove itself in work, work hard, continuous, unyielding. To two successive classes, 1904 and 1905, he says:

Let us go to our work. There is no use waiting for the big things to do. We do not even know for sure what the big things are. The widow who brought her two mites to the treasury gave more than they all. If there are any "big" things, they are probably those that lie next our door—namely *our duty*. The great thing is that we get to our work while it is yet day, and stay at it. Some people stop after every achievement to admire themselves and to celebrate the event —and so lose the advantage of the acquired momentum. After routing the enemy the thing to do is to pursue him, not to hold a feast.[22]

And also:

Stopping to look at one's self means loss of momentum, and in the race of life it is at any given time momentum more than distance that yields the reckoning; for in the things of the spirit it is tension and quality not weight and quantity that count. The leading runner in the dash dare not turn to watch his antagonist without periling the victory.[23]

In this life of hard work and of personal independence, the virtue of patience is to control in comprehensiveness of vision, of wisdom and of interpretation. He says:

[21] *Ibid.,* pp. 67-68.   [22] *Ibid.,* p. 49.   [23] *Ibid.,* p. 51.

In terms of the total result you will find that the patient doing of duty will count more than the brilliant strokes of wit. It is patience, patience, and yet again more patience that you will need; for your life is one long account, and you must give compound interest time in which to do its perfect work. . . . I tell you it is patience you will need; patience to do the little things thoroughly and well; patience to keep you digging on your own claim, to keep you at work on what comes next to your hand, to keep you from skipping over to glittering deceits beyond; patience to hold you to the gaining of results by processes that naturally produce them, and the winning of success by the plain and simple deserving of it.[24]

To all such counsels to both matriculating freshmen, graduating seniors, as well as to continuing students, a spice of wit is often added. As says the Spanish proverb, "in many a counsel he put in a 'bit of salt.' " To the freshmen in the opening of the year 1904-05 he says:

Some people are born prominent, some have prominence thrust upon them, but pray take my advice, and if you were born prominent, try to hold destiny in check during your freshman year. In general, keep your eyes as open as possible, and your mouth as shut as possible. Do not, however, take what I have said as an excuse for isolating yourself from the University life or moping in a corner.[25]

To his associates of state universities at their meeting of 1915, he says in his playfulness, "Agriculture

[24] *Ibid.*, pp. 53-54.　　　　[25] *Ibid.*, pp. 80-81.

leaves the door open and lets the cold air in, and, presenting a cheese or some other real thing as a thesis, brings pain to the metaphysicians." [26] Also, "I suppose that the spiritual university as set down in the New Jerusalem will have no Board of Regents —and for that matter, presumably no president." [27]

In the diverse and complete life which Benjamin Ide Wheeler was called on to lead, there is one principle which is fixed and permanent. It is his belief in a devotion to religion. In the rich manhood which was his it is the Christian purpose which dominates. In the many contributions which he makes to scholarship, it is the religious spirit which is felt as a permeating atmosphere. He did his work and lived his life as if he were ever in his "great Task Master's eye." "There is a truth and there is a lie; there is a right and there is a wrong; somewhere in the moral universe of God there is a heaven and there is a hell; there is a light and there is a blackness of darkness; the university casts in its lot with the light." [28]

The last words he spoke in farewell as president were a prayer. "May the blessing of the Almighty descend upon this University and abide within it. Amen." [29]

[26] *Ibid.,* p. 122.
[27] *Ibid.,* p. 127.
[28] *Ibid.,* p. 148.
[29] *Ibid.,* p. 75.

XXVIII
WOODROW WILSON

Born Staunton, Va., Dec. 28, 1856, of Scotch-Irish ancestry on both sides; died February 3, 1924; Davidson College, N. C., 1874-75; A.B., Princeton, 1879, A.M., 1882; grad. in law, U. of Va., 1881; practiced law at Atlanta, Ga., 1882-83; post-grad. work at Johns Hopkins, 1883-85, Ph.D., 1886. Associate professor of history and political economy, Bryn Mawr College, 1885-88; professor of same, Wesleyan University, 1888-90; professor of jurisprudence and political economy, 1890-95, professor of jurisprudence, 1895-97, professor of jurisprudence and politics, 1897-1910, president, August 1, 1902-October 20, 1910, of Princeton University; governor of N. J., 1911-13 (resigned); elected President, 1912, for term, 1913-1917, receiving 435 electoral votes; reëlected, 1916, for term, 1917-21. Left for France Dec. 4, 1918, at the head of American Commission to Negotiate Peace; arrived at Paris, Dec. 14; visited England, Italy; returned to U. S., arriving in Boston, Feb. 24, 1919; left New York on second trip to Europe, Mar. 5, arrived in Paris, Mar. 14; signed Peace Treaty, June 28, 1919; returned to U. S., July 8, 1919.

Author: Congressional Government, a Study in American Politics; The State—Elements of Historical and Practical Politics; Division and Reunion; An Old Master and Other Political Essays; Mere Literature, and Other Essays; George Washington; A History of the American People; Constitutional Government in the United States; The State-Elements of Historical and Practical Politics; Free Life; The New Freedom; When a Man Comes to Himself; On Being Human; also many addresses.

WOODROW WILSON

COLLEGE PRESIDENT

To the office of the college president Wilson brought noble resources and valiant forces. He brought an intellect rich in its disciplined powers, clear in its perceptions, logical in its processes of reasoning, gifted with the power of rational appeal, an imagination fertile and chaste, a taste based on the classical standards and aspiring unto the highest ideals, a will strong in its determinations, persistent in its processes and lasting in its impulses, a heart in which the will seemed to have a power quite as great as the emotions themselves, and a conscience which to itself was as commanding as Kant's categorical imperative. His was a personality in which self-respect was dominant, and in which a sense of victoriousness seemed to be masterful, or in which a certain masterfulness gave assurance of victory. Persuasiveness, too, was a constructive element. It was a personality vigorous yet self-controlled, warmly attaching certain personalities to itself, yet repelling other personalities quite as strongly. It was a personality in which contrasts fundamental, elemental and superficial prevailed.

Of all men, his contemporaries, engaged in public service the world over, I find no one who better illustrates the contrasts found in his character and career than Lord Curzon. Earl Ronaldshay, his biographer, writes thus of Curzon: "What gave to his personality its peculiar interest was its amazing contradictions and perversities. What more perplexing paradox could be imagined than that presented by the pomposity and the simplicity, the aloofness and the sociability, the broad-mindedness and the intolerance, the generosity and the pettiness, the exuberant affections and the implacable hates, the contemptuous arrogance and the strange humbleness of heart of this incalculable man?"[1] The contrasts which Ronaldshay notes in Curzon are not the contrasts which inhere in Wilson, but the fact of contrasts is equally dominant and evident in each man.

It was a uniquely rich preparation which Wilson had for a college presidency. Each element and force in his early life, education and training, as now seen in retrospect, was of highest worth. To the Princeton professorship he came from a life of pecuniary narrowness, personal and domestic, from constant disciplines, from hard work, from anxieties of the classroom and of the home, and from ambitions partly realized and partly unfulfilled. It was a great preparation for a great professorship in a great, historic college. Success had not weakened, nor had doubt or

[1] *The Life of Lord Curzon,* by the Rt. Hon. Earl of Ronaldshay, Vol. III, p. 384.

failure discouraged, him. He was virile, valiant, hopeful. The separate elements of such a preparation are evident. His undergraduate career—a student more or less lonely—in the sturdy North Carolina college, Davidson, the continuation of this career at McCosh's Princeton, his professional studies of law at the University of Virginia, and his graduate work in Johns Hopkins, all contributed to make a noble background and a strong force which only one student in a thousand can afford. Such opportunities for learning, for training, and for friendship were and are unique. His professorship, too, of three years at Bryn Mawr, of two years at Wesleyan, greatly prepared him indeed for his professorship of twelve years at Princeton.

His professorship, from 1890 to 1902, at Princeton, was also in its turn a noble preparation for a unique presidency. To learning abundant and diverse, he added the quality of inspiring students, both as a lecturer and as a teacher. To inspiration he added a sense of fellowship with undergraduates. His sympathy with them in their sports is a type of undergraduate feeling which ever appeals, not simply to the eleven and to the nine, but also to the whole student body. For instance, he coached in a dark season the Princeton eleven for no less a period than ten weeks. Year after year in the student poll he was voted as the most popular of all professors. He was one with the students, in mind and heart.

The oneness of Wilson with his students is only a

type and symbol of his intimacy with his fellow
teachers. Early he became a leader among the members of the progressive party of the faculty. For in
the first years of the 'nineties the progressive element among Princeton professors had its beginning.
The conservatives also were active. The progressives
were emerging as a vitalizing force, yet what they
called the dead hand still ruled. The want of vision,
the allegiance to, and the unquestioning belief in, the
old yet dominated. Wilson, as a progressive, felt the
power of the conservative force. He knew his antagonists of the faculty and he did not fail to recognize
the power of their opposition. Rifts and divisions
were soon to appear as cardinal and destroying
antagonisms.

Associated with the formal life of a professor was
an intimate fellowship of friends without as well as
within the academic walls. It was all a part of the
best life of the best people in one of the best of academic cloisters. Women, too, as well as college professors, were associated in close fellowship.

In all respects, personal, professorial, by associations of travel, by broad knowledge, Wilson seemed
fitted, gloriously fitted, to serve in the great office of
the presidency of Princeton.

It should also be said that the conditions at Princeton were nothing less than ideal for the incoming of
a president such as Wilson promised to be. For the
college was prepared for a progressive administrator.
Patton had been its president for fourteen years,

1888 to 1902. While president and professor Patton
was recognized and is still recognized as being one
of the most acute of philosophers. His mind is of the
metaphysical and theological type. His intellect is analytical, discriminating, profound. Its method of working was and is the method of Aristotle. But it was not
a mind of the executive type. Patton belonged to the
understanding intellect and not to the executive will.
Therefore, at the close of his term, Princeton was
prepared for a change in its government and control,
and in its administrative atmospheres.

The whole academic world, too, was ready to give
welcome to Princeton as a companion of Harvard in
the progressiveness of the educational movement.
Eliot was nearing the close of his great term of forty
years. But its enlarging power was yet dominant.
Johns Hopkins was still leading the higher scholarship. The heart of the higher education was beating
hard and fast for the incoming of a noble and progressive type of academic administration at the historic college of Princeton.

All elements, therefore, seemed to unite in and to
contribute for an administration under Wilson as its
leader unto the realization of well-founded and highest hopes, unto academic happiness, advancement and
achievement. A contribution to the progress of the
commonwealth of scholarship and of the higher learning seemed to be well assured. The prospect was filled
with a sense of rational hopefulness for richest results. Far more certain was it that these results

would be won than was the prospect which greeted
Eliot at the beginning of his presidency a third of a
century earlier.

Wilson moreover brought to the office of the college
president an understanding, large, wise, and sound,
of the place and function of the American college.
This understanding was unfolded in much fullness
and with great charm in an address given before the
Phi Beta Kappa chapter of Harvard University in
1909. Its subject was "The Spirit of Learning." One
does well to make liberal quotations. He says, "We
must re-examine the college, reconceive it, reorganize
it. It is the root of our intellectual life as a nation.
It is not only the instrumentality through which we
must effect all the broad preliminary work which un-
derlies sound scholarship; it is also our chief instrumentality of catholic enlightenment, our chief means
for giving widespread stimulation to the whole intellectual life of the country and supplying ourselves
with men who shall both comprehend their age and
duty and know how to serve them supremely well.
Without the American college our young men would
be too exclusively shut in to the pursuit of individual
interests, would lose the vital contact and emulations
which awaken them to those larger achievements and
sacrifices which are the highest objects of education in
a country of free citizens, where the welfare of the
commonwealth springs out of the character and the
informed purposes of the private citizen. The college
will be found to lie somewhere very near the heart of

American social training and intellectual and moral enlightenment." [2] "What we should seek to impart in our colleges, therefore, is not so much learning itself as the spirit of learning. You can impart that to young men; and you can impart it to them in the three or four years at your disposal. It consists in the power to distinguish good reasoning from bad, in the power to digest and interpret evidence, in a habit of catholic observation and a preference for the non-partisan point of view, in an addiction to clear and logical processes of thought and yet an instinctive desire to interpret rather than to stick in the letter of the reasoning, in a taste for knowledge and a deep respect for the integrity of the human mind." [3] "It is the duty of university authorities to make of the college a society, of which the teacher will be as much, and as naturally, a member as the undergraduate. When that is done other things will fall into their natural places, their natural relations. Young men are capable of great enthusiasms for older men whom they have learned to know in some human, unarti-ficial way, whose quality they have tasted in uncon-strained conversation, the energy and beauty of whose characters and aims they have learned to appreciate by personal contact; and such enthusiasms are often among the strongest and most lasting influences of their lives." [4] "My plea, then, is this: that we now

[2] *Representative Phi Beta Kappa Orations,* edited by Clark S. Northup, William C. Lane, John C. Schwab, pp. 468-469.
[3] *Ibid.,* p. 472.   [4] *Ibid.,* p. 478.

deliberately set ourselves to make a home for the spirit of learning: that we reorganize our colleges on the lines of this simple conception, that a college is not only a body of studies but a mode of association; that its courses are only its formal side, its contacts and contagions its realities. It must become a community of scholars and pupils,—a free community but a very real one, in which democracy may work its reasonable triumphs of accommodations; its vital processes of union.'' [5]

Under conditions wholly different from the Harvard Phi Beta Kappa address, in an address made at a momentous crisis, at the University of Paris, in December, 1921, Wilson also clearly and beautifully says of a liberal education as ''reminiscent of the high traditions of men, reminiscent of all those struggles, some of them obscure but others clearly revealed to the historian, of men of indomitable spirit everywhere struggling toward the right and seeking above all things else to be free.'' [6]

Above the minor purposes, above the secondary methods, above all lesser conditions, stand forth three supreme purposes which moved Wilson in his presidency at Princeton. Chosen president at the commencement of 1902, he resigned the office in 1910. These eight years were concerned chiefly with three movements, movements which have become both historic and historical. First, the installation of the pre-

[5] *Ibid.*, pp. 479-480.
[6] *The Messages and Papers of Woodrow Wilson*, Vol. I. With editorial notes and introduction by Albert Shaw, p. 577.

ceptorial system; second, the development of the graduate school; and third, a reformation of the social life of the undergraduates, an attempt to transform social clubs into democratic associations or colleges.

In the installation of the preceptorial system Wilson won a great victory, not only for Princeton but also for every university and college. In the discussion regarding the graduate school, debate came to center largely about the location of the principal building, although other elements were included. In this endeavor Wilson suffered defeat. The location finally chosen was one which the dean of the school, West, approved and promoted. In the matter also of the transformation or reorganization of the social life, he was partly victorious and partly defeated. This campaign, however—for it was hardly less than a long-continued war—was renewed from time to time. The debate still goes on, even at the close of his successor's term of twenty years.

The consideration of these three movements was not confined to trustees or to faculty, but was taken up by all who had special relationship to Princeton, students and graduates, by other colleges and indeed by multitudes interested in the progress of liberal learning and in academic administration. The debates were noted for their academic antagonisms, for the separations and divisions of participants who had been intimate and long-time friends, and they were also surrounded and pervaded by atmospheres of hatred and bitterness.

The details of all these ordeals are set forth in the

official life of Wilson by Ray Stannard Baker. It would be vain to seek to reinterpret. But it is not vain to ask what were either the primary or the superficial causes of this divisive, disintegrating, disorganizing, destructive academic storm, the effects of which are still visible, audible, and seem to be lasting.

The causes seem to me to be at least threefold. First, Wilson had the capacity of intense love and equally intense hatred; second, Wilson's mood and character lacked conciliatoriness; third, Wilson also lacked patience in administration.

Regarding the first quality of intense emotionalism, he himself recognized its strength and its weakness. There were friends, like Cleveland Dodge, who were attached to him and to whom he was attached with a devotion which belongs to few. He also was capable of great antagonisms, as is made evident in what is known as the "Pittsburgh speech" and other addresses. The Pittsburgh speech was an address to the Princeton Club of western Pennsylvania given in 1910. It has been called a "scathing" address, an unloosing of "his wrath." He struck at his academic enemies and other foes in terms which a college president, addressing his alumni and his fellow-graduates, should not use.[7]

[7] "As he wrote to Isaac H. Lionberger:
"'I hope—and believe—that the men who *heard* my Pittsburgh speech did not misunderstand, but in my deep excitement, I did not stop to think of how it would sound in the newspapers. I should have done so. Without interpretation, what I said about Lincoln is crude and badly reasoned.

Such emotionalism was also shown in his lack of a conciliative mood in administration. "Drastic," "dictatorial," were epithets which in certain periods of his career he seemed to deserve. Houston, however, after eight years of service in his cabinet, affirms he did not find him "dictatorial." Wilson once wrote the chairman of a committee of the Princeton trustees, "As long as I am president of Princeton I propose to dictate the architectural policy of the university." [8] Toward the close of his career at Princeton, he wrote, "We have no compromises to look back on, the record of our consciences is clear in this whole trying business. We can be happy, therefore, no matter what may come of it all. It would be rather jolly, after all, to start out on life anew together, to make a new career, would it not? Experience deepens with us . . . and with experience love, and I thank God with all my heart!" [9] His friend, and an interpreter of rare wisdom, Albert Shaw, interprets him as "uncompromising." In the controversy on the graduate school, Wilson wrote of the embarrassing position of the majority of a committee being obliged to coöperate

[7] "'I spoke too soon after a meeting of the Trustees at which the majority vote seemed to me to create an impossible situation; but that is only an explanation of my stupid blunder, not an excuse for it. I shall try to remedy the mistake when I can,—not by way of explanation, but by more just exposition of the matter.' (April 28, 1910.)" *Woodrow Wilson, Life and Letters—Princeton 1890-1910*, by Ray Stannard Baker, p. 341.
[8] *Ibid.*, p. 175.
[9] *Ibid.*, pp. 330-331.

with the minority of its membership. His convictions seemed absolute. As Dean Fine has said, ''They seemed to have for him the authority of objective unquestioned truths. It was apparently impossible for him to make allowance for the elements of doubt and uncertainty in the convictions of men in general.'' [10] He was indeed, as he said, the ''indomitable'' individual but not the ''defiant'' and ''impractical'' one.

In the large vision, made larger by the passing of time, it has become evident that the bitter divisions and deep antagonisms of the hour were not necessary. A spirit of conciliation could, should, and would have avoided them. A just appreciation of scholastic and of administrative values would have brought reconciliations and triumphs for great causes. The lack of conciliation resulted in a lack of coöperation and the lack of coöperation created disintegration. For, and with strongest emphasis be it said, every college president should find satisfaction in working with those who are in certain respects opposed to him or to his policies. He is to have those elements and qualities which Matthew Arnold attributes to Falkland, in his noble essay on the great martyr, sweetness and light, lucidity of mind, and largeness of temper.

Quite akin to the want of conciliatoriness, there was in Wilson also a lack of patience. He was unwilling to wait for conclusions. As his biographer says, ''He was too impatient with dullness; he was so swift

[10] *Ibid.,* p. 238.

and clear in his own mental processes that he did not explain enough; and half measures—'feeble passes'—irritated him sharply." [11] The virtue of patience, I heard President Eliot say at the close of his great career of forty years, was the chief excellence of his administration. Henry James in his biography of Eliot says that as presiding officer of the faculty "he tolerated wandering talk with a serenity that frequently exasperated everybody else except the talker. Years before he had remarked that a faculty 'is a ruminating animal; chewing a cud a long time, slowly bringing it into a digestible condition'; and that 'progress comes mainly from the Faculties' was what he said in the Inaugural. Everybody must be patient. What if the animal did sometimes stop chewing the cud and go a-wandering?" [12] This virtue and grace did not belong to Woodrow Wilson. It was said of him that "he drives too hard." "He was too intense"; he condemned the "human intractables" who restrained him. Near the close of his academic career he wrote, in the commencement season of 1910, "I do not feel that the fight here is hopeless. On the contrary, I think that a good deal has already been gained and that perhaps all that is necessary is a steady pressure, pressure, pressure in the right direction. That, after all, is the way in which all reforms are accomplished, and it seems to me the business of all men now interested in Princeton to see to it that the right sort of opinion is created and increased and

[11] *Ibid.,* p. 248.
[12] *Charles W. Eliot,* by Henry James, Vol. I, p. 305.

reinforced.''[13] Such sentiments he failed to make concrete. He neglected to put them into practice. He wished to hurry processes. He did not interpret college administration under the metaphors of biology. He preferred the metaphors of physics. Growth requires time; making things demands no, or only brief, time. He sought for swift achievement, and at heavy costs, terribly heavy costs. He was unwilling to wait for richest achievement through human and therefore slow processes.

These three elements of his character are consistent with the three forces which Henry White, his associate in the Peace Conference of 1922, says were the causes of his failure at that conference. ''Of course he failed most unfortunately at the Conference because (1) he does not know how to deal with men; (2) he has no idea of team-work, i.e., of how to devolve work on others and get them to work with him and each other; and (3) because he is a one-idea man, and thought the League of Nations would be the sovereign panacea for the world's tragedy.''[14]

Wilson's emotionalism, his lack of the spirit of conciliativeness, and his want of patience prevented him from knowing how to deal with men, as White intimates; they blocked his joining in team-work; and they also promoted his singleness of aim and of method.

[13] *Woodrow Wilson, Life and Letters*, by Ray Stannard Baker, p. 352.
[14] *Henry White, Thirty Years of American Diplomacy*, by Allan Nevins, p. 487.

But be it added there are other associates, some of whom knew him intimately and were personal friends, who found in him an element or elements still more fundamental than those to which I thus allude. They affirm that there was in him the element of selfishness. This element, they declare, was structural and comprehensive. Such selfishness, they affirm, was a primary weakness in his ethical and intellectual character. It was a disintegrating force. There are those indeed who believe that the good of Princeton University throughout his administration was not his supreme, dominant purpose. They further affirm, indeed, these intimate friends and long-time associates, that he was "ethically unsound" and "intellectually dishonest." Another friend, however, has said to me that after five years of almost daily co-working, he found Wilson "stiffly honest."

In considering interpretations so fundamental and so diverse I want to make certain remarks that may possibly help to explain. First, Wilson was a dreamer. He thought in terms of the imagination. His projects often seemed to him to be achievements; and his prophecies as historical. The visions of the future he brought into the present. Second, he was placed in the midst of complex conditions. Privately, he once said that he doubted the truthfulness of a method of interpretation of complex conditions by a simple method or process. Such a method resulted, he added, in either obscurity or untruthfulness. It promoted at least misunderstanding. Third, he failed to see things in relationships. He lacked the sense of proportional values. The location of a building of the Princeton Graduate School seemed to him as important as a fundamental principle of academic instruction. Fourth, the high cost of the Graduate School building seemed to him exorbitant, as it probably was. The cost of each individual room, as proposed, was from five to six times the cost of such a building built under fairly economic conditions. Fifth, with all these interpretations of causes and conditions of failure should be linked a further remark—ill-health. For his constitution was not robust. His temperament was of the nervous type. He usually worked his brain beyond the strength of the body to sustain hardest toil. In 1896, in 1899, in 1908 he broke down from overwork. In 1906 the doctors told him that he had hardening of the arteries and that henceforth he was to "live a quiet and retired life." [15] His life came to its end as a result of constant over-stress and over-strain. No man of his type could do, could endure what he attempted and suffered, without the causes for which he labored either coming to failure or he himself breaking under the strain. Some causes for which he labored succeeded; some failed. The great cause for which he labored in the final years is still unachieved. But its achievement does give, in the thought of most, either of gladness or of regret, a promised triumph. His own health failed—and the end came.

[15] *Woodrow Wilson, Life and Letters,* by Ray Stannard Baker, p. 201.

These five remarks seem to me to suggest conditions which promoted misrepresentations, which intimate causes of charges and recriminations, which, once launched, became larger and larger, which increased bitterness, and which gave a basis for judgments of selfishness, of moral weakness and unsoundness. These conclusions, sad though they are, are to me inevitable.

The presidency of Wilson at Princeton is to be contrasted with the presidencies of two predecessors, and also with the presidencies of two other great administrators, Eliot of Harvard, and Hutchins of Michigan.

The presidency of Wilson at Princeton was fundamentally unlike and fundamentally like the term of John Witherspoon. Wilson's Princeton service covered a period of eight years firmly set apart. It was distinct and individualistic. It was followed by the individualistic service as governor of New Jersey, and also as President. The individualistic political terms followed the academic. The term of John Witherspoon as president of Princeton was not a term set apart; it was a period contemporary and coöperative with his work as a statesman in the critical years preceding the Revolution, and also with the more critical years following. He was called the "absentee president." But though absent from Princeton, he was still her president while serving in Congress and in the Constitutional Convention. He was among the greatest both in the political and in the academic realm.

A second president of Princeton to be compared or contrasted with Wilson was James McCosh. McCosh's term from 1868 to 1888 was formative and reformative. Of it his successor, Patton, said in a memorial address, ''Beyond all question his was the most brilliant administration that Princeton has ever had. Everything contributed to add to the glory of that administration: the circumstances attending the Doctor's coming, the condition of the College when he came, what he was, and what he did. He found Princeton depleted by the war, yet already awakening to a new life. The money necessary for her equipment was ready and he came in time to give wise direction to its use. He brought to the service of the College a high reputation as a thinker, a commanding personality, and ripe experience as an educator: and with a purpose that was never daunted he bent himself to the task of making Princeton one of the foremost seats of learning in America.''[16] And again, ''As President of Princeton College he was enthusiastic, vigilant, and wise. He loved the College. He loved his pupils. He had the rare gift of being able to kindle and keep alive in others that zeal for philosophy which was so characteristic of himself. He was hospitable to new ideas, yet zealous also for the maintenance of the great Christian verities that are woven into the entire web of our College history.''[17]

[16] *Princeton College Bulletin,* Vol. VII, February, 1895, McCosh Memorial Number, p. 1.
[17] *Ibid.,* p. 1.

In comparison or contrast with the feeling of Princeton students toward Wilson, I want to quote a sonnet which Robert Bridges wrote at the time of McCosh's death:—

Young to the end, through sympathy with youth,
Gray man of learning! champion of truth!
Direct in rugged speech, alert in mind,
He felt his kinship with all human kind,
And never feared to trace development
Of high from low—assured and full content
That man paid homage to the Mind above,
Uplifted by the "Royal Law of Love."

The laws of nature that he loved to trace
Have worked, at last, to veil from us his face;
The dear old elms and ivy-covered walls
Will miss his presence, and the stately halls
His trumpet-voice. While in their joys
Sorrow will shadow those he called "my boys." [18]

Covering the eight years of Wilson's presidency and many more was the presidency of Eliot of Harvard. At the close of his term of two score years Eliot wrote to Edward Everett Hale saying that the "best fruits of my forty years' work" are:

"I. The re-organization and ample endowment of the Medical School.

"II. The re-making of the Law School under Langdell.

"III. The re-building of the Divinity School on a

[18] *Ibid.,* opposite portrait at beginning.

scientific basis with a Faculty containing members of several denominations.

"IV. The establishment of religious services on a voluntary basis under a board of preachers representing several denominations.

"V. The requiring of a previous degree for admission to all the professional schools except the Dental School, which is moving in the same direction.

"VI. The administration of the University as a unified group of departments—one undergraduate department and many graduate schools.

"VII. The perfecting of the elective system as a system.

"VIII. The increase of the endowments and of the number of students, due to the confidence of the public in the financial and educational management of the University during a period of remarkable development in the wealth of the nation.

"IX. The remarkable rise in the scholarly quality of the men appointed to teach in the University." [19]

Of President Hutchins of the University of Michigan, Earl D. Babst, an alumnus of the University, at a memorial service for Dr. Hutchins, said, "Of a multitude of side lights that touch Dr. Hutchins as he was seen and beloved by the alumni, I can mention only a few: his considerate and affectionate regard for 'Prexy' Angell; his whole-hearted devotion to his task; his singleness of purpose; his dignified common-man attitude; his refusal to be made a per-

[19] *Charles W. Eliot*, by Henry James. Vol. II, pp. 170-171.

sonage; his gifts of common sense, courtliness, and
firmness; his great respect for himself and for others
who were entitled to respect; his talent in exploring
ideas and fitting them into the pattern of his own
plans; his skill in attracting able men to his policies;
his methodical manner of curing administrative weaknesses; his unwillingness to make concessions to cheap
popularity; his ability to bring clashing interests into
harmonious action; his willingness to appear at Lan-
sing and to spend hour after hour in conference with
legislators, without loss of dignity or of influence;
his wisdom in dealing with the people of the State
and in avoiding entangling alliances; his early diffidence about his talents as a speaker and his later
confidence and effectiveness; his tireless energy in the
alumni cause; his arduous labors in visiting alumni
associations from coast to coast and calling on alumni
personally at every opportunity; his gift of remem-
bering names and of making the local associations
feel proud of his personal interest in their progress;
his assumption that the alumni were seriously interested in hearing about the intellectual and educational
progress of the University resulting everywhere in a
more earnest alumni attitude; the deep respect in
which he was held by his old law students; his reten-
tion of his undergraduate associations, even to the
extent of presiding as national president over his college fraternity; his modesty and reluctance about
accepting office, even for a limited term, though
judged by his personality and achievements he is

now acclaimed as a great university president, the success of whose administration looms larger in retrospect; his effacement of himself so that his successor might win his place of confidence and affection; and, lastly, the combination of talents and qualities, and their development while in office, which made his administration a fitting culmination of an exceedingly useful life."[20]

The similarities and the contrasts of Wilson's service as a college president with the service of Witherspoon and of McCosh, and also with the service of Eliot and of Hutchins, are deep, significant and impressive.

It may not be unfitting to point out that as the first years of Wilson's Princeton's presidency were characterized by the coöperation of academic forces, and by the happiness of Wilson's colleagues, so likewise the first years of his national presidency were marked by the co-working of the legislative and executive departments. Likewise, further, as the last years of the Princeton presidency were distinguished by discord, controversy, and division, so too the last two years of the national presidency were characterized by acrimony, bitterness, hostilities both personal and official. The similarities are strangely alike. Character, indeed, seems to be permanent under all ethical environments, in the midst of all administrative conditions, and in all intellectual climates.

[20] University of Michigan Official Publication, September 27, 1930. *In Memoriam Harry Burns Hutchins*, p. 17.

Therefore, by reason of these three elements, a college administration which should have resulted in structural, formative, whole and wholesome achievements became a partial failure. But it should also be said that under such conditions, such failure, finally resulted in a triumph and in a triumph of a wholly different nature from the academic conclusion. The way of escape from the impossible condition prevailing in the presidency of Princeton was found in the governorship of New Jersey. The governorship of New Jersey led to the Presidency of the United States. The eight years of the Princeton presidency finally lifted Woodrow Wilson into the national Presidency, also of eight years; and this Presidency transformed him into a force and personality of the world.

XXIX

DAVID STARR JORDAN

BORN Gainesville, N. Y., January 19, 1851; died September 19, 1931. M.S., Cornell, 1872; M.D., Indiana Medical College, 1875; Ph.D., Butler University, 1878; LL.D., Cornell, 1886, Johns Hopkins, 1902; Illinois College, 1903; Indiana University, 1909; University of California, 1913. Instructor in botany, Cornell, 1871-72; professor of natural history, Lombard University, 1872-83; professor of biology, Butler University, 1875-79; professor of zoölogy, 1879-85, president, 1885-91, Indiana University; president of Stanford, 1891-1913; chancellor, 1913-16. U. S. commissioner in charge of fur seal and salmon investigations; international commissioner of fisheries, 1908-10. Director of World Peace Foundation, 1910-14; president of World's Peace Congress, 1915; v.-p. of American Peace Society.

Author: Manual of Vertebrate Animals of Northern United States; Science Sketches; Fishes of North and Middle America (with B. W. Evermann); Care and Culture of Men; The Innumerable Company; Footnotes to Evolution; The Story of Matka; Book of Knight and Barbara; Imperial Democracy; The Strength of Being Clean; Standeth God Within the Shadow; Animal Life; The Philosophy of Hope; The Blood of the Nation; Voice of the Scholar; A Guide to the Study of Fishes; The Human Harvest; College and the Man; The Higher Sacrifice; The Religion of a Sensible American; The Stability of Truth; Unseen Empire; War and Waste; World Peace and the College Man; War and the Breed; Ways to Lasting Peace; Democracy and World Relations; The Days of a Man, 2 vols., and many others.

XXIX

DAVID STARR JORDAN

FOUNDER, PRESIDENT, SCIENTIST

DAVID STARR JORDAN was one of the great college presidents in an age great in presidents. It was the age of Eliot, of White of Cornell, of Gilman of Johns Hopkins, of Angell of Michigan, of Hadley of Yale, of Northrop of Minnesota, of Harper of Chicago, of Tucker of Dartmouth, and of Wheeler of California. Among them all stands forth Jordan.

Jordan also goes into academic and other history as the first president of Stanford University. But he was not only the first president. He was also in a sense the founder, or at least the co-founder, and, moreover, he was a saviour of the University.

Jordan's work at Stanford for twenty-five years bore the elements of his undergraduate career. He graduated at Cornell in 1872. In this career Andrew D. White had great influence. The nomination by White after his own declining was the exciting cause of the appointment by the Stanfords of Jordan as president. Following his graduation Jordan served as a teacher at no less than six institutions, including

439

high schools and the University of Indiana. While
serving as president at Indiana he was appointed to
the presidency of the newly organized university in
California. This appointment he heartily welcomed.
For, as he says, the educational ideals of Senator
Stanford "corresponded very closely with my own."
But his acceptance of the appointment and his entrance into the great opportunity was soon beset with all
manner of difficulties, legal, administrative, financial,
personal. Though the endowment which the Stanfords
had proposed to give to the university was supposed to
amount to no less than thirty millions of dollars, yet
debts, legacies, and defects in the charter granted by
California, and above all the suit of the United States,
brought the whole fortune into the peril of bank-
ruptcy, and the whole endeavor into the danger of
absolute collapse. Regarding this suit, Jordan himself
has said, "Near the end of the year (1893) the
United States, in the name of the Attorney General,
brought suit of the nature of an injunction to prevent distribution of the Stanford estate until $15,-
000,000, Stanford's share of the debt of $27,000,000
(now risen to $60,000,000 from accumulation of in-
terest) originally borrowed from the Government by
the Central Pacific Railway Company, should mature
and be paid. . . . Concerning the whole matter there
was much misunderstanding as well as wanton mis-
representation."[1] This suit, decided after three

[1] *The Days of a Man,* by David Starr Jordan. Vol. I, pp.
499-500.

years, in 1896, in favor of the University, ended the largest share of all the difficulties.

Throughout this long period of six years beset with obstructions of almost every nature, several heroes emerge. Perhaps the first of the little company is Mrs. Stanford herself, who gave herself and was willing to give all her possessions. With her stood Jordan, himself deserving a place, which if not first was assuredly next to the first. For if Jordan was the second, Mrs. Stanford's heroism would have proved unavailing without Jordan's endurance, and Jordan's endurance would have proved unavailing without her heroism. Mrs. Stanford's heroic sacrifice, evidenced for instance in her eagerness to sell her jewels of one-half a million value for the salvation of the university, would have been futile without the vision and the strength of the president. Mrs. Stanford and Jordan were the saviours of the university. The whole endeavor was characterized by forbearance, good feeling, patience, forcefulness, unity, the love of learning, and by the highest idealism.

The principles on which the university was founded and was administered for the twenty-five years of Jordan's presidency and chancellorship are well versed in his brief and weighty inaugural:

"The higher education should bring men into direct contact with truth. It should help to free them from the dead hands of old traditions and to enable them to form opinions worthy of the new evidence each new day brings before them. An edu-

cated man should not be the slave of the past, not a
copy of men who have gone before him. He must be
in some degree the founder of a new intellectual
dynasty; for each new thinker is a new type of man.
Whatever is true is the truest thing in the universe,
and mental and moral strength alike come from our
contact with it. We may teach the value of truth to
our students by showing that we value it ourselves.
. . . And above and beyond all learning is the influence of character, the impulse to virtue and piety
which comes from men whose lives show that virtue
and piety really exist. . . . Every advance which
we make toward the realization of the truth of the
permanence and immanence of law, brings us nearer
to Him who is the First Cause of all law and all
phenomena.'' [2]

Though his service as president of Stanford University is perhaps the most lasting and definite contribution to the world's betterment which Jordan
made: yet there are two other fields which are not
to be passed over in even a brief appreciation. These
fields are zoölogy and international peace. Diverse as
zoölogy and international peace may seem to be, yet
they have a common meeting point. That point is life
itself; its origin, continuance, preservation. A wise
interpreter once said to me that Jordan's place in
zoölogy was greater than his place as president. His
zoölogical field consisted largely of fishes, and fishes,
too, of many waters and many varieties. His re-

[2] *Ibid.*, pp. 688–690.

searches carried him far afield—from Japan, through Hawaii to Samoa. His publications, too, numerous and weighty, have lasting value. A fellow scientist says:

"Dr. Jordan was a real naturalist. He knew the animals and plants of the old farm on which he was brought up, and those of every region in which he later lived; not only the fishes (his first and abiding interest), but the birds, mammals, reptiles, amphibians, mollusks, crustaceans, lichens and the algæ not only of the fresh waters and damp places but of the sea as well." [3]

It is simply a continuation of Jordan's interest in life to say that he was among the most ardent of the apostles of peace among the nations. He was a member of the original board of directors of the Ginn Peace Foundation, and under its auspices he traveled far and much. He also wrote great tracts for the cause. In a confession of faith which he made for the students' paper of Stanford, he said that "fair play between men and between nations" is one of the three things that seemed to him "all-important." The other two were "clean living" and "sound education."

The great cause of peace was perhaps the most comprehensive of all his human interests. Writing in his autobiography and referring to the Peloponnesian Wars as leaving only cowards in Greece, he says, "The same story in one form or another has been repeated

[3] Article by Dr. Barton Warren Evermann, *Science,* October 2, 1931, pp. 327-329.

by all the civilized nations. For two thousand years this has been the most terrible fact in the history of Europe, the hidden cause of the downfall of empires, the basis of the problems of the slums, the basal cause of apathy, inefficiency, sterility, and the 'drooping spirit' of modern Europe. This matter needs most thorough and accurate investigation, and no scientific problem of the day surpasses it in interest and importance." [4]

Great as was Jordan's work as president, as a scientist, and as an apostle of international peace, yet his manhood was greater and was structural in noble human forces. One can almost change Emerson's remark to read that what you do is as nothing to what you are.

The power and achievement of Jordan in Stanford University came forth, as in the case of every great president, from his own personality. This personality had certain deep formative characteristics. For in Jordan was embodied a mighty sense of reality. The artificial seemed to have no relation to him. He belonged to the race of the rugged ones as the mountains belong to the landscape. In him was forcefulness, quiet indeed, but the quietness still evident in the midst of the manifestation of power. If quiet, this forcefulness was also persistent. In him was found the scientist's desire for facts, united with the philosopher's will to point out the significance of these facts

[4] *The Days of a Man,* by David Starr Jordan. Vol. II, p. 341.

and to reason about them. With a sense of self-complacency which he had a right to possess more fully than most men, was united a deep sense of humility. For he measured himself by the noblest and highest standards. At a comparatively early age he found his place in the universe and he never lost this appreciation. Like most achieving lives he was transparent and also he was translucent. He attained unto a sense of relations, seeing the great as great and the small as small. He lived both for the day and for the lasting tomorrow. An optimist, he saw the best in the better, the better in the good, and the good in things which were apparently evil. Freedom was his native air. Strong in himself, he was an apostle of democracy political, and also an embodiment of democracy social. Native to him there seemed to be a certain essential strength which the witnesses declare was characteristic of Daniel Webster. He himself testifies that one of his great works was his work as a teacher. Such interpretation was natural. For in him was found the teacher's altruism, and also the teacher's desire not only to convey knowledge, but to give one's self in giving knowledge.

In two respects his influence as an educationalist was fundamental. The first element refers to method. With Eliot he believed in an elastic curriculum. Freedom of the student in the selection of the subjects of study was dear to him. On becoming president of the University of Indiana, 1885, he introduced the elective system.

Likewise with Eliot he believed in the enlargement of the curriculum through the adequate introduction of the natural and physical sciences and the modern languages. The place for these sciences in the college was greatly enlarged through his influence.

Individualistic, yet Jordan was a conciliator. He worked with as well as for other people. I easily believe that there were in him great capacities for indignation and for wrath, but these capacities were well disciplined and their outbursts thoroughly controlled. In this control his keenness of wit and his humor gave constant aid. He once said: "I have lived three more or less independent lives: first, and for the love of it, that of naturalist and explorer; second, also for the love of it, that of teacher; and third, from a sense of duty, that of minor prophet of Democracy . . . if he had his days to live over, he would again choose all of the three." [5]

Associated with great men of the far Eastern world as well as of the near Western, he gave much to them and much also he received. His colleague of the Pacific coast, President Benjamin Ide Wheeler, on conferring the degree of LL.D., said, "Man of generous mould, in whom sympathy with men burst the bourn of natural science and reared a humanist. Teacher, founder, and preacher. A good neighbor." [6]

In the college year 1929-30 *The Stanford Quad* was

[5] Article by Dr. Barton Warren Evermann, *Science,* October 2, 1931, p. 329.

[6] *The Abundant Life,* by Benjamin Ide Wheeler. Edited by Monroe E. Deutsch, p. 332.

dedicated to him. At that time President Hoover wrote, "First president of our beloved university, creator of its oldest traditions, scientist of unquenchable thirst for truth and of unalterable integrity in its search, teacher of sympathy and imagination, friend of youth, wise counselor, believer in the inviolable sanctity and worth of the individual human soul, exemplar of the moral virtues, inspirer to the spiritual life, apostle and prophet of peace. . . ."

At the age of seventy Jordan wrote verses bearing the title "Men Told Me, Lord." I cannot bring this interpretation of a great soul to a more fitting close than by quoting a part of this poem:

Lord, here am I, my threescore years and ten
All counted to the full; I've fought Thy fight,
Crossed Thy dark valleys, scaled Thy rocks' harsh
     height,
Borne all the burdens Thou dost lay on men
With hand unsparing, threescore years and ten.
Before Thee now I make my claim, O Lord!
What shall I pray Thee as a meet reward?

I ask for nothing! Let the balance fall!
All that I am or know or may confess
But swells the weight of mine indebtedness;
Burdens and sorrows stand transfigured all;
Thy hand's rude buffet turns to a caress,
For Love, with all the rest, Thou gav'st me here,
And *Love is Heaven's very atmosphere!*
Lo, I have dwelt with Thee, Lord, day by day,
I could do no more, through all Eternity!⁷

    ⁷ *The Days of a Man,* by David Starr Jordan. Vol. II, p. 780.

XXX
SUMMARIES AND CONCLUSIONS

XXX

SUMMARIES AND CONCLUSIONS

THE interpretations of the great men of this volume and of the equally great men of a similar preceding volume, *Guides, Philosophers, and Friends,* give ground for certain conclusions. These conclusions may possibly have value touching some elements, conditions and relations of our common humanity.

As one reads in review the lives of these more than fifty persons, he is impressed with the number of their years. The average number of these years is no less than three score years and eleven. It exceeds the Scriptural limit. It makes a beginning into the eighth decade. The longest of all these lives are those of President Eliot and of Professor Edwards A. Park of Andover, each of ninety-two. Among the shortest are those of President Harper of Chicago of fifty years, of President Walker of the Institute of Technology of fifty-seven, of Dickinson of fifty-eight years, of Phillips Brooks of fifty-eight years, of Dr. John Phillips of fifty, and of Provost Pepper of fifty-five. The significance of the length of the average age is most impressive. For the normal working period of life is

451

desperately, pathetically short. About one-half of life is needed in preparation for the living and the doing of the other half. Most men of the commanding type do not reach the first years of their working period before the age of thirty. A larger number indeed come into this period after the age of thirty than enter it before this age. The working period normally ends in the seventh decade—with some at sixty, and with more at or before seventy. Many colleges and the pension foundations require retirement before the age of seventy. It is therefore important to make the thirty or forty years that remain just as remunerative as possible. For the callings which require administrative or executive skill the earlier years are the richest in achievement. For the service that makes special demands upon the intellectual resources of judgment, of weighing evidence, the later years are the richer resource. But in either case humanity is made happier and is the more blessed if the years lengthen out. By contrast I think of the resulting impoverishment of the race. Many are the friends of mine—doctors, ministers, teachers, lawyers, writers—who have died before their fiftieth anniversary and some even before their fortieth birthday. Why did such a physician as Francis Peabody, or such a scholar as Pease of Andover, leave us so early? We needed you so much and you had so much to give to us. Why did Arthur Hallam vanish, while still a boy, except that it may be said that his early death gave us one of the greatest of all poems.

The following lists sum up what I have just written, and give basis for subsequent conclusions:

Age

Charles W. Eliot	1834-1926	92
James Burrill Angell	1829-1916	87
Daniel Coit Gilman	1831-1908	77
Andrew Dickson White	1832-1918	86
Cyrus Northrop	1834-1922	88
Mark Hopkins	1802-1887	85
William Torrey Harris	1835-1909	74
William Rainey Harper	1856-1906	50
James Harris Fairchild	1817-1902	85
Richard Salter Storrs	1821-1900	79
Frank Wakely Gunsaulus	1856-1921	65
Henry Adams	1838-1918	80
James Bryce	1838-1922	84
John Morley	1838-1923	85
John Hay	1838-1905	67
Andrew Sloan Draper	1848-1913	65
William De Witt Hyde	1858-1917	59
James Monroe Taylor	1848-1916	68
Samuel Harvey Taylor	1807-1871	64
Edwards Amasa Park	1808-1900	92
William Jewett Tucker	1839-1926	87
George Herbert Palmer	1842-	at least 90
Phillips Brooks	1835-1893	58
George Edward Woodberry	1855-1930	75
Arthur James Balfour	1848-1930	82
William Howard Taft	1857-1930	73
Walter Hines Page	1855-1918	63
Thomas Wentworth Higginson	1823-1911	88
William Roscoe Thayer	1859-1923	64
William Everett	1839-1910	71
Talcott Williams	1849-1928	79
Henry Theophilus Finck	1854-1926	72
Francis E. Clark	1851-1927	76
Barrett Wendell	1855-1921	66
Edward Williams Morley	1838-1923	85
Richard Burdon Haldane	1856-1928	72
Henry Johnson	1855-1918	63
Charles A. Dickinson	1849-1907	58
Theodore Chickering Williams	1855-1915	60

Perhaps, however, the most common of all characteristics is the lack of (more than one or two) characteristics. The fact of diversities is indeed characteristic. Each of these men was an individualist. Each was himself. One had as a supreme gift, imagination, like Woodberry. One was a master of eloquent speech, like Storrs. One was primarily a scholar, like Morley, the scientist; and Wheeler, the classicist. One was a philosophic thinker, like Bowen and Palmer. One was an administrator, like Eliot. One was gifted with the quality of conciliatoriness, like Angell. One had a mind weighty, like Haldane. One was a diplomatist, like Hay. Each indeed was himself. Individualisms were found in each of these fifty and more individualists.

But more important and more constructive than the length of their years or the diversities of their personal character, was the fact that these men possessed, as an almost universal characteristic, intellectual understanding. They had the gift and the achievement of mind. By understanding and by mind, I mean the native gift, but not simply the native gift but also education and training. The native resources, the resources, too, achieved through the culture and use of the native powers, were conditions and forces that belong to each of these friends. Of course, the understanding may differ in its contribution to the original endowment or in the nature of the education and training received. Yet despite the differences, perhaps indeed by reason of the differences, the endowment and the subsequent culture were constantly present and were formative. There was in these men a presumption of brains. This presumption they made good. Their minds might be more distinguished by insight than by judicial competence, by comprehensiveness of knowledge than by imagination, by logical reasoning and metaphysical interpretation than by practical applications, by analytical than by synthetical qualities, by conservative than by progressive tendencies, by inquisitive than by acquisitive forces. But whatever differences might exist, as made by nature or by education or by training or by experience, there were in these men a great understanding and a unique mindedness. Their education might be based the more on classical models than on scientific principles and methods. Their culture might be quickened by great teachers, inspired by religion, enriched by rich friendships, might be symmetrical or tangential. But whatever may have been the origin, the nature or the

process of their education and training, they embodied
and they carried forth through all their years the
results of their education and of their training. Their
understanding was a deep, broad, structural power in
their life, in their character and in their achievements.

With these intellectual gifts and achievements were
associated life's ethical forces. These men embodied
the moralities. They stood for the cardinal virtues,
either the classical four or the Hebrew three. They
were just and brave. They were temperate and restrained in thought, feeling, language, action. They
interpreted the future in the light of the present and
of the past. Neither did they divorce the present from
the duties of the future, either near or remote. If
they were passionate, as some of them at times were,
or aggressive as most of them at most times also were,
they were also patient. They recognized that the laws
of biology and not the laws of physics are tokens of
the methods of the growth of moral character. In the
atmosphere of duty they lived and to life's duties they
were loyal. To the five great institutions of modern
society—the family, the church, the school, the government, and property—they were devoted. Regard-
ful of the rights of each of these institutions they also
had respect for the limitations of each. For the
Pauline virtues of faith, hope, and love, they had
constant regard. Kant's categorical imperative both
quickened and restrained. ''I ought,'' was the supreme command. Unconsciously they held and obeyed

Luther's judgment, "I can no other." The will for usefulness was regnant in their character as it was progressive in their service. Their ethical enthusiasms, though full of feeling, were solid and enduring. Their beliefs were well founded and well buttressed, and their principles of behavior and of conduct were altruistic, as their faith for humanity was optimistic. Love, they interpreted as both a sentiment and a good will, but more as a good will than as a sentiment. Friendliness was the atmosphere of their lives, and being friends themselves, they were endowed and blessed with friendships. Love for men was more characteristic of them than love for nature, though the love for nature was not lacking. High-minded, they were no less broad-minded and deep-minded. In some, individuality was the more formative, and in some conciliatoriness was the more constructive. Their moral elements flowered forth into associations and coöperations with their fellow men. They were rather selfward or even self-sacrificing than touched by selfishness. They were moral statesmen for the race. They were indeed patriots, but they recognized that "above all nations is humanity."

The union of the ethical veracities and of the intellectual verities led them to simple and regnant results: these men were wise and hard workers, and also were possessed of sound health. Laboriousness promoted soundness of health and soundness of health quickened and supported laboriousness. They were forces creative in literature, administration, church-

manship, medicine, law, government. Creative forces
represent laboriousness as well as endowment. They
were students, thinkers, teachers, doers. They worked
unto weariness and exhaustion. The body, the intellect, the heart, the will, the conscience, each contributed to their working power; and their working power
contributed to and flowered forth into achievement.
For they were neither amateurs nor dilettantes. They
had learned their trade and they followed it. They
knew their tools, and they used them. They had masters but their severest master was themselves. They
recognized that in their war was no discharge. Faithfulness clothed them as a garment. They spelled
recreation as re-creation. Of course, in such laboriousness they missed much—good fellowship, frolic-
someness, gleefulness. But they also gained much or
even more—richness of character, achievement, the
consciousness of having done their utmost and been
their best.

Of course, such a life of the seven labors was both
the result, the cause, and the condition of sound
health. They had respect for the laws of such health
and of such healthfulness. The three forces making
for health and healthfulness—food, sleep, exercise—
they recognized and worked with. Why did Byron die
at thirty-six, Shelley at thirty, and Keats at twenty-
six? They, these friends of ours, lived in obedience to
the laws of mind and of body. They wrought well.
They were not spendthrifts. They spent, but they
were thrifty in their spending. For their spending

they received much, more, most. They were savers and therefore they were saviours.

The characteristic of friendliness which I have noted invites to a more appreciative interpretation. For the sense and the practice of friendliness belonged to these men quite as completely as did any other faculty or function. They could not indeed be haters and enemies of the humanity of which they were a part. Their friendliness might take on different characteristics or characters, as special graciousness such as with Higginson, or faithfulness to the needy as with Hamann, or the sense of conciliatoriness as with Angell of Michigan, or of earnestness and of vision in service as with Brooks, or as a world imagination as with Hay, or of enthusiasm as with Pepper, or of love for youth as with Frank Clark, or of loyal human interest as with Talcott Williams, or of intellectual sympathy as with Bryce. But of each form and of all emphases and applications there was in each friendliness, friendliness to man and to men. Of course, such a character cannot be other than moral. Humanity was gathered up into them and from them there went forth unto humanity all they possessed. It was Greek philanthropy incarnated in sacrificing Christian love.

There was in these fifty and more men the spirit of the optimist, or at least the spirit of the meliorist. If they did not believe, as few can, that this is the best of all possible worlds, inhabited by the best of all beings, they did believe that this is among the better of all worlds, inhabited by a race which has many good qualities. They thought, however, less of the philosophical or psychological conditions of the goodness of this sphere than they unconsciously acted on the results of their thoughts and beliefs. For they knew and realized that optimism spells hope, pessimism despair; optimism gives assurance, pessimism despondency; optimism stands for courage, pessimism for cowardice; optimism creates expectation, pessimism dullness; optimism nourishes faith and faithfulness, pessimism doubt and faithlessness; optimism means constructiveness, pessimism, disintegration; optimism assures victory, pessimism threatens defeat. Optimists believe in the right, and optimists know that the right the day must win.

But there was one further element structural in their life and character! I refer to their religion. For fundamentally they were religious men. Their conceptions of religion of course differ. It may be a conception which Andrew D. White accepted in saying, " . . . the bringing of humanity into normal relations with that Power, not ourselves, in the universe, which makes for righteousness. . . ."[1] The conception also may be one to which President Eliot gave voice in writing of the religion of the future, " . . . monotheistic and the older conceptions of the Deity will be merged in it with the biological conception of a vital force, for it will deem the universe to be pervaded by the Infinite Spirit and will accept

[1] *Autobiography of Andrew D. White*, Vol. II, p. 568.

literally and implicitly St. Paul's statement, 'In Him
we live, and move, and have our being.' " [2] It may
also be a conception having for its basis a definition
of God as a personal being endowed with every excellence, infinite and perfect. These definitions at least
intimate, if they do not declare, that the Divine Being is personal. The conception may also be one of a
religion without a belief in a personal God. But the
first article of the creed, "I believe in God," was
usually characteristic and formative. With this belief
was found associated two other beliefs, freedom of
the human will and immortality. The belief in moral
freedom was common to them. The belief in individual immortality was fraught with doubtfulness on the
part of some. But be it said that these articles of the
one creed were of far less importance than the first, "I
believe in God," be that name spelled with a capital
or with a small letter. Yet with or without this central and controlling doctrine of divine personality,
religion of a sort belonged to these men. It seemed to
be fundamental. It was primary in their beliefs,
structural in their character, and directive in their
life. These friends may have had the faith and eccle-
siastic relations of Bryce, or the twilight beliefs of
Lord Morley as whispered in the beautiful epilogue
to his Recollections. They may give assent to the
creeds, an assent such as Tucker of Dartmouth and
Hyde of Bowdoin represented, who were ministers
and apostles of the faith. They may have been able

[2] *Charles W. Eliot,* by Henry James, Vol. II, p. 202.

also to sing the song of Henry Adams to the Virgin
of Chartres, or they may have knelt in adoration in
the sacrament of the communion, as Talcott Williams
requested his associates and students at the beginning
of every year of his School to do—in all events and
in all conditions these men were essentially religious.
Reverence was the substance of their being. If to
them religion was not as Walter Page once said to
me, "the only thing in life," it was at least formative. If it was not declared at the altars of the
church, it did breathe in their breath, and it moved
in their blood. They sought to obey the prophet
Micah's requirements of doing justice, loving mercy,
and walking humbly with their God. They could indeed unite in the prayer, common to all:

Our Father who art in Heaven, Hallowed be thy
name; Thy kingdom come; Thy will be done in the
earth as it is in Heaven.

THE END

INDEX

INDEX

"Abundant Life," of Wheeler, 392 ff.

Adams, Charles Francis, Sr., compared with Page, 97 ff.

Adams, Mrs. Charles Francis, Sr., allusion to, 154.

Adams, Henry, allusion to, 152, 167; prayer of, to the Virgin of Chartres, 462.

Alcott, A. Bronson, allusion to, 118.

Allen, A. V. G., quotation from "Life of Phillips Brooks," 24.

Alpha Delta Phi Society, 182.

Andover Theological Seminary, allusion to, 196-8.

Aristocrat and democrat in Wendell, 216 ff.

Arnold, Matthew, allusion to, 39, 393.

Artist, the, in Williams, T. C., 281 ff.

Arts, Fine, promoted by Raymond and Seelye, 348 ff.

"Atlantic Monthly," editorship by Page, 94 ff.

Austen-Leigh, allusion to, 61.

Author, Smith, E. F. as, 385 ff.

Authority, value of, to Balfour, 64 ff.

Backus, Professor, interpretation of Raymond by, 343.

Baker, Ray Stannard, "Life of Wilson," by, 421 ff.

Balfour, A. J., chapter on, 53-74; of the Cecil family, 55-6; Eton, allusion to, 56; friends of, 56; at Cambridge, 56 ff.; Sidgwick, allusion to, 56 ff.; his mother, 60; a thinker, 62 ff.; loyalty to authority, 64 ff.; acknowledgment of a Supreme Being, 66-7; loyalty to the Bible, 67; Christianity, ecclesiastical organization of, 67-8; Lady Frances Balfour, quotation from, 68; work for education, 69-70; defects of, 71; quotation from "Punch," concerning, 71; contrasted with Bryce and Morley, 73 ff.

Balfour, Lady Frances, quotation from, 68.

Batchelder, Mrs. N. H., sculpture by, of Williams, T. C., 286.

Berkeley Temple, allusion to, 271 ff.

Bible, loyalty of Balfour to, 67.

Birmingham, allusion to, 22, 28.

Black Regiment of Higginson, 114 ff.

465